HONEYTRAP

Twenty-five years ago, the world learned that a member of the government, Minister for War John Profumo, had been sleeping with a nineteen-year-old girl called Christine Keeler, who was seeing Soviet diplomat and spy, Eugene Ivanov. The Minister resigned, and attention focused on the prostitution trial of Stephen Ward, the osteopath and part-time artist, who had brought the couple together. Ward died, an apparent suicide, before the end of the trial, and Prime Minister Harold Macmillan resigned a few months later.

Honeytrap is the definitive investigation into the great sex and security scandal of our time.

About the authors

Anthony Summers is one of the world's leading investigative journalists. His three previous books, THE FILE ON THE TSAR, CONSPIRACY and GODDESS, were all world-wide bestsellers. His work on HONEYTRAP began when GODDESS research in American archives led back to aspects of the Profumo Affair.

Stephen Dorril contributed material for GODDESS and is co-editor of *Lobster*, a quarterly journal on political and intelligence affairs.

HONEYTRAP

Anthony Summers and Stephen Dorril

CORONET BOOKS
Hodder and Stoughton

Copyright © 1987 by Anthony Summers and Stephen Dorril

First published in Great Britain in 1987 by George Weidenfeld & Nicolson Limited

Coronet edition 1988
Second impression 1989

The authors thank the following for their kind permission to quote:
Warwick Charlton, for quotations from Stephen Ward Speaks.
Hod Dibben, for quotations from the late Mariella Novotny's unpublished manuscripts, 'The Government Chief Whip (Retired)' and 'The Girl who Paved the Way for the Permissive Society'.
Victor Gollancz Ltd, for quotations from The Trial of Stephen Ward, by Ludovic Kennedy.
A. D. Peters & Co. Ltd, for quotation from The Profumo Affair, Aspects of Conservatism, by Wayland Young.
Mandy Rice-Davis for quotations from Mandy.

British Library C.I.P.

Summers, Anthony
Honeytrap: the secret world of Stephen Ward.
1. Great Britain. Politics. Scandals.
Role of Ward, Stephen
I.Title   II. Dorril, Stephen
941.085'6'0924

ISBN 0-340-42973-9

Printed and bound in Great Britain for Hodder and Stoughton Paperbacks, a division of Hodder and Stoughton Ltd., Mill Road, Dunton Green, Sevenoaks, Kent TN13 2YA. (Editorial Office: 47 Bedford Square, London WC1B 3DP) by Cox & Wyman Limited, Reading, Berks. Photoset by Rowland Phototypesetting Limited, Bury St Edmunds, Suffolk.

'The System's just a story we tell to the people that aren't running it, and they're supposed to just mind their business and believe it . . .'

George V. Higgins

CONTENTS

ILLUSTRATION ACKNOWLEDGEMENTS

The photographs are reproduced by kind permission of the following: Associated Press: 4 (*below left*), 5 (*below left*); Camera Press: 3 (*above right*), 6 (*above*), 7 (*above*), 7 (*below right*), 9 (*centre*), 10 (*centre*); Epoque: 10 (*right*); National Film Archive: 4 (*below right*) © Miracle Films Ltd; Popperfoto: 3 (*below*), 7 (*below left*), 9 (*left*); Private Collection: 8 (*below*), 13, 16; Syndication International: 1 (*above*), 1 (*below*), 2 (*below*), 3 (*above left*), 5 (*above*), 5 (*below right*), 6 (*below*), 9 (*right*), 10 (*left*); Topham Picture Library: 2 (*above left*), 2 (*above right*), 8 (*above*), 10; Weidenfeld Archive: 4 (*above*).

ILLUSTRATIONS

ACKNOWLEDGEMENTS

The Honeytrap project was born in 1984. Anthony Summers was in California, working on *Goddess*, his biography of Marilyn Monroe. A friend gave him a copy of *Lobster*, a quarterly journal co-authored by Stephen Dorril, then working for the Probation Service in Yorkshire. It contained a long article on Mariella Novotny, the hostess at the infamous Man In The Mask Party, and her claims to have had sexual relations with President Kennedy. Summers was impressed by Dorril's work, and found that some of the research dovetailed with the Monroe research. Jim Lesar, the Washington lawyer who has become an expert on the Freedom of Information Act, was asked to look for official papers relating to Novotny. And so we came across the BOWTIE dossier, the FBI file on the Profumo Affair. Research began, with the notion that it might lead to a couple of newspaper articles. Nearly three years later, it has resulted in this book.

The detective work and writing has been conducted across the Irish Sea, because Summers lives in Ireland. He did most of the interviews in the United States. In England, Dorril eventually quit his Probation Service job and discovered that true journalism is based mostly on persistence and the hard slog of phones that do not answer, doors slammed in the face, and draughty night trains. In 1986, with a publishing contract secured, we hired two foot-soldiers. One was Claire Powell, an English graduate working on the Wolverhampton *Express and Star*. She left her job to work on *Honeytrap*. Gay Watson, who had worked with Summers in the sixties at the BBC, joined the team. Powell found herself trawling some of London's sleaziest backwaters in pursuit of the prostitutes and pimps of 1963 – and found some of them still busy. She proved to be not only a true gumshoe, but also a fine reporter. Watson made many difficult things elementary, even when her house burned down.

We are indebted to Anthony Frewin and Dick Brewis, respectively a personal assistant in the film industry and an academic, who ten years ago began their own citizens' enquiry into the Profumo Affair. In the United States, we thank Lori Winchester, of WCJ Incorporated, which provides investigative and protection services worldwide. It is hard to disappear if Winchester wants to find you. Robert Fink, a Washington investigative journalist with long experience of research in the labyrinth of US government agencies, did vital interviews in the last weeks of our research.

Of those crucial to the project, we thank **Palace Pictures**, producers of the television series *Scandal*. For Palace, Joe Boyd opened up difficult research roads.

In this case, before listing those who did help, we take pleasure in mentioning those who were not helpful: John Profumo, Lord Denning, Lord Wilson of Rievaulx, and Lord Home of the Hirsel. Profumo did not answer our letter.

Particularly generous with their time were the Hon. David Astor and the Earl of Dudley. We thank Mandy Rice-Davies, who cheerfully disinterred her youth; Mariella Novotny's husband Hod Dibben; and Christine Keeler's sometime lover Johnny Edgecombe. Ronna Riccardo, the prostitute who had the guts to retract her false testimony in 1963, bravely spoke up for the first time since then. Stephen Ward's friends, Jon Pertwee, Dr Ellis Stungo, and Warwick Charlton gave generously of their time. So did Robert Harbinson, better known as the travel writer Robin Bryans.

Of those who reported the scandal in 1963, most of whom remember the experience with disgust, we thank Peter Earle, then Chief Crime Reporter of the *News of the*

World, Trevor Kempson of the *News of the World*, Roy East, then Chief Crime Reporter of the *People*, Tom Mangold, then with the *Daily Express*, Brian McConnell, of the *Daily Mirror*, Barry O'Brien, of the *Daily Telegraph*, and Alastair and Sheila Revie, then freelance journalists, and Tom Tullett, then head of the *Daily Mirror* Crime Bureau.

Interviewees and correspondents included: former Police Commissioner Sir Ranulph Bacon; Michael Bentine; Paul Boggis-Rolfe; Derek Brook; John Broxholme; Mrs David Bruce; James Burge; Mrs Derek Cooper; Thomas Corbally (through his lawyer); Glen Costin; John Cummings (of the CID Officers' Association); the late Dr Eric Dingwall; Alfred Donati; John Doxat; Michael Eddowes; Walter Elder; Courtney Evans; David Floyd; Nina Gadd; John Grigg; Logan Gourlay; Lord Harrington; Brian Innes; Mandy Kearney; Lord Kennet; Angus Labunski; David Lewis; Paul Mann; John McCone (former Director of the CIA); Dr William McClurg; Bobby McKew; Michael Mordaunt-Smith; Frederic Mullally; Sir Godfrey Nicholson; Clive Nicol; former Detective-Inspector Thomas O'Shea; Serge Paplinski; Michael Pertwee; Jocelyn Proby; Chapman Pincher; Pelham and Philip Pound; 'Victoria Regine' (the pseudonym of a source on London sexual activity); the Right Honourable Enoch Powell; Max Robertson; Archibald Roosevelt (former CIA Station Chief, London Embassy); Gerharda Seedorff (of the Black Star Picture Agency); Harry Stevens; Donald Stewart (former FBI Supervisor); 'Sue' (prostitute); Sir Edmund Tompkins; Harry Alan Towers; Andrew Tully; Nigel West; and Mike Wallington.

We thank those members of the Intelligence Services, British and American, who helped but cannot be named here.

Of the institutions consulted, we thank especially the Huddersfield Public Library. Also the British Library, the

Canadian High Commission information service, Colindale Newspaper Library, the *Daily Telegraph* Information Service, Equity, the actors' union, Kensington and Chelsea Library, Eddie Pedda, *TV Times* Picture Department, *Queen* magazine, the staff of St Catherine's House and Somerset House, *Spotlight* magazine, *Stage*, Torquay Central Library, the Virginia Historical Society.

Sterling Lord, our agent, more than lived up to his name. At our publishing house, Weidenfeld and Nicolson, we respect Lord Weidenfeld for supporting a book on a subject that many British publishers shy away from, out of fear, or on the grounds that the privacy of 'Poor Jack Profumo' is more important than the pursuit of the truth. Our editor, Victoria Petrie-Hay, brought great skill and energy to a marathon finish. We also thank Rose Scott, Yvonne Holland, and Tomás Graves, who discovered obscure pictures. At Coronet, during major changes for this paperback edition, Peter Straus and Anna Benn helped us to become enthusiastic all over again.

Dorril's wife Stephanie gave infinite patience and real help, as a small house overflowed with research material. His mother was a mine of information on ancient scandals, and Marilyn Webb typed. Robin Ramsay, co-editor of *Lobster*, kept the journal afloat in Dorril's absence. Thornhill Machinery, of Holmfirth, and Cappoquin Chickens, in Ireland, kept the authors in touch through the new miracle of the Fax machine. Summers once again thanks Denise FitzGerald, the best typist in Munster, and Caroline Burrell, without whom it would have been impossible. His friends, Fanny Dubes, Paul Sutton, Kathy Castle, and Cecily O'Toole, helped more than they know.

A.S.
S.D.

PROLOGUE: THE DEATH OF CITIZEN WARD

Midnight, Tuesday, 30 July 1963, in London. A man in a white Jaguar drove through the streets of central London. He was fifty-one years old and tired, but looked much younger, spare and trim; his hair slicked back behind his ears. The man was now world-famous, but passed unnoticed that night. At about one o'clock he turned into a quiet road in Chelsea.

There, at Vale Court, in Mallord Street, the man let himself into an unpretentious flat owned by a friend. Then, after coffee and a last cigarette, he stretched out on the divan.

In the morning, at 8.30, his friend found the man still lying there, his face purple, hardly breathing, deep in a coma from which he would never recover. Beside him, near the coffee-cup and cigarette stub, lay several letters and an empty bottle of Nembutal sleeping-pills.

The dying man was Dr Stephen Ward. Six months earlier he had been an osteopath with a flair for portraiture, virtually unknown to the public. Now he was dying in a firestorm of notoriety. For Stephen Ward had become the focus of a crisis that effectively destroyed a British Conservative Government and rocked a society already off-balance, the sex and espionage scandal remembered as the Profumo Affair.

The Affair, to the avid millions whom it entertained, seemed a series of titillating sideshows around a seamy centrepiece. The British Secretary of State for War, John Profumo, aged forty-six, had conducted an affair with a

nineteen-year-old girl called Christine Keeler. On the very
weekend of their meeting, Keeler began an acquaintance
with thirty-seven-year-old Captain Eugene Ivanov, nominally a Soviet Assistant Naval Attaché in London but also
an officer in Soviet Military Intelligence, GRU.

Christine Keeler met both the Russian and the British
Minister as a result of her friendship with Stephen Ward.
Ward had met her when she was seventeen and working as
a showgirl at a London nightclub. He had introduced her to
John Profumo on 8 July 1961, at the country mansion of a
wealthy aristocrat, Lord Astor. The couple met at Astor's
swimming-pool, which Ward – who rented a cottage on the
Astor estate – was allowed to use.

The alarming fact of Keeler's simultaneous connection
with the British Minister for War and a Soviet spy remained
hidden for two years. It emerged only when the Minister's
girlfriend began talking about it – to the police, to Members
of Parliament, the press and others. As soon as she did so,
Captain Ivanov left London – presumably for Moscow.

The public scandal began in earnest in March 1963, when
Colonel George Wigg, MP, a close confidant of Labour
leader Harold Wilson, asked a question in the House of
Commons. Next day, after a dawn conference with a bevy
of high-ranking Conservatives, including the Attorney-
General and the Solicitor-General, Profumo told Parliament that there had been 'no impropriety' in his acquaintance with Christine Keeler. He made this statement flanked by the Prime Minister, Harold Macmillan, and other
ministers.

Within a week, Opposition leader Wilson sent a memorandum to the Prime Minister expressing concern about
national security. The memorandum was based on information supplied by Dr Stephen Ward. His version of the
affair supported Profumo's claim about Keeler, but stated
that MI5 – the domestic arm of British Intelligence – had
been briefed from the start on the fact that Profumo,
Keeler and the Russian had met each other. Ward's own
friendship with the Soviet spy, he said, had been 'used in
the interests of the country'.

The Prime Minister, pressed repeatedly by the Opposition, ordered an enquiry by the Lord Chancellor, Britain's senior judge. Within four days of the start of that enquiry, on 4 June, the Minister for War resigned. In his letter to the Prime Minister, Profumo admitted that he had lied to Parliament about his relations with Christine Keeler. He was found guilty of contempt of the House of Commons and was removed from his post on the Privy Council.

Aside from the Minister's personal disgrace, the Government now took a severe beating in a 'no-confidence' debate on national security. The Prime Minister came under pressure to resign – and was to do so in any case four months later, on the grounds of ill health.

Master of the Rolls Lord Denning, who headed the Court of Appeal, was ordered to investigate whether the Profumo case had endangered national security, and to examine the performance of British Intelligence. In autumn 1963, after an enquiry held in secret, Denning concluded that there had been no security breach and that British Intelligence had been competent. So ended a year-long crisis, the most public shaming a Government had endured this century.

Stephen Ward testified to Lord Denning but did not survive to read the Report, which vilified him in death while being hugely polite to the Minister whose folly triggered the trouble, John Profumo.

In the spring, just as Ward began supplying information to the Labour leadership, the police began an extraordinary investigation into his activities. This was, supposedly, prompted by anonymous letters sent to the police, claiming that Dr Ward had been living on the proceeds of prostitution. The letters have never been produced. The police pursuit of Ward began, however, within days of a meeting between the Home Secretary, the Commissioner of Police and the head of MI5.

In the weeks that followed, the police conducted interviews with 140 people, all in order to find evidence of poncing.

In early June, just as the crisis for the Government
became more serious, Ward was arrested. He was to be
charged with living on the immoral earnings of three
women, of procuring abortions,* and of conspiring to keep
a brothel.

In mid-July, when the Denning Enquiry was in full
swing, Ward went on trial at the Old Bailey on the immoral
earnings' charges. The trial, which held the attention of the
world for ten days, was a mockery of justice. Of two
prostitutes called to give evidence, one admitted in court
that her initial testimony had been false, and a second later
told a reporter the same thing. Both said the police had
persuaded them to give false evidence.

Christine Keeler admitted that she had received money
from men and that she had given some of it to Ward. She
said, though, that the cash had been given to Ward because
she owed him money, and that she usually owed him more
than she ever made.

Mandy Rice-Davies, an eighteen-year-old who had also
been Ward's protégée, said that she had taken money from
wealthy financier Dr Emil Savundra. Savundra slept with
her on several occasions, and would leave cash on the
dressing-table before leaving. Rice-Davies said she would
occasionally give Ward money to pay for food. Yet, like
Keeler, she also said she had been getting funds from
Ward.

The jury were not told of evidence that Keeler had
recently lied on oath in another court case. Like other
witnesses – both girls had come under enormous pressure
from the police.

Ward was clearly fascinated by sex, delighted in very
young women, and ingratiated himself socially by introducing them to affluent male friends with similar tastes. It was
nonsense, though, to suggest that this well-paid osteopath
and artist was living on prostitution. Nevertheless, after an
aggressive lecture from the judge on the precise letter of the

---

*The Abortion Act was not passed until 1967.

law, the Old Bailey jury found Ward guilty on the charges involving Keeler and Rice-Davies.

Stephen Ward never heard the verdict. By that time he was in hospital, being kept alive only by mechanical means, after the barbiturate overdose that was to kill him. As a distinguished observer wrote at the time, 'There were many people in Britain who, on hearing the news, felt a little ashamed, a little diminished . . .'

A few hours before the end, talking to a friend, Ward said, 'Someone had to be sacrificed, and it was me. One or two people can still vindicate me, but when the Establishment want blood, they get it.'

The writer Henry Fairlie defined the Establishment as 'A small group of men who use their contacts and influence to put a stop to the things they disapprove of, to promote the reliable, and to preserve the *status quo*.'

The British Establishment has been described as time-hallowed, but longevity has left it with the odour of corruption as much as of sanctity. It provided the principal villains in the Profumo Affair, and this is a story still relevant a quarter of a century later. Today, though it has been forced to adjust its mask, the Establishment has not lost its grip.

An élite, bred to the exercise of privilege and power, still directs the nation's affairs. Its champions justify the British Establishment – as once the British Empire was championed – for its preservation of the common good and the just. Yet the Establishment is first and foremost venal and hypocritical. That truth is at the core of this shabby story of 1963. This book will examine how Stephen Ward was used, then made a scapegoat, and why.

In summer 1963, there was a growing threat that more top names would be tarnished. Allegations to be considered in these pages suggest that a Cabinet Minister offered to resign at the height of the affair, out of concern that investigations would reveal his relationship with the Duchess of Argyll, the subject of a recent sensational divorce. And then there was the Royal Family.

Ward, as a fine artist, had sketched no fewer than eight members of the Royal Family in 1961. Prince Philip he knew already; they had been acquainted since the forties, and Philip had attended a party given by Ward. Philip's cousin and close friend, David, Marquess of Milford Haven, had cause for fear. There is evidence, to be examined in this book, that Ward provided women for the sex parties he gave.

During Ward's trial, a London art gallery held an exhibition of his sketches, including those of several members of the Royal Family. No sooner had the exhibition opened than a mysterious emissary bought up all the Royal portraits.

A high point of the Profumo furore was a story about an orgiastic dinner at which one distinguished male guest waited on the others dressed only in a waitress' apron and a black mask. There has been speculation ever since about his identity. We shall show, to a virtual certainty, who he was – a member of a famous aristocratic and political family, now dead.

In 1963, then, there was a cause for panic in the ranks of the Establishment. That, though, does not explain the decision to try Ward on trumped-up charges. There was, indeed, the risk that prosecution would goad Ward into exposing those he had imagined to be his friends. Yet the risk was worth taking. Why?

Putting the osteopath on trial meant that many matters became *sub judice*. There was a strict limit on how the scandal could be discussed in the press, and even in the House of Commons. Most important of all, Ward's sexual peccadilloes – dressed up as crimes – created a diversion. The lurid headlines, the bedroom revelations, titillated as many people as they outraged. It made Ward and his girls, rather than John Profumo and the Government, the focus of public attention. It diverted attention from the real issue – national security.

Harold Wilson was right when he told Parliament, just before Ward went on trial: 'What concerns us . . . is whether a man of high trust, privy to the most secret information available to a Government . . . imperilled our national security or created conditions in which a continued risk to our security was allowed to remain . . .'

Wilson understood something the authorities preferred the public not to think about – that the Minister for War had laid himself open to blackmail. It did not matter that he had supposedly terminated his affair with Christine Keeler long before the scandal became public. The very fact of the affair left him vulnerable until the moment of his resignation.

Some tried to calm such fears by suggesting that Profumo did not, in any case, have access to much sensitive material. As we shall show, he did.

Lord Denning's report made light of one specific allegation: that Ward, prompted by Ivanov, had asked Keeler to get information from Profumo on 'when the Americans were going to supply the atomic bomb to Germany'. Put like this, it was a nonsense: there never was any question of giving West Germany 'the bomb'. In 1961, though, there was real Soviet concern as to whether the US Sergeant and Crockett missiles were to be armed with nuclear warheads for use in Germany and, if so, when. The alarming possibility of active espionage in the Profumo case was not considered in any depth in the Denning Report. Nor were a string of questions concerning the role of British Intelligence.

According to the Denning Report, MI5 did not learn until early 1963 that Profumo and Keeler had been lovers. In fact, as we shall show, MI5 officers knew of the affair much earlier. What was British Intelligence up to? The answer lies in the title of this book – *Honeytrap*.

'Honeytrap', in intelligence parlance, is the entrapment of an espionage target through sexual compromise. If there was a honeytrap in the Profumo Affair, who was hunting whom? Lord Denning considered only that the Minister for War was lured into folly as part of a Soviet plan to sow disunity between Britain and the United States. The British, at the highest level, would appear to be unreliable

partners and Washington's trust would be eroded. If that
was the plan, it succeeded to some extent.

What was Ward's true role? He spent a good deal of time
with the Soviet attaché and sometimes aired sympathies for
the Soviet Union. During the Berlin Crisis, and later during
the Cuban Missile Crisis, he acted as an intermediary for
Soviet diplomatic initiatives. Was he simply a naïve dupe of
the Russians? Was he a witting traitor? Or was he acting on
behalf of British Intelligence?

The Denning Report did not pursue this last possibility,
that the British were the hunters and the Soviet attaché the
target. We can now piece together the way Ward was
effectively recruited by MI5, two years before the scandal,
in the hope of softening up Ivanov as a potential defector.
Profumo's affair with Keeler may have been – to MI5 –
only an unforeseen hitch in an operation that lasted long
after the affair was over. That was something British Intelligence wished to keep to itself, not least when the scandal
broke.

Today there is fresh evidence on Ward's Soviet connection.
We have discovered that a second Soviet, a diplomat, was
in touch with Ward. His calling card was found in Ward's
pocket after his death. Meanwhile, our enquiries have
located another prostitute, not identified in 1963, who now
admits that Ward sent her British MPs and Americans as
clients. This raises new questions about Ward's true alle-
giance and leads us into an area that escaped notice in 1963
– the American connection.

It was known at the time that three American airmen,
based at the US Third Air Force Headquarters in Britain,
were recalled because of their association with Christine
Keeler. It was decided that there had been no security leak,
and the men returned to England.

Today, with access to the files of the US Air Force and of
the FBI – the Bureau's dossier was code-named BOWTIE –
we know about a fourth airman, who had had sex with a
prostitute Ward knew, at his flat. The prostitute first gave

false evidence at the trial, then admitted she had done so following police pressure, and subsequently fled to the United States.

The next – and potentially the most extraordinary – piece in the puzzle lifts the story into the stratosphere of scandal. According to a combination of human sources and official documents, the Profumo Affair touched the President of the United States, John F. Kennedy.

At least one woman linked to Ward may have met and had sex with Kennedy. Mariella Novotny, then eighteen, claimed she did so, immediately after Kennedy's election, but before the inauguration. We have established that this is a story she told at the time, and have obtained a memoir in which she describes the experience in detail.

We have also obtained a mass of US official documents on a young actress called Suzy Chang, who attracted intense federal interest at the time of the scandal. On the day an American newspaper publicly linked her with 'one of the biggest names in American politics', the President was in England visiting Prime Minister Macmillan. He at once assigned his brother, Attorney-General Robert Kennedy, to mount a ruthless damage-control operation.

Mariella Novotny saw Stephen Ward the day before she flew to the United States on the trip during which she allegedly met John Kennedy. Later, she was to say that she believed she had been a pawn in a plot to compromise the President-elect. Novotny's alleged encounter with Kennedy took place – as did all the central events in the Profumo case – at the very height of the Cold War. Just as the British Minister of War was compromised by his mistress's link to a Soviet spy, so too there were efforts to link Novotny, the daughter of a Czech father, with the communists.

At the height of the crisis, Harold Wilson referred darkly to 'evidence of a sordid underworld network, the extent of which cannot yet be measured'. Wilson's chief adviser on the Affair, George Wigg, claimed flatly in Parliament: 'There are three gentlemen actively connected with blackmail on an international scale who got out of London as quickly as they could when they knew that Dr Ward had been arrested.'

Who were these 'blackmailers' and what really triggered the Profumo scandal? We shall be analysing the strange circumstances in which the story broke surface, and the odd way Profumo's lover, Christine Keeler, suddenly started pouring out her tale to anyone who would listen. She did so partly because of one man's personal vendetta against Dr Ward. But was there, in 1963, a plot within a plot, one which sought to destroy even the President of the United States?

What is not in doubt is that this was a graver international drama than was ever understood at the time. A former Deputy Director of the FBI has told us: 'This was a time when there was a feeling that we had been deceiving ourselves, that we had felt more secure than we should have done, not least because we depended a great deal on the security capability of the British. And then to find that the President was perhaps involved with somebody involved in the British security scandal. Nobody was grinning . . .'

The truth behind the Profumo Affair was obscured at the time. In many ways, the authorities deliberately misled the nation. Today British files remain closed, and former officials tight-lipped. Even in the United States, the Freedom of Information Act is thwarted by heavy censorship. As late as March 1987, in the House of Lords, a group of peers made an astonishing attack on the BBC, which had recently dropped plans for a documentary about Stephen Ward. Lord Grimond, former leader of the Liberal Party, said it had been 'extremely irresponsible' for the BBC even to have considered making such a programme. Lord Denning himself, speaking like some aged headmaster, deplored the way the BBC had been re-examining past court cases. 'Does not this conduct,' said Denning, 'tend to shake people's confidence in the courts and in the police, and is it not therefore to be condemned?'

The debate gives the Profumo Affair a new relevance. We live in a time when probing journalism is discouraged, when broadcasters are intimidated by Government – again a Conservative one – as never before. When a Liberal peer castigates the BBC for merely thinking about a programme, the day of Orwell's Thought Police looms frighteningly closer. Such talk ignores entirely the fact that long after all other appeals have been exhausted, books and broadcast programmes have exposed serious miscarriages of justice. Living men have walked free, dead men have received posthumous pardons. Sometimes, literature can be the court of last appeal.

'Over twenty-three years ago,' Lord Denning said recently, 'I heard all the evidence . . . and was quite satisfied that there was no miscarriage of justice at all.' We must not tremble before such bombast – from the man who in 1963 produced the only public report on the Profumo Affair. Lord Denning devoted only two paragraphs to the Ward trial, in a report of more than a hundred pages. Our investigation, conducted over three years, suggests that the public never learned the true facts about the Profumo case, and remained woefully uninformed about the role of British Intelligence.

We have reached these conclusions by compiling our own dossier, based on many dozens of fresh interviews. Apart from the new American documents, we have been permitted – for the first time – to see official transcripts of the Ward trial, a record that has always been denied to researchers. Finally, we have obtained a typewritten outline for a memoir, assembled by Ward himself shortly before he died. Part of it was written by hand in Brixton Prison, and taken out in sections by a visiting friend, part was apparently dictated into a tape-recorder. We quote from it here for the first time in Britain.

'Seek ye the truth, and the truth shall make you free,' is an ancient exhortation that has been allowed to become something of a cliché, in Britain and in the United States, countries that wrongly take their freedom for granted. This book is an effort to provide, for the first time, a window on history that, in this most secretive of Western nations, has been denied to the British people for nearly a quarter of a century.

ONE

LEARNING THE GAME

'The story must start with Stephen Ward,' Lord Denning was to write at the beginning of his report on the Profumo Affair. There was no reason why his report should start thus. The focus should have been on Minister for War John Profumo. Let us nevertheless, like Denning, open our story with Dr Ward. Who was he?

He was born Stephen Thomas Ward on 19 October 1912, the year the *Titanic* went down. One of those who perished in the shipwreck was millionaire Jacob Astor. His relative, young Bill Astor, who would one day become Lord Astor and Ward's patron, was about to start school. John Profumo, the son of a line of Italian aristocrats, would not be born for another three years. Harold Macmillan, future Prime Minister, was about to go to Eton, the launchpad for political stardom and marriage to the daughter of a duke. Beside these lucky inheritors of privilege, Stephen Ward's silver spoon seemed somewhat dull.

The baby Stephen was born to Arthur, a Hertfordshire vicar, and his wife Eileen. Reverend Ward, described by his bishop as 'a forthright preacher of fiery sermons and modern ideas', was scholarly and somewhat austere. Eileen Ward enhanced the social clout of the family. She came from the Vigors family, of County Carlow in Ireland, landed gentry who had produced a steady stream of clerics, magistrates, High Sheriffs and officers for the British Army.

Later, Stephen Ward would make a point of telling

people he was Irish and from a 'good' family. He had social aspirations, and his mother supplied excellent credentials. She doted on her boy and thought he was 'brilliant'. There were prayers at Stephen's christening for 'a happy and holy life', and Eileen told a close friend: 'One day my boy will be famous.' She did not live to know the irony in the remark.

Ward's father moved his family, as vicars must, from parish to parish, eventually settling amidst the genteel seaside folk of Torquay. The Reverend Ward's church was St Matthias, still flourishing today. Young Ward had two brothers and twin sisters. He was educated first by a private tutor, then at a private 'prep' school, and finally sent to the empire-building academy of the British class system, a public school.

Just as Ward was born to an upper middle drawer, rather than the top one, so his public school was – as a luckier acquaintance later sniffed – 'second-rate'. Canford, in Dorset, was for those whose parents wanted their sons in a privileged school, but had to settle for less than the best. Stephen wanted to impress his father. 'I wanted to be good at everything,' he would one day tell his close friend Warwick Charlton. 'I wanted to pass exams brilliantly, to be noticed for my fine mind. I also wanted to be good at games.'

It did not happen. In a world of achievers, Ward was not especially good at anything. He was lazy, a bit of a dreamer, but he could not dream his way out of what public-school enthusiasts like to call their 'code'.

Forty years later, at the height of the Profumo Affair, Ward told Charlton about an incident in the dormitory at Canford. Someone, not Ward, had hit a boy who was snoring during the night. In the morning, the boy was found unconscious with a fractured skull.

'Someone,' Ward said, 'had to be punished. If no one confessed, then the entire dormitory had to be punished. I knew who it was, but one was not supposed to tell. There would have been great fury if I'd said anything and in any case I was completely indoctrinated. I had a horror of being a sneak. The upshot was I was taken away and thrashed in front of the whole school and I jolly well nearly got the sack, too. Of course, all the other boys thought I was a famous fellow. I'd done the right thing. I hadn't split . . .'

Long afterwards Ward asked one of his former masters whether he and his colleagues had really believed he was the culprit. 'No,' came the reply, 'but someone had to get whacked. It just happened to be you.'

During the Profumo Affair that episode was still a bitter memory. 'I suppose they expect me to go along with this stupid public-school convention that good chaps don't tell. Well, I didn't tell once. But not this time. If I'm going down then they're going with me. I promise you that.'

When it came to it, Ward died without splitting on his friends. At one stage he even lied in public to protect John Profumo. Like so many of its victims, the public-school code bound him to the end. Good chaps don't tell.

After the dormitory incident, at the age of seventeen, Stephen Ward told his father he wanted to leave school and get a job. 'He was puzzled,' Ward recalled. 'In my father's world young boys simply did not chuck up their schooling and get jobs for which they had no apparent training. Gentlemen's sons didn't behave like that.'

Gentlemen's sons, in the twenties, certainly did not take jobs at the Houndsditch Carpet Warehouse. That, however, is where Ward first worked, and it is here that he takes up his own story – in the memoir written before he died.

'I was paid twenty-seven shillings a week and no over-time,' Ward said of his spell at the warehouse. 'It was rather amusing . . . I spent the day turning over carpets and taking wholesale buyers to various departments. I wasn't there very long, I think the Christmas rush finished me.'

Within months, Ward was off to Germany and a return to something closer to a gentleman's existence. An uncle found him a job as a translator for Shell Oil in Germany, though his German was poor. He played football for a Hamburg team, joined the local British tennis club, and took long weekend trips on the river. He went out with Liese-Lotte Peters, the Swedish consul's daughter.

Hamburg, according to Ward, marked the start of his sex life. He recorded, without elaboration, how he 'explored the extensive night life of the famous Reeperbahn'. The Reeperbahn was, and is, Hamburg's brothel district.

The job in Germany ended the day 'I imprisoned my very fat boss behind a door and made him yell for mercy. Paris was next on the list.' Ward went to join a young friend, Paul Boggis-Rolfe, who had gone there to study. Boggis-Rolfe, who remembers Ward as 'a delightful person, awfully nice', gave Ward a bed in his room at a Left Bank *pension*.

Ward registered at the Sorbonne for a 'Civilisation' course, but did little studying. He supplemented his allowance by giving English lessons, guiding tourists and working in a nightclub called Chez Florence. The writer John Doxat, 'Britain's foremost thinking drinker', met Ward in Paris at this time. He remembers him as 'an ebullient character, a bit of a laugh. He was doing a stupendous amount of drinking. I was just beginning, he was a past master.'

In later years Ward drank little. Life in the Latin Quarter, though, formed some traits that would last. There he cultivated good conversation and the easy charm that would later make him popular in London. In the boulevard cafés, Ward perfected the insouciant pose, the white shirt rolled up to the elbow, the Gauloise cigarette at the lip, the black coffee in hand. He now knew he had a gift for portraiture, especially in chalks, and in Paris he practised a lot – drawing girls.

Ward took parties of tourists to Le Sphinx, a famous brothel where 'the girls were all naked and danced with the customers'. As he put it later, 'It didn't take me long to find out that people were more interested in real live girls than in the Mona Lisa.' Oddly enough, as Boggis-Rolfe remembers it, Ward himself showed little interest in actual sex with girls. That was how it was to be in the early sixties. He gathered girls around him, he drew them and he introduced them to his wealthy friends. But, many noticed, he had little sexual appetite for them himself.

Boggis-Rolfe stayed in France and went on to become a

soldier, then a member of MI6 during World War II. In 1932, Ward, now twenty, returned to England. The improbable jump from Paris to Torquay did not slow him down. The Bohemian returned, he breezed into County society and a whirl of hunt-balls and parties. Now he was home, Mummy proved generous with funds, and Ward acquired a red two-seater MG sports car. Then came a family crisis. The vicar's son had a blatant affair with a married actress, a former Ziegfeld Follies girl performing at the Pavilion. Ward's mother cut off his allowance, and he left home for a while. Then – for the first and perhaps only time – he fell in love.

The girl was a beauty called Mary Glover, the daughter of a local insurance man. She recalled in 1963, 'At first I thought Stephen rather arrogant, vain and snobbish, but as time went on I found myself in love with him.' Ward said, 'Mary gave me the confidence that I could accomplish anything I set my heart on.' There was talk of marriage, but Ward had no job and no money.

In London, Ward had an influential godfather, his uncle Edward Vigors. Vigors, an Examiner of Standing Orders to both Houses of Parliament, decided it was time to intervene. He introduced Ward to Jocelyn Proby, an aristocratic friend who was then at the forefront of introducing osteopathy to England. He had just returned from the United States, where osteopathy originated, and suggested Ward go to America to learn the profession. Ward, who saw that he had to 'make good' for Mary Glover, agreed.

So it was that, in autumn 1934, Ward found himself aboard the ss *Mauretania*, in third class, watching the towers of Manhattan appear on the horizon. He travelled on by Greyhound bus to Kirksville College in Missouri, the home of osteopathy, and there began medical studies that were to last four years.

In England, during the Profumo Affair, the press suggested that Ward was a quack doctor who had performed poorly at college. It was not true; Ward worked hard and passed his examinations with credits. In the United States, an osteopath must qualify fully in conventional medicine,

and Ward devoured pathology, gynaecology and surgery.
His British mentor, Jocelyn Proby, now nearly ninety, says
that Ward 'could memorise whole paragraphs of Gray's
Anatomy at one sitting'. The young doctor discovered that,
in America, there were ample bodies available for dissec-
tion – the corpses of negroes, purchased from the poor for
fifty dollars apiece. 'When we did obstetrics,' he recalled,
'we were often taken to remote farms, sometimes in winter
over deep snow and on snow shoes. We did surgery on
kitchen tables and deliveries of the most abstruse type
without help.'

   Soon came a severe blow, a letter from home telling him
that his sweetheart, Mary Glover, had decided to marry
someone else. Ward hurried back to England, desperate to
stop the marriage, but failed. He took it badly: 'This was
my first brush with pain. I wondered how anyone could
possibly reject me like that . . . I decided that I would never
again become so seriously involved with anyone.' Significantly, Ward never did have a stable, long-term affair with
a woman.

   Back in America, Ward threw himself into his studies
and into exploring the continent. He travelled to Mexico
and to every state in the Union. He hitchhiked to Florida
and survived an attack by a bear in Wyoming. He began a
lifelong fascination with show business when he went to
Hollywood to meet the film-star Madeleine Carroll, who
was a relative by marriage. He went to Chicago and met the
gangster Ralph Capone, Al's brother, and, following a
pattern he would keep to in every great city, he made for
the red-light district.

Ward liked game-playing in sex. He told his friend Warwick Charlton that he had vastly enjoyed the 'petting' ritual
then much practised in America. 'You touch the girl's
hand. She must make a sign of withdrawal. Never take this
seriously. From the hand you move to the lips. You kiss.
The lips, of course, are closed. Once you have kissed, then
you caress. More expertly, more lingeringly. You may
touch the body. But petting must be staggered over a

period. There's an art in this sort of stimulation. I found it an exciting emotional experience.' Years later, Charlton noticed, 'Stephen had refined the art of petting until it became almost a perversion. Consummation was never supremely important to him. A sort of body closeness, a hint of dangerous pleasures to come, a smoothly placed hand, a dextrous slip of silk against skin. These were the delights of Stephen Ward. Pleasure was always to be round the corner. Never to be taken now.'

In 1938, still only twenty-six, Ward brought his experience home to England. He was now Dr Stephen Ward, a gifted osteopath, and he began by setting up a practice in Torquay, close to the clock tower on the Strand. He became sought-after for his medical skill, and once again his social charm made him a favourite in the County set. The records of the South Devon Debating Society show that, in January 1940, Dr Ward spoke at a debate on 'Modern Sex Problems'. One female acquaintance remembers first hearing about him because 'he had young girls staying in his tent' during a Dartmoor camping holiday. Ward might have stayed in West Country obscurity but, just as it changed the lives of so many others, World War II intervened.

Ward volunteered for the Royal Army Medical Corps as soon as the war broke out, but was rejected. The Army did not recognise osteopathy. He was conscripted instead into the Armoured Corps, and sent for training at Bovington camp. It was now that Ward's beguiling manner, combined with his osteopathic training, got him his own way – as it would throughout his life. Among those who discovered his talents was the colonel in charge of the regiment, and Ward was soon running an unofficial clinic from his own Nissen hut. It did not last long. The actual Medical Officer, who was also called Ward, complained, and Stephen Ward was given a commission and transferred to the Medical Corps. He was where he wanted to be, but banned from practising medicine because his qualification had been obtained abroad. The frustrated Ward now started a campaign for the Army to recognise osteopathy.

The young doctor took his fight for acceptance to the
limits, appealing to the very top. He believed, however
naïvely, that an individual could beat the system, that
justice would be obtained if he took his case to higher
authorities. It was a notion that would remain with him
until 1963, when he fired off letters to the Home Secretary
and other public figures. It failed to save Ward then, and it
failed him in the war.

In March 1945, Ward was aboard ship on the beginning
of a posting to India. There were compensations – three
thousand young women on a vessel carrying only three
hundred men. 'The longer it took,' said Ward, 'the happier
we were.' Once in India, and with the war winding down,
Ward was in his element. His prowess at osteopathy won
him friends in exclusive clubs and in Maharajahs' palaces.
When Ward treated Gandhi for a stiff neck, the Indian
leader greeted him with the remark: 'It is strange to have a
visit from a British officer who has not come to arrest me.'
'Pity you didn't twist it right off,' Winston Churchill was to
tell him years later, when he in turn became a patient.

Meanwhile, Ward's tussle with the Army bureaucracy
never ceased. When the Army continued to ignore his
qualifications, and then used him merely to draw anatomic-
al specimens for other doctors, he became obsessional in
his fight to have osteopathy recognised. By the end of his
military service, Ward had appealed to Churchill, and even
to the King – all in vain. Eventually he suffered some sort of
nervous collapse. According to Dr Ellis Stungo, a psychiatrist who knew him in India and later became a good friend
in London, he was shipped home in 'an anxiety state'.

In October 1945, Ward reached England aboard a hospital ship and then spent three days in hospital. When he
was allowed off base to go to art classes at Oxford, he later
confided to a friend, he was accompanied everywhere by a
military policeman. The record shows that Ward was soon
allowed to leave the Army – 'on account of disability'.

Dr Jocelyn Proby, the osteopath who originally encouraged Ward to become a doctor, thinks his protégé was
seriously disturbed during this period. He believes Ward

'may have attempted suicide'. Dr Stungo knows of no suicide attempt at this time, but knew from first-hand experience of one a few years later. If Proby is right about the 1945 attempt, it was the start of a trend. Ward's was a fragile ego, and his reaction to rejection was always extreme. Serious instability was hiding beneath the smiling charmer the world saw as Stephen Ward. Jocelyn Proby, who liked Ward and continued to help him, was one of the first to understand this. With hindsight, he describes a man who remained 'utterly irresponsible and emotionally immature, someone who could not settle down and was largely ruled by the impulse of the perverse'.

In 1946, with Proby's help, Ward began to practise as an osteopath in London. At first he was employed by the Osteopathic Association's clinic at Dorset Square. His starting salary was ten pounds a week; his clients those not wealthy enough to go to a private consultant.

Ward was not patient for long in this humble post, but not only because of the lowly pay. 'I believe that in medicine, as in all things,' he was to say, 'you finish up as you start. If you want to finish up at the top, you've got to start at the top. Get one or two good patients and, if you're any good, you'll soon be treating nobody but top people.'

The man with the impulse of the perverse was on his way.

TWO

PYGMALION AND THE POPSIES

One morning in 1946, a few months after Ward began working in London, the telephone rang at the Dorset Square clinic. He happened to answer the call and found himself talking to an official at the American Embassy. The official wanted the name of an American-trained osteopath, 'the best in town', to treat an important dignitary.

Ward grabbed the opportunity. 'Our best man is Dr Stephen Ward,' he told the caller. 'I'll get him to phone back.' After a pause, during which he arranged to borrow a consulting-room at a smart Park Lane address, Ward fixed an appointment. The important patient turned out to be the American ambassador in London, Averell Harriman. 'He told me he always visited an osteopath every week,' Ward wrote. 'It was the only thing that kept him going . . . I decided to let him in on my prank. He thought it was a terrific joke.'

Years later, at the height of the Profumo Affair, Harriman was to say he could 'not recall' his treatment by Ward. This, though, was at a time when all Ward's famous acquaintances were running for cover. The American ambassador to London in 1963, David Bruce, accepted as a fact that Ward had treated Harriman – as one of his diary entries shows. Ward always spoke of Harriman with gratitude. He 'dropped my name in high places,' he said, 'and soon I began to get private patients.'

'He was very clever, very knowledgeable, and he was

considered a good and talented osteopath, rightly much sought after.' So says Dr William McClurg, and his comment is typical of several osteopaths and doctors we asked about Stephen Ward. Shortly after the Harriman visit, Ward took over a practice in Cavendish Square, just round the corner from Harley Street. 'Pretty soon,' he later said proudly, 'my patients included King Peter of Yugoslavia, several maharajahs, six members of the Churchill family, Elizabeth Taylor, Ava Gardner, Danny Kaye, Frank Sinatra, Mary Martin, Mel Ferrer and dozens more. My appointment books read like the invitation lists to film premières.'

Ward treated Winston Churchill a dozen times at his home. 'He hopped out of bed to get on to my portable treatment table,' the osteopath remembered, 'forgetting that he was wearing only the top half of his pyjamas.' Ward and the former Prime Minister seem to have got on well: they discussed their mutual interest in painting and Churchill showed Ward some of his canvases. Ward's name had been recommended to the great man, he said, by his daughter, Diana Duncan Sandys.

Ward lived above his consulting rooms, in a large first-floor flat. For the next two years it became open house for his friends, including a procession of young women. One became Ward's second real love. This was Eunice Bailey, a red-headed beauty from Bexleyheath who went on to marry the son of Sir Harry Oakes, the millionaire victim in a famous Caribbean murder case. Rejection by Bailey was a shattering blow for Ward. Probably for the second time, he tried to commit suicide.

Ward was rescued by the friend he now called 'Pops', psychiatrist Dr Ellis Stungo, after taking an overdose of barbiturates. Stungo administered a lifesaving injection, and Ward woke up in the Middlesex Hospital. The psychiatrist, who admired Ward professionally and liked him personally, thought this more of a cry for sympathy than a serious attempt to kill himself.

In the summer of 1949, at the age of thirty-six, Ward got married, to a twenty-one year old model and former beauty queen, Patricia Baines. It was a calculated decision, for by now Ward was collecting women the way some men collect butterflies. 'I decided at the very first meeting that I wanted her,' Ward·later reminisced. 'I worked it out quite calmly. She would grace the practice. She would be useful. She was also desirable.' The new wife, according to a friend, bore an astonishing physical resemblance to Ward himself.

There were rows even on the honeymoon in Paris, and it was an unhappy couple who headed back for England on the boat train. The marriage was over, bar the legalities, within six weeks. Years later the former Mrs Ward said, 'I was desperately unhappy with him. He was virtually a stranger to me, and he was a very unhappy man. But he did have a lot of charm. I think basically he was in conflict with himself most of the time . . . I was left at home while Stephen was out socialising.'

For his part, Ward said of the marriage: 'She was always wanting things, and pretty soon I couldn't stand the sight of her. Soon she had divorced me on the grounds of adultery, which wasn't difficult.'

Michael Eddowes, a wealthy former solicitor who will later play a role in this story, met Ward at the time of his marriage. Now in his eighties, Eddowes offers a hilarious and revealing anecdote on the episode that brought Ward's marriage to an abrupt halt. 'Ward,' says Eddowes, 'always had a penchant for street-walkers. He was always disappearing from the flat where they lived, for a couple of hours at a time, and Pat didn't know what he was up to. One evening she decided to find out and hid in the back of the car – the boot opened into a sort of jump-seat. When the car stopped she jumped out, to find Ward chatting up a prostitute!'

The end to this sad tale is provided by the actor Jon Pertwee, later to become 'Dr Who' in the famous television series, who was a loyal friend to Ward from the forties until Ward's death in 1963. Ward's enraged wife, he relates, 'came out over the back of the car like an avenging angel, and practically gave Stephen a heart attack. The poor prostitute fled in a state of terror, and fire and brimstone was poured on his head.'

Ward had always patronised prostitutes. Now, with the vast London market in girls at his disposal, whores became a very regular diversion – some would think it an obsession. Michael Eddowes remembers visiting Ward at his flat on an evening when several other men were drinking there. 'Ward disappeared out,' he says, 'and returned thirty minutes later with a couple of real tarts. He put one in the consulting room and one in the bedroom, then disappeared into the consulting room and came out a few minutes later, laughing and doing up his flies. He then went into the bedroom and, presumably, had the other one too.'

The prosecuting counsel at Ward's 1963 trial was to call him 'a thoroughly immoral man'. It was a hypocritical slight, for tens of thousands of men, now as then, regularly seek sex for hire. Prominent amongst them, not least because they can afford it, are the well-heeled upper-class customers daily seen ducking into red-lit doorways from Mayfair to Soho. It was the exposure of the carnal antics of some of those customers, though not triggered by Ward, that was to lead to his eventual ruin. What set Ward apart from the rest was his dedication to the sport of sex, his sheer resourcefulness in always having a girl on hand – whether pretty protégée or professional whore. It was a facility that made him the toast of hundreds of well-placed London males.

'I suppose I have been one of the most successful men in London with girls since the war,' Ward said with relish in his memoir. 'I am the proof that you don't have to be handsome or rich to get the best girls. My technique has been never to force them. Just be gentle, interested, and they come . . .' That was the boast, but – as friends noticed increasingly, especially after his rejection in love and marriage – intercourse itself was not a priority.

'I don't think he was interested in sex *per se*,' says Jon Pertwee. 'He was fascinated by women, fascinated by sex, but not particularly by the act. One of his girlfriends

complained rather bitterly that he treated her like a piece of
wood . . . As a lover he was a disappointment.'

From now on, though he had affectionate relationships
with some women, most became commodities to Stephen
Ward. A great number of them would be prostitutes, or
close to it. 'He was what we call passively aggressive,' says
Dr Stungo. 'He was like a spoilt child who gets his way, in
Ward's case thanks to his charm . . . without regard to
convention, propriety or suitability.'

Dr Stungo had no small experience of the sex habits of
the famous – one of his patients was Errol Flynn, another
Judy Garland. Though Ward was not his patient, he
thought him something of a voyeur, one who cheerfully
owned up to his fetishes. This distinguished Ward from so
many of his English fellows, for he indulged his kinks and
admitted to enjoying them. He had a special fixation about
legs and loved to have a girl pose in underwear, stockings
and suspenders, and high-heeled shoes.

Ward was a keen photographer and accumulated a large
collection of photographs, some just 'girlie' pictures, some
blatantly pornographic. Most of the pornography showed
straightforward sexual intercourse, but Dr Stungo remembers that one set of photographs showed a girl grinding her
stiletto heel into a young man's penis. Those pictures
particularly excited Ward. Another friend, antique dealer
Hod Dibben, recalls Ward indulging his shoe fetish at a
party. 'One thing he liked,' says Dibben, 'was to have a
high-heeled shoe tied around his nose.'

In psychiatric terms, an individual like Ward gradually
becomes more attached to the idea, or to the symbol of sex
– as expressed in the pictures – than he or she is to the
reality of the partner. The longer Ward indulged, the less
he was interested in real live women, and the more intense
his passion for the bizarre.

The easiest way to satisfy such a need is through prostitutes, which is not to say that Ward treated them badly. The
contrary was true. Their services aside, he liked the company of whores and befriended many. According to Dr

Stungo, if Ward saw a loitering prostitute on the street being hustled by the police, he would rush up with an 'I'm sorry I'm late dear' to get them out of trouble. He became something of a connoisseur, as Jon Pertwee says: 'Stephen had a fascination for prostitutes . . . he used to pick them up and talk to them. He used to drive around the park in his car, pick up a girl and sit her in his car, smoke a cigarette and talk to her . . . find out why she did it and all that sort of thing. He was fascinated by the subject.'

Ward fancied himself as an amateur psychiatrist and admired the girls who were good at their trade. 'They knew more than any psychologist what was needed by certain types of men,' he told Warwick Charlton. 'These girls accepted sex as sex. To them it was a job. Whippings, beatings, the lot – what did it matter to them? I really believe they felt they were performing just as good and necessary a service as a doctor. Perhaps, indeed, they were.'

Ward's apartment at Cavendish Square, with its spacious old-world rooms, became the venue for much partying. Often these were impromptu affairs – Ward's osteopath mentor, Jocelyn Proby, on a visit to London one night, was woken by Stephen erupting into the flat at three in the morning with a bevy of girls from the Windmill Theatre.

Ward earned well enough, but was usually broke. When he gave a party, guests were expected to bring their own bottle. He would supply the glasses and perhaps the tonic for the gin. He himself never drank hard liquor. Dr Stungo, again, remembers dining at the RAC Club with Ward and two female companions – Joan Collins, today's star of *Dynasty*, and her sister Jackie, the best-selling author of sex sagas. When the bill came, Stungo had to pay, because Ward had left his wallet at home.

Dr Stungo hastens to say that Ward was not a sponger: he was simply not sufficiently well-off to 'stand his whack' along with the rich men he was making his friends. A journalist friend, Frederic Mullally, puts it down to the young osteopath's 'heavy overheads – and a chronic reluctance to have the thrill of the chase constrained by excessive hours working over obese matrons' vertebrae'. Since the outward appearance – good suits and a fast car at the kerb – belied this truth, Ward quickly became known as one of the tightest men in town.

'Ward's objective was esteem,' says Dr Stungo. 'He wanted to impress his acquaintances and be accepted in society.' Ward found himself accepted, and quickly, thanks to his osteopathic and artistic skills. These twin keys brought him both distinguished and raffish friends. One of the latter was the portrait artist Vasco Lazzolo, who had met Ward at the end of the war, in Oxford, where Lazzolo was at the Slade School of Art.

'Latin' Lazzolo came to his role as society artist after years of commercial art in Soho, when one of his mistresses married into the aristocracy. He was, like Ward, in his mid-thirties, and he shared many of Ward's characteristics – not least the predilection for young women and prostitutes, and the world of show business.

Ward was often called to the Hippodrome Theatre, off Leicester Square, to look after dancers with pulled muscles. Michael Bentine of *Goon Show* fame, who had heard of Ward's reputation as 'the best physio in town', met him at the theatre. He remembers Ward as 'a very handsome man, with his black hair combed back very tightly, and smelling eternally of aftershave. He was a charming person, a very good conversationalist and witty . . .'

His two closest friends, though, apart from Lazzolo, were both photographers. There was Anthony Beauchamp, born Entwhistle, who married Sir Winston Churchill's actress daughter, Sarah. He was currently breaking through into top-flight portrait photography, and at first spent a good deal of his time in the United States. He preferred the London nightlife, though, and it was there that he and Ward became close. 'Like me,' Ward said, 'he knew no barriers of class in his relationships with men and women. He took his friends from all walks of life.' Beauchamp's wife Sarah remembered his catholic tastes in another way, as his 'wild, insubstantial infidelities'.

The other photographer in Ward's life, who had by far the greatest influence, was known simply as Baron. Born Baron Nahum of Italian ancestry, he used a studio above Lazzolo's in Belgravia. He had come to prominence before the war and, as Court photographer and bright light of the London scene, became a legend. His success was assured when, with the support of Louis Mountbatten, he began taking pictures of the Royal Family.

Ward deliberately cultivated Baron and became a familiar visitor at his unpretentious flat in Brick Street, off Piccadilly. 'I knew he was on the way up,' the osteopath recalled. 'Everyone seemed to know him, and I felt I had a certain rapport with him.' One reason Ward knew he was on the way up was the identity of two of Baron's close friends – the young Battenberg cousins, David, Marquess of Milford Haven, and Prince Philip of Greece, the present Duke of Edinburgh.

The twenty-five-year-old Prince came to London after the war to stay at the Belgravia home of his uncle and mentor, Louis Mountbatten, and renewed a childhood friendship with the Marquess of Milford Haven. Now, running around town in Philip's red MG sports car, the two young men sowed their wild oats.

In 1946, it was Baron who dreamed up the Thursday Club, which for years afterwards convened for lunch on that day of the week in a private upstairs room at Wheeler's Oyster Bar in Soho's Old Compton Street. The meal was a ritual of oysters and lobster claws, washed down with copious quantities of champagne and Guinness. One member, *Daily Express* editor Arthur Christiansen, was seen to drink the champagne out of one of his own shoes. The membership included the Battenberg cousins and Iain Macleod, who was to be Leader of the House of Commons at the time of the Profumo Affair. Also members were the artists Vasco Lazzolo and Felix Topolski, Baron's barrister brother Jack, Pip Youngman Carter, editor of *Tatler*, Sam Boal, *New York Post* correspondent, and, from the world of show business, Peter Ustinov, actors James Robertson Justice and Michael Trubshawe, Gilbert Hard-

ing and Larry Adler, the harmonica player. The Knightsbridge solicitor Michael Eddowes, who was to play an
interesting role during the Profumo scandal, also belonged
to the Club.

Stephen Ward was not a full-time member, but a frequent guest and associate of almost all those who were.
One of them, Felix Topolski, remembers airily, 'I have a
drawing of Ward having intercourse with a woman.'

The Thursday Club was a strictly male affair. Lunch, a
euphemism for a booze-up that often lasted into the evening hours, was the occasion for the telling of long, funny,
and often bawdy, stories. A Club rule dictated that Baron
himself, though one of London's best raconteurs, was
never allowed to finish his stories. Each month, the members elected one member 'Cunt of the Month', honouring
the man who had made the biggest fool of himself in recent
weeks.

Ward's friend Anthony Beauchamp was keeper of the
Club records, a set of visitors' books filled with the *bon
mots*, yarns and caricatures that kept the membership in
belly laughs down the years. According to Fleet Street
artist member, Tony Wyzard, the books were 'very near
the knuckle. Whatever the main topic of conversation, the
scandals of the day and so on, people would write relevant
verse and I would provide the illustrations. Not for publication, as you can imagine!' Ward's other intimate friend,
Vasco Lazzolo, became custodian of the records when
Beauchamp died, until they were finally transferred to the
safety of a bank vault.

There was a Friday Club, too, founded by Savoy Hotel
press officer Jean Nicol after Thursday Club drinking left
Baron and the Marquess of Milford Haven too plastered to
turn up for one of her cocktail parties. The glamorous Nicol
was married to intelligence officer Derek Tangye, who at
that time headed the MI5 section charged with 'monitoring
the mood of people in influential circles'. His wife, he later
wrote, was 'an important link in the chain of my work'. Ward
was a friend of Nicol's. He also frequented the Steering
Wheel Club, nominally a watering hole for motor racing

aficionados but also home to a much wider clientele, including the last woman to be hanged in Britain, Ruth Ellis, and her racing driver lover David Blakely. The film-star, Douglas Fairbanks Jr, whose name would come up years later at Ward's trial on prostitution charges, was another regular, as were a number of MI5 officers.

Clubmanship aside, the members of this fraternity became celebrated for their party-giving. The gossip columns regularly reported the parties held by Baron at his Piccadilly flat. He later gave others, that went unreported. Those, as Vasco Lazzolo was to recall, were wild affairs, some attended by 'girls dressed only in Masonic aprons'. Ward was a regular at Baron's parties.

Association with the Thursday Club circle must have proved embarrassing to Prince Philip when his wife Elizabeth became Queen in 1952. He was on the organising committee and a regular dinner guest at Baron's flat. Through Baron, Philip found himself backstage at the Hippodrome Theatre, being introduced to singer Pat Kirkwood, whom Michael Bentine describes as a 'gorgeous, uninhibited, outgoing Northern lass'. Baron was in love with Kirkwood for years, but his passion was unrequited.

After the Coronation, there were rumours about Philip's past, of his alleged affairs and of wild goings-on with his Thursday Club cronies. One of those who had met Philip in the forties was Stephen Ward, and the Prince apparently attended one, and possibly two, of the parties Ward threw at his flat in Cavendish Square. In his memoir, Ward drily mentions Philip's appearance at one of the parties 'with a very attractive girl called Mitzi Taylor'. Taylor was a Canadian model, whom Baron had often photographed. Dr Stungo says he met Prince Philip at Ward's place on a couple of occasions, and Michael Eddowes also remembers Philip being present – the Prince danced with Eddowes' wife.

Stephen Ward liked to say he knew Prince Philip, but sneered a bit when expounding on high society to Warwick Charlton, shortly before his death. 'I've always found them schoolboyish,' he said of Philip's jokes. 'I don't see much fun in turning hoses on photographers and that sort of thing. You see, the superior person should never do that. It is part of the rules that only small fry may take liberties, and balancing the degree of liberty and daring is the whole art of the business. Usually the big people know this and play up to the people who do it cleverly. Philip wants to hold the stage himself. He acts like a little person when in fact he should try to be a big person . . . That's how society works.'

Philip's cousin, David, Marquess of Milford Haven, knew Ward very well indeed. The Marquess cut a lurid path through London society in the forties and fifties, and his intimacy with Prince Philip caused tremors of panic at Buckingham Palace in years to come.

The Marquess of Milford Haven once gave Ward one of the moments he pathetically coveted, to 'make a break-through' in society. The setting was an open-air luncheon at Les Ambassadeurs, in Park Lane. 'I knew,' said Ward, 'that one could never afford not to be noticed at these events . . . How to be bright and yet not put one's foot in it? That was the problem. David was talking about shaving. I remember he thought shaving a bit of a bore, and to demonstrate the point he fingered a small cut on his chin. He said he had cut it that very morning. Suddenly I said, without thinking, "Well, what are you worrying about – wasn't it blue?" . . . Everyone thought it was very funny and even David smiled. So that was it, I told myself. The moment. The moment when everyone laughs at something you said . . . You will certainly be remembered as the man who dared to say something daring to someone like Milford Haven . . .'

The Marquess of Milford Haven was thoughtless enough, from the Royal Family's point of view, to marry a Mrs Simpson, like the Duchess of Windsor – by comic coincidence – an American divorcée. A Mexican divorce followed, and he then set up house with the Hungarian actress Eva Bartok.

After leaving the Marquess, Eva Bartok wrote bitterly of the 'misuse of sex' and of wanting to marry a man who 'is not guilty of the frightful sin of having lost his birthright, his title – the only title I respect – a human being. Someone who is not an empty shell in a human shape . . .' In the mid-fifties, Milford Haven played host at specially organised sex parties in Mayfair. Selected men would be invited to the Marquess' flat at 35–37 Grosvenor Square. The evening would begin with card-playing and then, when the drink had flowed for a good while, girls would be brought in. Then the betting would be on the women, in games with names like 'Chase the Bitch' and 'Find the Lady'. Winners won the obvious prize – intercourse in one of the luxurious bedrooms. According to Brian McConnell, former *People* reporter who investigated the stories, several of the girls were brought to the flat by Stephen Ward.

According to Warwick Charlton, a number of prominent people attended other early sex parties. One was a member of the Royal Family, another became a Conservative MP. Vasco Lazzolo and the photographer Baron were also participants. So also, though perhaps later on, was the American singer Bing Crosby.

The Marquess and Stephen Ward shared an intense interest in pornography. The Marquess had inherited one of the largest private collections of pornography in the world. Along with a multitude of books, there were seven albums of erotica, some embossed with the Milford Haven family crest. Album 7 – described by former Curator Dr Eric Dingwall as 'Leaflets, booklets . . . advertising dirty books, tickler condoms, dildoes, photographs and so on' – ended up in the Private Case at the British Museum when, shortly before the Profumo scandal broke, the Marquess decided to get rid of the family collection. Two other albums were acquired by the University of Texas, while yet more material reached the British Museum thanks to the Profumo Affair and a friend of Stephen Ward.

According to Dr Dingwall, police raided the homes of several of Ward's friends at the height of the Profumo Affair in 1963. One of them was Beecher Moore, a wealthy American who had lived in London for many years. The dawn raid at his home was a heavy-handed affair which reportedly included threats that Moore's wife might be charged with running a call-girl racket. Although there was no foundation to such a charge, Moore was much alarmed by the invasion and donated his erotica to the British Museum. Some of it has been retained, some passed on to the Kinsey Institute in the United States.

The police also descended on Vasco Lazzolo. He too had erotica, but later said with satisfaction, 'I didn't, of course, keep any of the pornographic drawings there. They were elsewhere, thank God. The police said it wouldn't look good if the man who was painting Prince Philip had anything to do with a scandal.' Lazzolo had been commissioned to paint the Prince's portrait at the time the Profumo Affair broke, and had also painted the Queen. No doubt he recalled an earlier occasion, when he and Milford Haven had visited the French Riviera. Prince Philip, on the Royal yacht anchored off-shore, is said to have snorted when Lazzolo phoned to suggest he come aboard with Milford Haven. 'Not him!' sighed the Prince. 'I've got enough problems already.'

Stephen Ward maintained his own collection of pornography, mostly photographs. In 1986, after a complex series of telephone calls that led to a meeting on Liverpool Street Station with a 'Mr Melton', we were shown many of these Ward pictures. Melton produced enough information to satisfy us that the photographs were the genuine article, and some of Ward's girls are clearly identifiable. Some of the photographs, with alterations for decency's sake, are published in this book.

In 1956, Baron, the man who had given Ward his entrée to high society, died. This death, and that of the playboy photographer Anthony Beauchamp, was a blow to the osteopath. He tried to fill the gap by becoming more of a party-giver himself. For years now he had been exploring the possibilities of sex parties and recruiting girls he could supply for them. Ward was laying the foundations for the disasters of 1963.

Ward's first introduction to full-scale orgies, he said, had been 'a rather amateurish affair in Hampstead. There was abandon all right, and the sight of naked bodies all over the room . . . It was at this gathering that I met for the first time one of the more determined organisers of these parties in London. I was standing rather bemused when he came up to me and said, "If you are surprised at this, come round to my flat one day and be really amazed." This was temptation and I went.'

'The only excuse I can make', Ward claimed 'is that I really was curious in a sort of detached way. I would be a humbug if I did not confess that I looked forward to it too. There was the start of one of the strangest experiences of my life . . . Looking back one sees how easy it is to be drawn into a situation out of simply weakness, to be horrified to start with and later to accept it all as normal behaviour or nearly so.'

'These parties,' Ward continued, 'nearly all started in the same way, a few drinks, rather formal introductions, and one or other of the girls would start the ball rolling . . . It was always the girls that seemed most eager – usually one would offer to do a strip-tease or a belly dance. That was enough. Someone would then suggest what was called "costumation", which was dressing up in a scanty loincloth, a pretence of fancy dress but in reality a "clearing of the decks for action".'

They could last for days: 'One could go to a party like this on Saturday, go home and come back to the same scene on Monday with very few of the personnel changed. How was it achieved? I found out at about the third one I went to. I came across the host grinding up pills in a bowl which he put into everything we drank, whether it was gin, whisky, or just coffee. Benzedrine or Methedrine was used . . .'

At one Belgravia party, hosted by the man Ward had originally met in Hampstead, the telephone went wrong. The host, evidently no longer thinking straight, threw a message out of the window, begging whoever might pick it up to call the telephone engineers. He wanted to use the telephone to send for more recruits for the party. An alarmed passer-by duly called the police, who found themselves confronted by a naked girl at the front door. 'It's girls we want, not men,' she snapped and slammed the door.

Ward liked to play the psychiatrist and was still doing so when he wrote his memoir at the height of the Profumo Affair. 'The people involved,' he said of the parties, 'never forced any situation . . . the married couples were invariably happy and contented. Possibly this open infidelity prevented anything being hidden and consequently removed one of the biggest obstacles to happy marriage normally encountered . . . I have never known a couple involved to split up or go off with anyone else. Curious but true . . . I have seen well-known psychiatrists at these parties . . . The other thing, of course, was that a lot of the people were not sexually normal, and such parties allowed them to indulge in anything their mood dictated.'

At two points in the memoir Ward proceeded, without naming names, to describe parties devoted to masochism and sadism. 'I remember one dinner party,' he said, 'where all round the room were girls and men tied and gagged in various attitudes and they so remained during the entire meal. Suffering was an essential part of their enjoyment. No cruelty was done – I myself never saw any cruelty, though I certainly heard of it being practised . . .'

'It is a kind of ritual sado-masochism,' Ward explained. 'One of the most noticeable things about these people is the high standard of intelligence among them . . . rather like an intellectual cocktail party. The ceremonies usually started as follows – a large collection of chairs, straps and apparently fierce instruments would be produced and laid out in a formal manner on a low table. A beautiful girl would step forward and remove her clothes. The master, as he was called, would sit on a kind of throne. The girl would kneel before him and kiss his feet . . . finally she would be dressed in a wide, studded black leather belt, high-heeled black shoes and straps around her wrists, neck and ankles, and each time they were offered to her master a ritual punishment was administered. Finally, long bars were fastened to hooks in the straps . . . in such a way that the legs were widely separated . . . and a gag was placed in her mouth. Drinks would now be brought and the secured girl would be left lying or standing while the guests stood around discussing the finer points . . . When this was over everyone looked normal again . . . There we were back at a normal cocktail party again.'

Then there were the satanic rituals: 'At one such party in Kensington, there was a huge and obscene priapic emblem in the middle of the room. All the girls, and there were about a dozen, knelt down round it and made obeisance . . . the spontaneous way in which it was done made me realise they had all done it many times before . . .'

Who were these people? According to Ward they were 'quite normal' individuals. 'Of necessity, most of them are attractive . . . The men tend to be older than the girls who are nearly all very beautiful . . . Many of them are rich and many famous – many faces that are seen in public life and on television. If their public could only see them like this!'

'The two lives of Stephen Ward gave him knowledge of many secrets,' his friend Warwick Charlton has said, 'for many highly placed men shared his sexual likings . . . He participated in the pleasures of his circle and that circle was suitably wide . . . He gained confidences from his patients in his consulting room . . . If a few patients had their sexual needs attended to at the same time, by way of a few little parties and introductions, well, that was life, wasn't it?'

By the mid-fifties, that was indeed Ward's life, one that gave a new impetus to his habit of marking out girls as another man marks his race-card. Increasingly, he concentrated on the cultivation of women to his own special design.

In 1963 Ward would be dubbed a Pygmalion. The label, of course, was given because of the London stage-show, *My Fair Lady*, but the classical Greek original was a god who carved a statue of a maiden, and then fell in love with his own creation. Ward no longer fell in love with his discoveries – nor did his relationships necessarily include sex. He genuinely liked women as people and he continued to have purely affectionate friendships with many.

A Ward protégée in the fifties was one Anita Wimble, a taximan's daughter from Essex. A well-endowed young woman, still remembered for going bra-less in a succession of angora sweaters, she came to London at the age of fifteen. Somewhere along the line she got a part in a Tommy Trinder revue, changed her name to Pat Marlowe and met Stephen Ward. 'I've decided on my career,' she was to say, 'I'm just going to get rich.' Under Ward's tutelage, she succeeded.

Marlowe now forgot about being an actress and plunged into the high life. The word jet-setter had hardly been invented before she was flying endlessly to New York and Hollywood, to Paris and Monte Carlo. Prince Aly Khan, producer Jack Warner, and Billy Wallace – Princess Margaret's escort of the day – were her friends. She had use of a Manhattan apartment when Mike Todd was in town, made news when she stripped off at one of Warner's parties in Monte Carlo, and held parties for prominent homosexuals in London. She had flings with Ward's friends – one, she claimed, with Lord Astor, and one with the lusty old bandleader Jack Hylton. She had a baby by entertainer Max Bygraves, who recently admitted paying Marlowe £10,000 to keep quiet. The child was a boy, and Marlowe named him Stephen.

Millionaires used Marlowe as a front for projects they did not want to be publicly associated with, and the press described her as 'the shrewdest businesswoman in the West End'. Ward had helped her to become rich, but not to be happy. In August 1962, not long before the Profumo scandal, Marlowe was found dead in bed at her Mayfair flat. The man who found her, one of her homosexual friends, said, 'Pat talked to me yesterday about Marilyn Monroe. She knew her well . . . from Hollywood . . . said she could understand why she did it.' Monroe had died just a couple of days earlier, like Marlowe, from an overdose of barbiturates.

'There are always these silly girls around,' Ward told reporter Peter Earle, 'who take some pills, have a drink, and then forget they have taken them, and so take some more.' Ward's girls were to be of a pattern. Most were long-legged and – with the odd exception, like Mandy Rice-Davies – ample-bosomed. They usually came from a lower-middle or working-class background. Ward would teach them how to speak and eat correctly, and even how to improve their sexual technique. Speaking properly was especially important, for Ward wanted his girls to be acceptable in London society. Like Professor Higgins, he taught them how to iron out their working-class accents.

Girl after girl was now to come off the Ward production line, little painted statues fashioned in coffee-bar conversations and late-night drives. Frederic Mullally, Ward's journalist friend, remembers 'a constant self-renewing flow of them, passing through that benevolently bogus *ashram* in Devonshire Street* . . . Most, when they took shelter there, were nonentities. At a personal count – and I was too often away from England to know the true score – three of them went on to titled marriages in England or on the Continent, five to international fame as actresses or top models, and four found sterling-millionaire or dollar-millionaire husbands . . .'

The prototype, in about 1952, had been a girl called Vicki Martin, whom Ward met on the streets – the easiest place to find a girl in London in those days.

'I met Vicki in a shower of rain at Marble Arch,' he recalled in his memoir. 'Blonde with large eyes set wide apart, and with probably the most exquisite smile you have ever seen, revealing perfect teeth. I used to try to keep her laughing just to see it . . .'

The osteopath had no difficulty persuading Martin to take a taxi with him to his flat. There he dried her hair by the fire and dressed her in clothes left behind by his ex-wife. After several years, he had still not got rid of them. He

---

*Ward had moved his practice from Cavendish Square to Devonshire Street.

discovered that her real name was Valerie Mewes, that she was not yet twenty and the product of a broken home in Staines, Middlesex. She had left school at fourteen, tried nursing and then been diverted by dreams of becoming a film star. At seventeen she was in London, working as a hostess at the Court Club in Mayfair.

The Court Club was known as a fashionable nightspot, but it was the next thing to a brothel. Its owner was known as the 'monster with the Mayfair touch', who expected the girls to sleep with the customers. A mix of the English upper class and racketeers, they 'looked after' the girls who did. Ruth Ellis turns up again in the story here, for she was a hostess at the club and Vicki Martin's best friend. They made trips together to the country to stay with Ellis's men friends, and milked the wealthy ones for money and gifts. Martin was young, but no innocent.

Stephen Ward told her she could do better, and she stayed with him for more than a year. He did not sleep with her at first, and may have not have done so ever. He was truthful enough when he said, 'I really do love girls for themselves and not purely for a sexual reason . . . I have always tried to help them along – often with very good results.'

The result, for Martin, was a quick breakthrough as a model. She posed for Court photographer Baron in 1956 – the year he died – and Vasco Lazzolo painted her portrait around the time he undertook a commission to paint the Queen. Soon, groomed and coached by her Pygmalion, Martin was being invited to high-society dinners and parties. Her name began to appear in the gossip columns, and she was dubbed the 'Golden Girl'.

Soon one of Martin's lovers, a well-known and wealthy man, undertook to set her up in a Mayfair flat. When he reneged on the agreement, Ward brought pressure on the man to pay up, or be exposed in the courts. The money came through. Then the Golden Girl thought she had really struck gold, with one of Stephen's Indian friends, the Maharajah of Cooch Behar. There was travel, much jewellery and talk of marriage – until the Maharajah discovered that marrying a non-Indian would mean forfeiting his princely allowance.

Martin loved fast cars. She had hobnobbed with Ward's friends at the Steering Wheel Club, and made headlines with the Maharajah in 1956, when he crashed at high speed in Hertfordshire. That same year, in another car, at four in the morning on the Maidenhead road, she died in a head-on collision. Hundreds of people attended her funeral, including the Marquess of Milford Haven. 'One man well-known in London', Ward was to say, 'was so overcome he had to go into a nursing home.' Ward himself went to visit her relatives, and did so for years afterwards.

Ward was saddened by Martin's death, but she was replaced by another girl, then another, and yet others. With her he had set a trend, and a dangerous one, for in truth Martin was, if not a whore, a tramp verging on whoredom. Ward felt no guilt and saw no peril.

As a fellow osteopath, Dr William McClurg, says, 'Ward had no necessity for financial gain from girls. He earned well, and was busy.' Dr Stungo is emphatic: 'He never lived off the girls or ran a call-girl service. He often had three or four girls staying at his place, because he was so generous and wanted to help people.'

Dr Stungo himself once experienced exactly the sort of Ward introduction that would one day have the lawyers bickering over the fine line between poncing and putting a pretty woman a friend's way.

'Shortly after my divorce,' he says, 'Ward phoned me one evening and asked if I was doing anything. I said I wasn't and Ward said that in that case he was sending over a young girl, a "popsy", because he, Ward, had been called out.'

Had Dr Stungo accepted the offer, and then 'looked after' the girl when she left his bed, the law – as interpreted in the 1963 trial – might have judged her a prostitute. And if she gave some of the money to Ward, it could have been said he was living on immoral earnings. They might even have said that of Ward and his first Golden Girl.

'When she was broke,' Warwick Charlton said of Vicki

Martin, 'Stephen sometimes lent her money. When she was affluent she would repay him or make some contribution towards their joint living expenses. It did not occur to Stephen that there was anything wrong in this.'

It did not occur to anyone, until 1963. 'The accusation that he was this sort of monster who lived off the immoral earnings of women, as far as I could see,' says Ward's friend Michael Pertwee, 'was the most abject rubbish . . . though it would be wrong to paint him in any way as an admirable figure . . . He was known as a man who knew a lot of pretty girls. He was a snob and a social climber, and this was a passport into the kind of circle he liked . . . He was, if you like, a social pimp.'

The girls themselves, says Frederic Mullally, all loved Ward, 'as a girl might love an elder brother or a father . . . Stephen used girls. But he never abused them, which is more than can be said for many of his betters. In Stephen's London – then as today – young girls were pressing their noses to windows screening the merchandise of luxury and fame. Stephen's sin was to show them the way in from the cold. That he enjoyed himself in the process, that he flourished in the sensual hothouse of a home forever strewn with discarded nylons, lip-printed tissues, cosmetic debris, these were the bounties of a prodigious expenditure of enthusiasm and compassion on the female sex.'

In the oddest way, Vicki Martin was a marker for the quicksand of Ward's future. Three years after her death, when Martin's name came up in conversation, another young protégée would exclaim, 'I was at school with her sister!' The girl's name was Christine Keeler.

But these were still the fifties. A young Queen was on the throne, and post-war England had only just begun to feel the soft touch of affluence. Those who felt it first, as always, were those already at the top of the social pile. One day, an MI5 officer was to write in a report, 'From what I hear of Ward and his dealings with women and his enormous circle of friends, I strongly suspect that he is the provider of popsies for rich people.' This was precisely accurate and, for many years, it suited everyone nicely.

THREE

OSTEOPATH BY APPOINTMENT –
WOOING THE ASTORS

'Stephen was a specialist in lost souls, and Bill Astor was a lost soul.' So says David, the brother of Lord William Waldorf Astor, the third Viscount – most definitely a rich person, and one who encountered any number of Ward's popsies. For the boy from a 'minor' public school, Ward's entrée to the Astor family was the most important single feat in a lifetime of social climbing. It was disastrous social alchemy, a fatal mix that would lead to Ward's death, John Profumo's ruin and dishonour for the house of Astor.

Lord Astor, Bill to those who knew him, inherited his title in 1952, when he became the last of the line to live at Cliveden, the monstrous family home in Buckinghamshire. The family's rise to wealth had begun in the eighteenth century, when a Spanish butcher called Astorga emigrated to Germany. He dropped the 'ga' on the end of the name, and sent his sons to seek their fortune even further afield. They found it. Two went to London to make musical instruments and another to America. In New York, the Astors sold flutes brought from London, started the American Fur Company, became property moguls and ended up almost as rich as the Rothschilds. One of the heirs came to England at the end of the nineteenth century, supposedly hoping for a peerage. Wealth works wonders, and he got one. William Waldorf, who became the first Viscount Astor, bought Cliveden from the Duke of Westminster for nearly ten million pounds at today's value. Not satisfied with that, he also bought Hever Castle in Kent and built a village nearby for the guest overflow.

Bill Astor was the eldest child of the second Viscount and his formidable wife Nancy. Born in 1907, he came to adulthood during the Astors' British heyday. Cliveden, set in four hundred acres, and with the big house overlooking the River Thames, was the scene of lavish entertainment on a scale barely imaginable today. 'Dinners for between fifty and sixty were very frequent,' said a former staff member. 'Two or three balls for anything up to five or six hundred would be given during the season.' There was an army of servants – the garden alone employed fifty men.

The guests at the Astor table, between the wars, included kings and queens, ambassadors and high politicians. One of them, in the thirties, was the man who would be Prime Minister at the time of the Profumo Affair, Harold Macmillan. He was then in his thirties, a World War I veteran and a fledgling MP, recently married to the eldest daughter of the ninth Duke of Devonshire. The Astors' American money brought to Cliveden an aristocratic style that had become virtually extinct after 1918.

Yet some felt uneasy at Cliveden, in the dusk of a summer's evening on the paved terrace overlooking the river. It felt out of place, as though it ought to be in the Mediterranean – but the fireflies and the grasshoppers were missing. 'To live here would be like living on the stage of the Scala theatre in Milan,' wrote diarist Harold Nicolson. 'Its beauty is purely scenic . . . There is a ghastly unreality about it all.' The Astor children had cause to agree.

Bill Astor's parents' view of the world was dominated by the idea of 'doing good'. It was a fine idea, but not necessarily good for their brood of six. The father was a remote figure, and the mother unable to bend the rigid code in which she imprisoned herself. 'She felt it her bounden duty,' said Bill's brother Michael, 'to chastise, in and out of season, those weaknesses and uncertainties that beset young men and women as they begin to grow up . . . Trying to do "bad" . . . I came to discover in myself forces which did not recognise these absolute distinctions.'

The two in the brood whose lives would most entwine with that of Stephen Ward were Bill Astor and Bobbie Shaw, his stepbrother by Lady Astor's first marriage. The latter was programmed for disaster more than all the rest. 'Don't bother about the new baby [Bill],' his mother wrote to a friend, 'look after Bobbie . . .'

Bobbie was the cuckoo in the Astor nest, born to an alcoholic American father, and, of course, with no rights of succession to the Astor peerage. As if to compensate, his mother smothered him with love and cold-shouldered the unfortunate Bill. Bobbie first depended on her to an unnatural extent, then came to resent her. After serving in the trenches in World War I, when he should have gone to university, he entered manhood psychologically maimed. He was handsome as a god, witty and charming – and a human disaster.

The real downward spiral began in 1929, when, at thirty-one, Bobbie was drummed out of the Royal Horse Guards for being drunk on duty. Two years later he was caught committing a homosexual act, and spent four months in prison.

Years later, when Lady Astor was trying to write her autobiography, another son told her the truth would be too horrifying. 'What d'you mean, horrifying?' asked her ladyship. 'Because you are so possessive,' he responded. 'That's why we are all cases of arrested development. Though I admit . . . Bobbie is the only one of us actually to have been arrested.'

To the writer Christopher Sykes, a friend of the family, Bobbie was 'a cynic and secret debauchee'. He remained, all his life, a homosexual and alcoholic. His meeting with Stephen Ward, probably at an osteopathic consultation, led to a long relationship. David Astor remembers his surprise, years later, when Bobbie adamantly refused to accept attention for a poisoned arm from any doctor other than Ward, an osteopath. 'Ward,' says the younger Astor with distaste, 'liked to have people on strings. There was no reason why he should want to control Bobbie, except for the lust for power and influence.'

Some wondered whether Ward himself was homosexual. 'There was a precision about him that seemed significant,' American columnist Dorothy Kilgallen observed during his trial, 'a soft reluctance in the way he used his fine hands. He did not strike me as a man who would be attractive to a woman except as a friend who would be kind and amusing, and always ahead of the game in knowing which Greek island will be fashionable next year . . . They send flowers and thoughtful notes on birthdays, they can be funny or wicked or nice, but they are not usually interested in women in the conventional way. The evidence at the trial, however, indicated that I was wrong, or that there were two sides to the defendant . . .'

Ward was aware of the impression he made. Once, when he was stripped to the waist shaving, Warwick Charlton commented on his soft, pale skin. First Ward made a joke of it. 'You mean my ambidextrous look, eh?' Then he added quickly, 'Hair on the chest isn't a sign of virility, Warwick.' Ronna Riccardo, a prostitute who testified at Ward's trial, said that Ward 'couldn't manage normal sex'.

Ward had numerous male friends whose sex interests were not confined to women. One was Robin Drury, an avowed bisexual, a publicist who 'managed' Ward's protégée Christine Keeler at the time of the scandal. Ward was very close to another bisexual, John Hamilton-Marshall, in the early sixties. He was friendly with Toby Roe, proprietor of the Rockingham, London's first overtly homosexual club.

The travel writer Robert Harbinson, who writes under the name Robin Bryans, knew Ward and Bill Astor's stepbrother Bobbie Shaw for years. Himself bisexual – and disarmingly open about it – he has no doubt that the homosexual society was another of Ward's secret worlds. Harbinson says that Ward took a great interest in the Bloomsbury art set. The osteopath sat as a model for the prominent artist Frank Slater, who in 1953 painted the first portrait of Queen Elizabeth, and Harbinson comments, 'Stephen was a very vain person. That's why he posed for Frank – he was very proud of it.'

Ward also associated with the Scots painters, Robert Colquhoun and Robert Macbryde, familiar kilted figures in Soho, and was a hanger-on in their Bohemian circle. 'It was a very gay group,' Harbinson recalls. 'Not only gay but extremely wild. The sort of orgies that Stephen was supposed to have gone to, these people were there.'

Ward was friendly with the homosexual writer Godfrey Winn. Mandy Rice-Davies, who with Christine Keeler was one of the two female stars of the Profumo Affair, says they were dinner companions. Winn, a poseur and hypocrite, promptly dumped Ward as soon as the scandal broke in 1963 and excoriated him in print.

Thanks to the Astor connection, Bobbie's friends became accessible to Ward, including Sir Malcolm Bullock, Conservative MP and Chairman of the Sadler's Wells Society. Ward now also had friends among homosexuals of influence. He made an important connection in the Very Reverend Monsignor Hugh Montgomery, a controversial churchman who, according to Harbinson, was a lover of the man who eventually became Pope John Paul I.

Ward often met with another of Monsignor Montgomery's male lovers, the very distinguished Sir Gilbert Laithwaite. Laithwaite, who died recently aged ninety-two, was a former British ambassador and a powerful businessman. He was a regular visitor to Cliveden and was especially close to Bobbie Shaw. When Ward knew him, through Bobbie, he was Permanent Under-Secretary of State for Commonwealth Relations. Laithwaite used to invite Ward to the Travellers' Club, of which he was Chairman. There, in that hallowed watering-hole of diplomats and Intelligence officers, Ward and Laithwaite, red carnation in buttonhole, would hold earnest conversations over lunch. Laithwaite was an extreme right-winger, and Ward would goad him to fury with socialist comments.

Ward's Astor relationship had thus moved him into a strange eddy of the social stream, the so-called 'Gay Establishment'. It was the world of upper-class homosexuality, and of the generation that produced Britain's most infamous traitors this century: Burgess, Maclean and

Anthony Blunt. Sir Gilbert Laithwaite was a friend of the by then Sir Anthony Blunt, the highly respected Surveyor of the Queen's Pictures. Monsignor Montgomery's brother Peter was Blunt's lifelong homosexual lover. Robert Harbinson cheerfully admits having sex with Guy Burgess. Ward was at one remove from the enemy within and, as we shall see, was also moving around perfectly loyal people in the world of Intelligence. It was another fateful development, heavy with implications for the scenario of 1963.

Ward was as close to Bill Astor as he was to Bobbie, perhaps closer. Like Bobbie, Astor had had a miserable childhood. 'Though one of the most privileged children in the world,' observed John Grigg, a biographer of Lady Astor, 'he was therefore, in a sense, cruelly disadvantaged and deprived.' He emerged from Eton and Oxford a shy, awkward figure, by no means handsome, with a receding hairline and a baby-face complexion. Pressed into politics by his mother – who was Britain's first female MP – Bill won the Conservative seat of Fulham East in 1935, when he was twenty-eight.

In the Royal Navy, during World War II, Bill Astor served for three years as an Intelligence officer. He was frustrated about being based on land, so his friends nicknamed him 'No Ships'. In his unit, the A Force, he was regarded as an intellectual lightweight. Astor ended his war with numerous Intelligence connections – and they would prove most pertinent to the story of Stephen Ward and the Profumo Affair.

Astor came home to a changed situation. In 1942, with the family's agreement, his father had made over the Cliveden mansion and estate to the National Trust, under an arrangement that opened the place to tourists during holiday periods, but allowed the Astors to remain in residence. Meanwhile, Bill had been distressed to learn that he had been passed over as Chairman of the *Observer* newspaper, a family property, in favour of his brother David.

In 1945, as befitted the man who was to become master of

the house of Astor, Bill was bridegroom at the first lavish, peacetime society wedding. He married Sarah, daughter of Baron Grantley, a prominent film producer. Lord Mountbatten was a family friend, who had hosted Sarah's coming-out party, and Astor's bride was a personal friend of Prince Philip. She had also been very close to Kathleen Kennedy, the sister of the future US President, who had married the son of the tenth Duke of Devonshire.

Astor and his bride were not happy, and their divorce, in 1953, was the latest in a cycle of mounting pressure. His father had died the year previously, making him head of the family and the new Lord Astor. Close at hand, and offering support, was Stephen Ward.

The man who was now Lord Astor had met Ward three years earlier, in 1950, when he went to him for treatment following a hunting accident. The two men became close cronies.

'Bill fell into Ward's clutches,' says his brother David, 'at a time of great vulnerability and distress. Bill had difficulties in human relations. Ward gave Bill psychological support and introduced him to girls.' At the same time, Lord Astor attracted Ward like a magnet. He held the keys to the social kingdom of Cliveden, and threw it open to Stephen Ward.

Many thought that World War II had sounded the death knell of the aristocracy. It was one of many parts of the apparatus of the British state that seemed anachronistic, useless in a modern country. It may well have been both, but the aristocracy refused to lie down. The fifties saw the great houses still open and the company of lords and ladies the bench-mark of social success. As the decade wore on, seven years of Conservative rule kept them at the top of the social hierarchy. This was the Indian summer of the nobility, and Stephen Ward basked in its warmth. It began, for him, with dinner invitations to Cliveden.

'The Visitors' Book,' Ward recalled in his memoir, 'reads like *Who's Who*. After changing for dinner, the guests usually meet in the Long Drawing-Room. Champagne and cocktails are always served here . . . and the guests nearly always include at least one duchess. Dinner is announced by the butler, and the guests drift into the huge and ornate dining-room, once a room in Madame de Pompadour's hunting lodge. The flower decorations are superb and there are always dishes of grapes, nectarines and peaches, from the outhouses. Course follows course and wine follows wine, until the ladies leave and the men can draw their chairs together and pass the port and walnuts and, of course, tell each other the latest joke from White's or Boodles's . . .'

The Canford boy was unabashed among the dukes and duchesses, industrialists and politicians. Ward had a fund of dinner stories, mostly borrowed from others. He retold the one about the young Winston Churchill informing an irate field marshal that he was entitled to wear a certain medal because his godmother had given it to him. His godmother, he explained, was Queen Victoria. Another of his stories was about Picasso's trick on a dealer who had been pestering him to sell a picture. The great painter waited until he was asleep in the sun, lightly drew on his chest and stomach, and then woke him to announce he was the possessor of a genuine Picasso.

It was Ward's medical skill, though, that made him *persona* very much *grata* at Cliveden. He was now osteopath by appointment to the Astor household. Lord Astor's widow, Bronwen, the last of his wives, says, 'Every guest, no matter who, on a Saturday night was asked, "Would you like a free session? Stephen's coming up, and if you've got any aches and pains . . ." Bill hunted nearly every Saturday, and part of his relaxation, especially if he had a fall or something, would be to have a massage.'

'In this way,' Ward was to write, 'I treated Duncan Sandys . . . a frequent visitor with his red dispatch-boxes from the Ministry . . . and Peter Thorneycroft, later Minister of Defence in the Macmillan Government, Lord Hailsham and several others.' Among the many other notables that Ward would meet during this period was the man who would become Minister for War, John Profumo and the film-star Valerie Hobson, who was to become Profumo's wife.

Lord Astor introduced Profumo to Stephen Ward in 1956, when he took him round to the osteopath's consulting rooms in Devonshire Street. Profumo was then forty-one and increasingly successful, true to family tradition. The Profumo family, as the name indicates, was Italian. His grandfather, an Italian baron, settled in England at the turn of the century, and the Profumos became English squires, with a country seat at Avon Carrow, near Stratford-upon-Avon. Even after the scandal in 1963, John Profumo would still be styled 'Fifth Baron of the late United Kingdom of Italy' in his *Who's Who* entry, surely an indication of pretensions to grandeur. The family motto is 'Virtue and Work'.

Profumo went to Harrow and Brasenose College, Oxford, where he distinguished himself as a horseman. His was a hunting family, and the Profumo horsebox always turned up for the hunt behind an immaculate Rolls-Royce. He was born to Conservatism, the whole gamut – polo, horse shows, house parties and fêtes. After Oxford, his barrister father sent him round the world, to the Soviet Union, the Far East and the United States. He met Bill Astor before the war, when – at the remarkably tender age of twenty-one – he became Chairman of the Conservative Association in East Fulham, where Astor was MP.

By the time he met Stephen Ward, Profumo already had an impressive career behind him: governor of two London hospitals at twenty-four, Conservative Member of Parliament for Kettering at twenty-five. Already he had the sharp features and the smarmed-back, receding hair that would become familiar in 1963. Some thought him a potential Prime Minister.

Profumo went into the war as an Army lieutenant and came out as a colonel with an OBE. In the fifties, as MP for Stratford-upon-Avon, he rose steadily in government: Secretary at the Ministry of Transport and Civil Aviation under Churchill, Under-Secretary of State for the Col-

onies, Minister of State for Foreign Affairs – and finally, of
course, Minister for War. In all of these posts, the Prime
Minister under whom Profumo served was Harold Macmillan.

A Conservative Party official noted that Profumo 'believed in the ruling class', and he ran his social life accor-
dingly. He was a member of the Other Club, which had
been described as 'perhaps the most exclusive dining club in
the world'. Founded by Churchill, its sixty members included Harold Macmillan, Selwyn Lloyd, a Foreign Secretary in the fifties, and Colin Coote, Editor of the *Daily
Telegraph* and the man who would one day introduce Ward
to a Soviet spy.

Until the scandal that ruined him, little was known
publicly about Profumo's love life. He was rumoured in the
press to have had an involvement with 'a widowed member
of the Royal Family', probably the then Duchess of Kent.
To his friends Profumo was something of a blade, with a
weakness for nightlife. 'Jack was the sort of chap,' says a
former fellow Conservative MP, 'who would go around the
nightclubs with another chap who was in Parliament, and
who's now a peer. And they would like to sit with these
hostesses, which I must say I found rather painful whenever
I sat with them. I'd have wanted to be paid to sit with them.
But this is what Jack liked . . .'

'I was in the motorboat', Ward was to write coyly in his
memoir, 'with a famous actress (the female lead in *The
King and I* – I've forgotten her name), Lord Astor, and the
second Lady Astor . . .' The female lead in the London
stage version of *The King and I* was the actress Valerie
Hobson. Hobson was in her mid-thirties, the veteran of a
string of films, including *Kind Hearts and Coronets*, *Great
Expectations*, *The Spy in Black*, *Unpublished Story*, *Bride
of Frankenstein* and *Lovers, Happy Lovers*, her last film
before retiring to marry John Profumo in 1954.

The day Stephen Ward went on his motorboat trip with
Profumo's future wife, was the day he spotted Spring
Cottage, a country hideaway that was still capable of

sending him into raptures, years later, at the worst moments of the Profumo Affair. It was larger than it sounds, with half-timbered walls, a turreted roof and a carved wooden balcony. In the grounds of Cliveden, to Ward's delight, were 'temples, statues and grottoes, caves, cliffs and streams. It was here, in probably the loveliest corner of all, and one of the most secluded, that my cottage lay . . .'

It became 'my' cottage when Harold Macmillan's goddaughter Philippa Hunloke, for a while to be Lord Astor's second wife, took notice of Ward's enthusiasm. The cottage had long been abandoned, and she persuaded Astor that Ward could bring it to life again and use it as a weekend place.

Ward laboured long and hard to restore Spring Cottage, working much of the time with a young woman called Margaret Brown, perhaps the most beautiful of his many girls. She rose to become a top international model while under Ward's wing, and was probably the last woman to have his full attention.* 'She painted while I dug,' said Ward, remembering the happy days fixing up the cottage.

Lord Astor gave Ward his idyll at a peppercorn rent of one pound a year, on the understanding that he provided his osteopathic services virtually free. It was an easy arrangement, and Astor was easy with his money. He lent Ward a thousand pounds in the fifties, and that too was written off to occasional osteopathy.

Soon Ward was down at Cliveden nearly every weekend, and the big house had become open house. After the gardening, Ward wrote, 'I always remember the rush to get the dirt off and change into my dinner jacket to get to dinner with Lord Astor . . .' The butler, Mr Lee, found Ward 'an affable and friendly gentleman'.

Suddenly Ward was more than an egregious osteopath – he was himself fashionable. 'The cottage is big enough to entertain Ward's friends,' drooled a national gossip columnist in 1958, 'and what a lovely line they can shoot at

---

*Brown later married the composer, Jule Styne.

dinner parties . . . the Cliveden tag makes the Ward retreat unbeatable in the U-stakes!'*

Cliveden's butler did not fail to notice the number of girls Ward brought down from London, and confided to Lady Astor's maid that he thought they were Windmill girls. 'I treated them,' said Mr Lee, 'just as I would any other guests, and so far as I know – and I should have known if they hadn't – they conducted themselves properly when they were in the house.'

And when they were in the cottage? The then Labour MP, Woodrow Wyatt, remembers walking by the river at Cliveden with Lord Astor one weekend. 'I let Stephen Ward use that house,' said Astor, pointing out Spring Cottage. 'Then,' says Wyatt, 'he giggled a lot . . .'

'If you create an evil atmosphere then other people pick it up,' Astor's widow says today. After the Profumo Affair, a new incumbent of Ward's weekend cottage committed suicide by drowning himself in the sink. Lady Astor was so concerned about the aura hanging over the place that she brought in a priest to perform an exorcism. Today Spring Cottage is still there, refurbished by new tenants who lease it from the National Trust.

Some still alive know the nature of the sex games Ward orchestrated on the Cliveden estate. Certainly, John Profumo was not the only man to be drawn into folly there. There are ageing men in England, once powers in the land, who no doubt still fear the disclosure of ancient indiscretions. Others have been accused and simply deny – like Douglas Fairbanks Jnr.

The American actor and producer, best known for *Dawn Patrol* and *Sinbad the Sailor*, never could challenge his famous father. He made few films after the war, and came to live in London. He was already a famous Anglophile – his father had introduced him to the Mountbattens as a young man – and in the fifties he became a scion of society.

*'U' or 'Non-U', the fifties slang for fashionable or the opposite.

He and his wife are among the few foreigners ever to have entertained the Queen and Prince Philip at home.

Fairbanks had known Lord Astor since before the war, and one of his daughters had her coming-out party at Cliveden in 1957. 'I did, of course,' he told us recently, 'know Dr Ward, whom I went to for a serious bursitis attack. And I did meet him through the late Lord Astor.' The osteopath himself was never to talk publicly about his famous friends, but he could not control the tongues of his girls. Unfortunately for Fairbanks, one of them brought up his name at Ward's trial. Mandy Rice-Davies was asked by the prosecution about activities at the flat she shared with Christine Keeler in 1961. To the question, 'Were you having intercourse with any other man or men at Comeragh Road?', Rice-Davies replied, 'Douglas Fairbanks.'

Fairbanks denied the allegation in 1963. Rice-Davies, however, has since offered detail. 'I was seriously thinking,' she says, 'of becoming an actress. It was one step on, I thought, from modelling, and making commercials had given me an idea of how to work with cameras and lights. I met Douglas Fairbanks Jnr with his wife and daughter, Melissa, at Cliveden, and was able to talk to him about the film business. I was flattered by his interest when he telephoned me a few days later and invited me to lunch at the Dorchester.'

Rice-Davies, who was sixteen at the time, goes on, 'Even then, in his fifties, he was a remarkably good-looking man as well as being an amusing companion. After lunch he suggested we go upstairs . . . and I did. We went to bed. There were several of these little afternoon interludes. I was genuinely fond of him, and I imagined he felt something similar for me . . .'

Christine Keeler goes further. She has described joining 'a jolly threesome' with Douglas Fairbanks. She thought it great fun to cavort with a star. Rice-Davies says she and Keeler posed for pictures taken by Fairbanks.

Lord Astor was another famous casualty when matters came to court in 1963. His name first surfaced in the most unfortunate way, for him, when Mandy Rice-Davies was asked who had paid the rent at the Comeragh Road flat. She truthfully answered 'Lord Astor', although she had not even met him at the time. Stephen Ward, who made the arrangements, was simply using a cheque Astor had given him as a loan. They did meet later, though, when Ward took Rice-Davies along with him to Upper Grosvenor Street. He had been called in by Bronwen, Astor's third wife, to treat her stiff neck.

According to Rice-Davies, in testimony and in recent interviews, she went to bed with Lord Astor in November 1962, at Wimpole Mews. It was not a commercial exchange. Ward was in the other room while she had intercourse in her bedroom. That startled the trial-judge in 1963 but Rice-Davies responded perkily, 'It's quite normal, isn't it? There's nothing wrong with it?'

Another of the girls around Ward, Mariella Novotny, was a frequent visitor to Ward's cottage at Cliveden. Lord Astor, for his part, attended parties given by Novotny and her husband at their flat in Hyde Park Square. According to Novotny, whose role in the story will later be examined in detail, there was a darker side to Astor's sex life. This emerges from an unpublished manuscript, obtained by us after Novotny's death in 1983. It is relevant, because Astor's preferences must have left him wide open to blackmail and pressure.

At first, Novotny wrote, Lord Astor simply took her out to dinner: 'Bill made a great fuss of me. We dined, gossiped leisurely . . . he could be an amusing partner when he forgot to be pompous. Then he said he could show me something really exciting if I wanted a special scene.' Astor then took her to a Mayfair brothel catering especially for sado-masochists. There was an elaborately equipped torture chamber, according to Novotny. 'Every type of whip and cane was neatly displayed. Bill selected a cat-o'-nine-tails with fine thongs of leather, and showed me how to manipulate it . . .' A coloured girl was selected from several candidates and strapped to rungs set in the wall. 'I tentatively lashed her buttocks,' Novotny continued, 'Bill told me I was just playing at it. He provoked me with derogatory comments. The girl's gasps of pain and Bill's derisory remarks got me going. I lashed her backside with all my strength . . . I ignored the blood running down her legs, and her shrieks simply made me more and more sadistic. Finally . . . Bill grabbed the whip and said I'd gone too far – he had to pay fifty pounds instead of the usual ten.'

This allegedly took place in 1960, when Novotny was eighteen and Lord Astor fifty-four. Is it true? Certainly Novotny was deeply involved in sado-masochism within a year or so: she was the hostess at the notorious 'Man In The Mask' orgy, which will be described later. A witness at the Ward trial, an Austrian girl identified only as Miss R., testified that Ward asked her 'to go to a party given by a woman, Mariella . . . he said that at this party I would see girls being tied up and whipped.'

It is hard to know whether Mariella Novotny was telling the truth about Lord Astor. There may be a strong clue, though, in an intriguing *roman-à-clef* called *The Last Temptation*, published in 1984. It features a character called 'Lord Asterisk' and contains the following conversation between two men at a party:

'Well, certainly I was warned about Bill Asterisk and all the boots and spurs and things. But I didn't expect to have to dress up as a policeman.'

'Policewoman, surely, darling.'

'No. That is the whole point. *Not* a policewoman, a police*man* with a helmet and a truncheon . . .'

Asterisk is almost certainly a coded reference to Lord Astor, and the subject and authorship of the book make it almost indisputable. *The Last Temptation* is a thinly veiled account of the life of Guy Liddell, a close friend of the traitor Guy Burgess, and Deputy Director of MI5 in the late forties. Liddell kept a journal, which was entitled 'Wallflower' for the purposes of secrecy, which was looked after following his death by the MI5 Director-General, Roger Hollis. Hollis eventually ordered its destruction, but, according to another MI5 officer, it made the rounds before being returned to the archives. *The Last Temptation* may be linked to 'Wallflower', but it is the identity of its author that provides a firm link to Lord Astor.

The Last Temptation was written by David Mure, a former Army Intelligence officer who served with the same units as Lord Astor during World War II. Mure, whose memory was legendary, worked first with the A Force, organising deception operations against the Germans in the Middle East. He then headed the 31 Committee in Beirut, which specialised in double-crossing the enemy.

Astor was the Naval Intelligence representative for the Committee, and thus came into regular contact with MI6 and MI5 officers in the area. The MI5 man in Jerusalem was Lieutenant-Colonel Henry Hunloke, father of Philippa, who was to become Astor's second wife. In 1943, Astor returned to London to continue working in Intelligence at the Admiralty. Soon afterwards, he met his first wife, Sarah, who was a document translator for MI6 at Bletchley, where the ENIGMA code was broken.

Astor's service colleague Mure used pseudonyms to describe his Intelligence contacts in two books, *Practise to Deceive* as well as *The Last Temptation*. In both he refers to the wartime MI6 station chief, Charles Dundas, as 'Fergie', and, in *The Last Temptation*, he calls Guy Burgess 'The Duchess'. 'Fergie,' Mure writes, 'frequently attended the Duchess's parties with his friend, Lord Asterisk, the prominent whipman.' In 1955, after Burgess and Maclean defected to Moscow, Lord Astor made a speech in the House of Lords denying that he had ever met Guy Burgess. Time, perhaps, will show whether he was telling the truth or whether his old comrade, Mure, was spinning vicious lies.

Stephen Ward, for his part, had his own strange connection with the world of diplomacy and Intelligence. He and royal photographer Baron used to visit the Gargoyle Club where Burgess and Maclean regularly got drunk. As we have seen, he consorted with the homosexual diplomat, Sir Gilbert Laithwaite, and with Monsignor Montgomery, whose brother was Anthony Blunt's lover. In the fifties, according to Robert Harbinson, Ward was also close to two remarkable women who had served in Intelligence during the war – Gwen le Gallienne and Princess Dil de Rohan.

Gwen le Gallienne, an accomplished portrait painter, was a lesbian, a blonde who wore short, mannish hair, and sometimes a monocle. She had been the lover of Louise Bullitt, sometime mistress of socialist writer John Reed, hero of the film *Reds*, and wife of the first American ambassador to the Soviet Union. The Bullitts socialised with the Astors.

According to Harbinson, who knew them all, 'Ward hated to be thought gay, except in the company of Gwen le Gallienne, when it was all chaps together. There were terrible scandals about her, which Ward was fascinated by. Stephen, of course, was a mine of information on all this.'

Princess de Rohan, also lesbian, came to London after marriage to a German prince, and a heyday as a Berlin hostess of the thirties. She worked for the British Ministry of Information during the war. Both de Rohan and Gwen le Gallienne worked with Tomas Harris, the left-wing associate of Burgess, Blunt and Kim Philby.

In the mid-fifties, the Princess lived at the home of the painter, Sir Francis Rose. Rose had been the close friend of the leader of Hitler's S.A., the Brown Shirts, Ernst Rohm; had met Hitler himself and was close to Italy's pioneer frogman, Prince Doria. In 1953, when Doria came to England, he stayed at Forest Farm at Windsor, as guest of his relative, the Duchess of Newcastle. Ward was present, giving osteopathic services and taking a great interest in Prince Doria, and underwater warfare.

Sir Francis Rose's 'soulmate' in London, according to Harbinson, was a man whose disappearance made world headlines and an enduring mystery, World War II frogman hero, Commander 'Buster' Crabb. In 1955 Crabb was used by British Naval Intelligence to examine the hull of the Soviet cruiser *Sverdlov*, while it was on an official visit to Portsmouth. A year later, Crabb disappeared while attempting a similar operation against the Cruiser *Ordzho-nikidze*, also on an important official visit. Crabb's operation had been vetoed by the Prime Minister, Anthony Eden, but was executed anyway by Naval Intelligence, with the connivance of MI6.

Stephen Ward, according to Harbinson, seemed a fund of information on Buster Crabb. As late as 1962, according to Mandy Rice-Davies, he was still deeply interested in submarine warfare. Was it an entirely casual interest?

MI6, as we shall examine in detail later, had an interest in Ward from the early 1950s. It also concluded that MI5 was using the Astor estate at Cliveden for 'Honeytrap' operations, to entrap intelligence targets by compromising them sexually. One establishment MI6 officer, speaking in 1970, said that Lord Astor was 'on friendly terms with senior members of MI5, and was happy to help them, and in his view the country, when asked to do so . . . When they needed to make use of Ward, to provide suitable women for visiting heads of state, they went through his friend Lord Astor.'

Which British Intelligence service was doing what at Cliveden, given Lord Astor's connections? The truth is elusive, because of the internecine rivalry between the two agencies. It seems most likely that this was the operational territory of MI6, which has indeed pandered to the sexual needs of visiting dignitaries. Greville Wynne, who was the contact man for Soviet traitor Oleg Penkovsky, revealed that MI6 maintained a group of high-class whores available for the use of chosen guests. Norma Levy, the leading lady of a later sex scandal, the 1972 Lord Lambton Affair, said she had entertained foreign diplomats on the say-so of a 'Mr Whitehouse' of the Foreign Office. The Foreign Office is responsible for the activities of MI6.

If Cliveden was the location for Honeytrap operations, it was hardly coincidence that Stephen Ward was conveniently on hand, the purveyor of female bait.

At New Year 1959, on a trip to St Moritz, a friend told Lord Astor about a stunningly beautiful model called Bronwen Pugh. Back in London, Astor got word to Pugh, through Ward, that he would like to meet her. They were married the following October, when he was fifty-three and she was twenty-eight. The new Lady Astor did not like Ward.

'I knew about him already, from another model girl,' she says today, 'and when I heard that he had a cottage on the estate, I was just horrified. I could sense who was taking my husband for a ride, and when it was innocent and not so innocent. I felt that Ward was manipulating Bill, and I was there to marry Bill not to manipulate him. The whole beginning of my life at Cliveden was marred by the presence of this man.'

At Christmas 1960, Ward was a Boxing Day guest, taking dinner at the big house alongside Astor's family, Lord Palmer of biscuit fame, and the young Lord Gowrie, who later became Margaret Thatcher's Minister for the Arts. Astor's friend Maurice Collis, who was also there, thought him amusing, 'quite at home in good society'. Lady Astor, who was not amused to find Ward there at all, henceforth banned him from the dinners. Ward continued to come up to give massages, though, and – as we know from his bedroom adventure with Mandy Rice-Davies – Lord Astor continued to see the osteopath behind his wife's back.

At a bridge party hosted by Lord Ednam, the writer Godfrey Winn watched Ward carefully and sized him up. Winn remembered 'this tallish man, with a face free of fat to match his thin body. I suspected he was already in his forties,* though his manner was consistently more youthful, at times almost coquettish, though in an entirely masculine way. His facile smile turned on and off like a light in a dark room – in momentary repose the skin of his face had a peculiar emanation of deadness; above all, his elaborate attentiveness gave the impression of someone who, though eager to please through not being absolutely sure of himself, yet at the same time had an equal desire to manipulate the company, even to command.'

Some people, like Lady Astor, were troubled by the fact that Dr Ward manipulated not only bodies but also human lives. They were troubled, but there was little to be done

---

*Ward was, in fact, nearly fifty.

about it. Things had already gone much too far. And besides, the rich men Ward cultivated had no wish to part company with him. Without him, after all, how in the world would the chaps find the girls?

It was too late now. Stephen Ward was a loose cannon on the deck of history.

FOUR

A RECIPE FOR SCANDAL

'Nowadays,' says William Shepherd, former Conservative MP and friend of John Profumo, 'if you go to the best places you are quite likely to meet the worst people. Well, there are one or two places left . . . there's the Stork Room and there's Eve's, a place Jack Profumo used to go to quite a bit – but nobody who's anybody ever goes to them now.'

London nightlife of the fifties and early sixties was a phenomenon of the era. 'London was a much smaller place in those days,' Jon Pertwee remembers. 'The social scene was a mixture of the characters of London. Something to do with the war bringing everybody down to a certain level. It wasn't like now, with the Dickies and the Dianas separated. I mean, today, people who go to Tramp would never dream of going to Stringfellow's, or wherever, downmarket. The social scene in our day ranged right across from the Berkeley to the Nuthouse and Boogie Woogie . . .'

Stephen Ward's London after dark was a post-war melting-pot. The idle aristocrats were there as always, along with Members of Parliament filling in time during an all-night sitting, and actors winding down after the last curtain. Fresh in their ranks, though, were a more raffish crowd, *nouveau riche* millionaires, art dealers and salesmen with money to burn. Not everyone now spoke with a public-school accent, though many pretended. They had one thing in common, of course – lust.

'An older man,' says Pertwee, 'had absolutely no problem in finding a pretty young lady to accompany him. A

Bentley, an old banger of a Bentley I mean, or an old sports car, and your fifty-year-old would have no problem getting his twenty-year-old girl.'

Stephen Ward was entering middle age in the fifties. The teeth were false, but they smiled well. The blue eyes of the boy from Canford School had not dulled much, and the soft baritone was practised at seduction. When he was in a club, there was always the sports car parked round the corner – on hire purchase, but who was to know? In the clubs, Ward cultivated his upper-class pals, but he also bumped up against the new infiltrators, and made friends of them, too. Their Bohemian ways were amusing, and, besides, they were useful. One such was Horace – 'Hod' to all who knew him – Dibben.

Hod Dibben, now eighty-two and proud of his past as a rogue, was born the son of a Southampton ironmonger, a member of the Plymouth Brethren. The repressive religious background predisposed him to sexual rebellion. In the thirties, locked in a dull job and a duller marriage, he began pursuing a female associate. One night, having followed her home, Dibben peered through the curtains and saw something strangely exciting. She was with another man, and she was whipping him.

Soon, Dibben was tied to a tree in the woods, himself being flogged with briars until the blood flowed. Pleasure followed pain, and Dibben went on to become an ardent sado-masochist. Today, he is frail and has fallen on hard times, an old man in a dirty cardigan with gold chains and an Egyptian medallion dangling round his neck. He cheerfully admits his bizarre sexual past, and cheerfully provides a stream of ancient gossip. Gossip, someone has said, is history, and Dibben appears to be truthful in old age.

Like Ward, Dibben was something of a Pygmalion. At the end of the war, when the RAF let him go, he put an advertisement in the papers: 'Intelligent young girl required for antique business. Must have knowledge of art.' (It was genuine enough – Dibben had become an acknowledged restorer and expert on eighteenth-century antiques.) The girl he chose, Patsy Morgan, was out of place in the salesrooms with her provincial accent, so Dibben sent her to a finishing school run by the Countess of Devon. A year or so later, re-educated so that the join hardly showed, Morgan joined Dibben at Lytescary Manor, in Somerset. The aristocracy and the not-so-smart began flocking to their parties, which were numerous. 'The sweet life,' as one magazine put it, 'had begun.'

In London, 'everyone' knew Dibben and his girl Patsy. Dibben went bankrupt, not for the first time, but that did not cramp his style. Patsy was forever in the newspapers, attending first nights, being photographed – heavily made-up – in all the fashionable nightspots. By the mid-fifties she was running one herself, the Torch Theatre Club, alias Esmeralda's Barn. It was, she said, 'a place where everybody went, the Duke of Kent, jazz singer Josh White, Lord Suffolk, the Earl of Warwick and John Huston.' The launch of the club, with interior design by Annigoni and a bugle blast of publicity, soon brought the young Guards officers, the debutantes and the celebrities running. Lord Astor was one of them, accompanied by Stephen Ward. Patsy, who was assumed by most to be Dibben's daughter, was ever-present, smiling her painted smile and calling everyone, be they peer or jumped-up peasant, 'Sweetie'. Then, she disappeared for a while.

When traced to the home of an Argentine millionaire in the Bavarian Alps, Patsy said she was hiding from someone. According to the newspapers, she had left behind a diary containing 'notes about love affairs with high-placed personalities, the names and peculiarities of so-called refined people, and tales of narcotics and degenerate impulses'. 'If I talked,' Patsy said she was told by her lawyer, 'it would make things worse, and he advised me to stay abroad.' Seven years later, when Christine Keeler headed for Spain, people would again be wondering what was being hushed up.

Patsy was soon involved with a new beau, old Etonian Michael Mordaunt-Smith, nephew of Lord Oranmore and Browne. 'Hod was a voyeur,' says Mordaunt-Smith, 'the only thrill he got was from watching other people screw. He would sit in the corner of a semi-darkened bedroom and . . . just watch.'

Dibben had lost his Patsy, but there were more where she came from. One, indeed, was to be directly relevant to the Profumo Affair.

Stephen Ward had known Dibben for years by this time. 'He came to supper every Thursday,' says Dibben. 'It was a regular thing. He had often been to the Thursday Club during the day. Later, we saw him mostly at Cliveden. John Profumo was a regular visitor.' Ward's Thursday dinners with Dibben took place at the Belgravia home of a mutual friend, Dr Edward Sugden, who was a gynaecologist and quite a character.

'Teddy Sugden had a paralysed face,' says Jon Pertwee. 'He was horrific looking, one side of his face was permanently down, and he kept alligators, and lizards and snakes in his surgery . . . When you went to see him you saw these horrifying animals all crawling around in their cages. He was weird, but a most loved man. His morals were not quite as people would expect them to be, but he was generous and nice . . .' Dibben agrees: 'You couldn't have met a nicer man.'

Some things about Sugden were not so nice. He liked his female companions to simulate sex with one of his pet snakes. On a visit to China in the 1920s, according to one acquaintance, he had filmed the torture and rape of a group of Russian ballet dancers who had fallen into Chinese hands. The footage pleased Sugden so much that he had several frames enlarged and reproduced as stills to show his friends.

Sugden's main line of business, in the fifties, was as an abortionist. Abortion was illegal before 1967, and – while poor girls tried gin and knitting needles – girls with connections went to the likes of Dr Sugden. Sometimes he helped young women free of charge, and he could afford to. On a commercial basis, several sources confirm, he was performing ten to fifteen abortions a day, at one or two hundred pounds a time. Among his long-standing friends had been the Messina brothers, the notorious Sicilian pimps. When Messina prostitutes got pregnant, Dr Sugden dealt with the problem. None of this bothered his friends in the fifties – least of all Stephen Ward – for Sugden gave just the right kind of parties.

'At the end of every week,' Dibben says, 'Teddy used to go round to the wine merchants and load up his huge Bentley with drink. I used to sit in the front with him, and off we'd go . . .'

'Teddy had a house on an island in the middle of the Thames, near Ham I think,' says Jon Pertwee. 'He was a great nudist . . . and everybody used to go down and wander around in the nude in the sun. It was quite jolly.'

Sugden held his most exotic parties at a place known as 'Teddy's hut', which, Dibben recalls with glee, 'was next to the sewage department of Windsor Castle. The Queen had allowed him to build a bungalow on the banks of the Thames, and he enclosed it completely with a very high fence. Every summer Teddy would open the bungalow and everyone would go down . . . We would take off all our clothes when we got there, and didn't put them back on until we had to go back. People tried to bore holes in the fence to see what was going on. Local fishermen were desperate to get permits to fish on the banks facing the bungalow so they could see what was going on . . .'

'Teddy had an unlimited supply of girls,' Dibben says, 'because all the actresses and models in London came to him for their abortions, and then he'd ask them down to Windsor. The odd thing was, Teddy's wife never let him join in – he could only watch.'

Dr Sugden squared things with the local police and invited one local officer to visit. 'We asked him in and gave him some whisky,' says Dibben. 'He was lying on the grass watching the naked bodies cavorting about when one woman popped her head up and said "Hello!" It turned out that she was his daughter . . .'

'The first time Stephen came,' says Dibben, 'he arrived by boat – he'd borrowed one from the Astors. He brought a load of girls with him, four girls. They had just arrived from

Australia and were coming to work as models, and Stephen had just met them at Southampton. He had taken them to Cliveden and brought them on to Teddy's. Three of the girls were absolutely delighted with what they saw – a load of naked guests – but the fourth left and went straight on back to Southampton . . .'

On these occasions, says Dibben, Ward always kept his clothes on. He even had his clothes on in bed once, at the Cliveden cottage, when Dibben blundered in on him in bed with —————— ————*, a well-known model.

On rainy weekends, the Star Tavern in Belgravia was a favourite haunt. 'London Lotharios pulled their sports cars up to the door to display their latest girls,' recalled an American associate of Ward at the time of the Profumo Affair. 'Dr Ward invariably showed up with the envied beauty.' The Star, in those days, was a hang-out for the better class of criminal, including Charles de Silva, 'Dandy Kim' Caborn-Waterfield and Bobbie McKew. Old Etonian Caborn-Waterfield was a former lover of Diana Dors, another of Ward's circle, though she denied it. He served two years in prison for robbing Jack Warner's house on the French Riviera. McKew, dubbed the 'Chelsea Scallywag' in the fifties, was also involved in the Warner heist. He was the man who found the finance for Dr Emil Savundra, later infamous for perpetrating the biggest car insurance fraud of all time.

Savundra, Ceylonese by birth, gave himself the title of 'God's own lounge lizard turned swindler', and pursued sex as avidly as he did money. He had a love-nest at Marble Arch provided by a criminal called James Pyper, who also supplied him with telephone numbers for call girls. It was McKew, though, who introduced Dr Savundra to Dr Ward. He liked blondes and redheads 'with long legs and very white skin', and Ward was able to oblige. The evidence of one of those blondes was to cost Ward dear at his trial in 1963.

The next part of this story is a sad saga of three young

_____
*Name deleted for legal reasons.

girls, of three teenage virginities lost, and three trips to London that would bring the girls to Ward and his friend Dibben, and eventually to starring roles in the Profumo scandal.

Christine

One day in 1957, a girl in Staines, Middlesex, went to the lodgings of a Ghanaian student, a sweeper in the dress shop where she worked, to help him with his homework. The Ghanaian told the girl how lonely he was, and she listened. When he began kissing her, she did not object. When he asked her to get into bed, she said it was time she was leaving – then she gave in. 'Of course,' she said later, 'once he started he went the whole way. I was not very stimulated . . . on the train home I began to feel guilty and full of secret shame for what I had done.'

The girl was Christine Keeler, and she was fifteen. Her father had left home long ago, and much of her childhood had been spent with her mother and stepfather in a converted railway carriage. Keeler's mother took her to see a psychiatrist because she hated the stepfather so much. She was molested, she says, early on, and – at twelve or thirteen – saw her mother and stepfather making love. 'I was afraid,' she said, 'that what went on might happen to me.'

When it did happen to her, Keeler had little time for home. By the time she was sixteen she was hanging around a pub called the Angel, picking up American GIs from the several US bases in the area. She had a preference, one that was to prove durable, for black men. Soon she was in a swanky American car, heading for the NCOs Club at Langley Airbase. There were bottle parties, an early encounter with marijuana – not yet a common indulgence in England – and a second lover.

One of the GIs was a hard-faced, black sergeant with a crewcut, about twenty years older than Keeler. She remembers him as Jim. He swept her off her feet, and became the first man to enjoy Keeler's favours for a whole night.

Jim was long gone, back to America, when she discovered she was pregnant. 'I then did all the usual things,' said Keeler in her book *Nothing But* . . . 'gin and hot baths, castor oil, and finally the horrible self-probing with the knitting needle.' It worked, but in a horrendously botched way. Keeler was alone in bed when the damaged baby arrived, 'a slimy mauve and red head, there, not there, and there again. Mum heard my call and cycled away for the doctor.' Keeler's child was born alive, but died six days later in hospital. He was a boy and, during his brief life, he was given the name Peter. That summer of 1959, just turned seventeen, Keeler stole a car – by slipping a piece of silver paper into the ignition – and headed for London.

She was working as a waitress in Baker Street when an Irishwoman, Maureen O'Connor, told her that she could make good money at Murray's Cabaret Club, in Soho. Soon Keeler was being introduced to Percy Murray, a pseudo city gent, in spectacles and a double-breasted suit. Murray's boast was that most of Europe's nobility had sat at his tables, and that Winston Churchill had been a customer during the war. Princess Margaret had favoured Murray's with her presence, and King Hussein of Jordan was a regular. The clientele were a mix of aristocrats and commoners, gathered amongst the potted palms to drink, watch the costumed dancers and flirt with the 'showgirls', who performed topless.

Keeler was hired as a showgirl. She teetered on to the stage for the first time wearing high-heeled shoes, a shiny *cache-sexe* and a fantastical assortment of feathers and sequins. Keeler was red-haired and slim, but more ample-bosomed than met the eye when she was clothed. It was the profile that made her beautiful, as the great British public would later discover in myriad photographs. 'She had the face of Nefertiti,' one female friend would say, and it was fair enough.

Like other Murray's girls, Keeler was soon sitting with male customers between acts, encouraging them to buy more drinks. Each order brought her a commission, and there were tips, too. Murray's had strict rules about sex with customers, but Keeler says they existed only to protect the reputations of the customers.

Percy Murray himself set the real tone. 'He used to bed me once or twice a week, and there was always an extra fifteen quid in my hand afterwards,' she says.

'I think I would divide the girls between those who did and those who didn't,' says William Shepherd, a former Conservative MP and an habitué of Murray's. Christine Keeler was one of those who did. She was soon a hit with an old Etonian and ex-Guards officer called Michael Lambton, a cousin of the Lord Lambton who was to figure in a later sex scandal. Lambton was a rich young publisher with a drink problem. One of Keeler's friends would recall how Lambton was prone to saying, ' "Pass the potty, dear" – and one would lean over for the baby's pot kept in the back seat of the Bentley like an aircraft sick bag.'

One night another friend of Keeler's came to Murray's, a rich Arab student from the London School of Economics called Ahmed. With him came a film starlet – and a second man. His name was Stephen Ward.

'You were delightful in the show,' is supposed to have been Ward's opening gambit. 'Will you dance?' – 'What are you doing later?' he asked. According to Keeler, she tried to avoid him at first. Then, much to the irritation of the Arab, he wormed her phone-number out of her. Notebook in hand, he jotted it down. Then Ward wished everyone a very good night, and departed with his starlet.

The next day Ward called Keeler, not once but three times. When she fobbed him off, he turned up at her home in Staines one weekend to charm her mother and stepfather – Ward made a habit of cultivating the parents of his girls. Soon Keeler was closeted with him in a Marylebone coffee-bar, and – at their second date – Ward asked her to move into his flat.

In spite of the age difference, Ward had much to offer Keeler. She felt highly vulnerable in London, a lonely bird of paradise in the big bad city. Ward offered undemanding friendship. 'I felt,' she said later, 'that there would always be Stephen.' Keeler could not know then just how much, as long as she lives, there will always be Stephen.

Unlike most other men, Ward did not pester Keeler for sex. He made a few passes, at the beginning of their friendship, but only in a half-hearted sort of way. Soon, she has recalled, they were living like 'brother and sister'. Although they sometimes slept in the same room, they never did have sex together. Sex, though, was all around. Stephen Ward found great amusement in introducing his young discovery to upper-class sex orgies. He confided that he personally found himself impotent at sex parties, but liked to watch. He took Keeler to swapping sessions in Maida Vale, then hosted one of his own at the cottage on Lord Astor's estate. Keeler looked on in youthful surprise as a husband and wife – she refers to them pseudonymously as 'Bertie' and 'Mary' – had sex with other partners in each other's presence. The husband's main concern, she observed, was that his wife should enjoy herself as much as possible.

Ward explained the philosophy used to justify such diversions. The thinking, he told Keeler, was that group sex stimulated marriages rather than causing upset and unhappiness. 'It makes you think, little baby,' he mused, 'perhaps that's what it's all about.'

Keeler became a regular weekend guest at the cottage. Once they were joined by another girl, whom Keeler has called 'Barbara'. Barbara's sexual preference was bondage. She lay tied to the bed, shrieking hysterically, laughing one moment, crying the next. 'Leave her there,' Ward said as solemnly as possible, '. . . that's what she deserves.'

The flat Ward had in London at that time was small, and he wanted to move. He had a friend in property, one who could produce any sort of accommodation if he wanted. This was Peter Rachman, one day to be exposed as London's worst property racketeer.

'Rachmanism' was eventually to enter the *Concise Oxford Dictionary*, defined as 'exploitation of slum tenants by unscrupulous landlords'. He was an expatriate Pole, aged forty-one in 1960, who started his career in Britain as a scorer at Jack Solomon's billiard hall in Soho. Rachman started in property finding rooms for prostitutes, then helped the Messina brothers – the clients of Dr Ward's abortionist friend Dr Sugden – as 'an investment consultant'. By 1960, though the British press ignored him, Italian newspapers already referred to him as the 'King of Vice'. Somehow the police in London never pulled him in – his money looked after that.

Rachman became a property mogul in Notting Hill and Bayswater at the right time, during a wave of immigration from the West Indies. He found them accommodation, but at an extortionate price in high rents and overcrowding. He employed thugs to enforce his rule, including Michael de Freitas, better known as Michael X, later hanged in the West Indies for the savage murder of his white English mistress. In the seventies, another of Rachman's henchmen supplied the guns for the Spaghetti House siege in Knightsbridge. Rachman owned clubs as well as living accommodation – and the slum rents alone were making him £78,000 a year, a fabulous sum in the late fifties.

In 1960, Rachman told a friend he would soon be 'one of the richest men in England'. He would do it 'honestly', transferring his property to surrogate owners, and taking a major stake in property about to be used for the building of the M6 motorway. The tipoff about this project came from cronies who were Members of Parliament, one of them Ernest Marples, the Conservative Minister of Transport.

Ward and Rachman shared a mutual friend in Dennis Hamilton, husband of glamour girl Diana Dors. On Rachman's behalf, Hamilton would pull out his 'fish book', a list of girls available to service him and his friends at his London flat in Bryanston Mews, or his country place, the Penthouse, in Maidenhead. At the Penthouse there were cameras to film orgies, picture albums memorialising sex parties attended by celebrities, tape-recorders hidden under beds, and a two-way mirror in the ceiling through which guests could watch others having sex. The mirror was moved to Bryanston Mews when Hamilton broke up with

Diana Dors, shortly before his death from syphilis. Rachman then acquired the flat, but – contrary to later press reports – the infamous mirror was smashed long before he rented the flat to Stephen Ward.

While Ward and Keeler were house-hunting, Rachman invited them to dinner at the El Condor Club, then run by Diana Dors' boyfriend of the moment. It was a trendy place, patronised by Princess Margaret, the Duke of Kent, and the usual coterie of nobility and military has-beens. The invitation on this occasion was a pretext, a chance for Rachman to tell Keeler he fancied her.

Keeler was at Bryanston Mews the very next day, visiting Rachman and the current female incumbent. She was at once hugely tempted by the millionaire's overtures, and guilty about letting Ward down. Temptation triumphed, and Keeler abandoned Ward within a few days. She packed her bags, and moved to Rachman's flat. He took her to bed, without preamble, as soon as she arrived. From that day on he had her daily, as a matter of course, usually after lunch. Rachman made no pretence at passion.

'Sex to Rachman,' according to Keeler, 'was like cleaning his teeth and I was the toothbrush . . . I never saw his face while we had sex, as he always made me sit on top of him facing the other way.'

Ward was furious, in a way that now sounds very funny indeed. He thought Keeler's reputation would suffer from being seen in the company of a man like Rachman. Keeler took no notice at first, but soon got bored with Rachman anyway. It was time for fresh adventures, with a new female friend – and the friend would look after Rachman.

Mandy

'I was slower than most finding out about sex,' says Mandy Rice-Davies. 'I knew about horses. I had read *Forever Amber* and believed fervently in the agony and ecstasy of love – red, violent and blood-splashed.'

She was sixteen in 1960, born – as Marilyn – to Welsh

parents. Her mother was a miner's daughter, her father an ex-policeman now working for Dunlop. She grew up in Solihull, near Birmingham. As she entered her teens she was interested in a pony called Laddie and Roman Catholicism. At fifteen, but looking much older, she was modelling mink for fashion shows at Marshall & Snelgrove.

At this time she had a flirtation with a trapeze artist in a visiting circus. She lost her virginity before she turned sixteen, 'in the room over the sweet shop next to the Odeon cinema'. The man was a graduate of Trinity College, Dublin, helping out in the summer holiday. 'I was an enthusiastic participant,' she says, 'in what struck me as a perfectly pleasant way to spend an afternoon. I had expected, afterwards, to feel in some way fundamentally changed by my experience, but in this respect was disappointed. Oh, so that's it, I thought, as I set off home.'

Soon after, following a meeting with a talent-spotter in the street, Rice-Davies was in London, posing as a model at the launch of a new car called the Mini. The pay for the week was £80, and there was no keeping her in Birmingham after that. She gave her notice at Marshall & Snelgrove, bid goodbye to her glum parents and took the train to Paddington. An advertisement in the *Evening Standard* brought her to Murray's Cabaret Club, a role as a dancer dressed up as a Red Indian squaw, and a meeting with a twelve-month veteran, Christine Keeler.

'It was dislike at first sight,' Rice-Davies recalls, and Keeler felt the same. Nevertheless, partly because Rice-Davies got on well with Arabs, and they both ended up at the same parties, the two became companions. They functioned well together in company – partly, Keeler thought, because Rice-Davies had a good head for money, while she was vague about it.

The partnership also worked well in the bedroom. Though there were no lesbian overtones, the two girls took part in 'threesome' sex scenes with men. Keeler says this became something of a speciality, that it excited the men so much that they forgot any desire they might have had for a two-woman show. She says neither of the girls was a bit bothered by group sex – it was amusing, and it brought in money for clothes and partying. Rice-Davies confirms that the threesomes took place.

Unlike Christine Keeler, who looked better in photographs than in life, Rice-Davies was to survive the 1963 scandal still looking 'fresh as a milkmaid'. She had 'a hard cat-like face,' said one observer, 'but a very pretty one.'

In her two months at Murray's, Rice-Davies found many wealthy admirers but – at that stage – not much sex. She started with Azis, a friend of Keeler's Ahmed, and then discovered Walter Flack, a partner of property magnate Charles Clore. Clore was to have sex with Keeler for money. Flack, on the other hand, wined and dined Rice-Davies but never propositioned her.

Eric, Earl of Dudley, seemed a good bet. He showered Rice-Davies with flowers, sent a case of pink champagne and took her out in his ancient Jaguar. He told Rice-Davies how to address the Queen should they meet, and actually took her to dinner with the woman who missed being Queen, the Duchess of Windsor. Lord Dudley at one point proposed to Rice-Davies, but then he quarrelled with her over Aziz and went off to marry Princess Grace Radziwill.

The next nightclub Croesus was millionaire Robert Sherwood, a machine-tool manufacturer from New York, the husband of an actress in *Cat on a Hot Tin Roof*. He told Rice-Davies at Murray's, 'This is no place for you. Go back before it's too late.' Rice-Davies did go back to Solihull, but only for Christmas.

On New Year's Eve 1960, Mandy Rice-Davies and Christine Keeler moved to a flat at Comeragh Road, in unfashionable Baron's Court, thanks to rental arrangements made by Stephen Ward and Lord Astor. Ward brought his cousin Tim Vigors, a Battle of Britain fighter pilot, to the house-warming party, and he made a play for Keeler. Keeler's old boyfriend, Peter Rachman, was there too. He left with Rice-Davies' telephone number and called a couple of days later. On and off, for nearly two years, he was to be her lover and the fount of all good things

– and money seemed a very good thing to the sixteen-year-old from Solihull.

Mariella

On the night of 29 January 1960 Ward's friend Hod Dibben found himself in an unaccustomed predicament. He had got married that day to a girl he hardly knew, and – in bed that night – discovered she was still a virgin. She wanted to be 'de-virginised', as she later put it, but the process took a full month to achieve. Once the deed was done the bride thought, 'What a fuss people make of so little! . . . I suspected there must be more to it, set about finding out, and am still discovering fresh games to play.'

Dibben's latest acquisition was eighteen-year-old Mariella Capes, and – under her father's name, Novotny – she would become notorious for the sex games she tried out on London society. In 1963, there would be sensational rumours about the Man In The Mask Party, a masochistic orgy attended by mysterious, unnamed prominent people. Mariella Novotny was the hostess at the orgy, yet her name and Dibben's do not appear in the Denning Report.

Today, with access to an unpublished manuscript written before her death in 1983, it is evident that Novotny was much more involved in the Profumo Affair than has ever been understood. Even her origins are interesting – her father was Czech, a factor that, we shall see, had troubling security implications in 1963.

She was born Stella Marie Capes, according to the birth certificate, in May 1941, close to Sheffield, in Yorkshire. The certificate names her mother as Constance Capes, a shorthand typist, but does not identify the father. There is no record of her attending schools in the area. To fill the gaps, we must fall back on Novotny's own account, written in long sloping handwriting across fifty pages of an exercise book, on her mother and her husband Hod Dibben, and on the fragmentary official record. 'My father was a Czech in the RAF,' Novotny was to say in 1963, but she and her mother had given much more detail years earlier, when she made her debut as a topless dancer at London's Latin Quarter. Interviewed by a reporter looking for personality features, mother and daughter said Novotny's birth was the result of a relationship – perhaps a marriage – between Mrs Capes, who is part Spanish, and a Czech called Anton Novotny, then serving at a Lincolnshire airbase.

According to Mrs Capes, the family travelled to Czechoslovakia after the war. She returned to England when the communists seized power in 1948 and her husband, who was in the anti-communist underground, attempted to follow with nine-year-old Mariella in 1950. Mariella said she and her father became separated after fleeing to West Germany, and then spent harrowing months in a camp for displaced persons. Years later, to prove it, Mariella would produce a childhood photograph of herself standing in a breadline. She said she later rejoined her mother in London.

Who was the father, and what became of him? Novotny said her father was 'first cousin' to President Antonin Novotny. 'I am ashamed of my relationship,' she said. 'It is something I have tried to hide all my life.' The Novotny she was referring to was a Khrushchev protégé who came to power in 1957. Josef Josten, a Czech journalist who came over to the West after the war, has confirmed Novotny's blood relationship with the Czech leader. It is clear that the British Government long knew about Novotny's father, and was sensitive about him entering the country. One document shows he was refused a visa to enter Britain in 1948, but Mariella's mother says he did eventually come to London.

When he did arrive, Mrs Capes has said, 'my husband acted very strangely. He was asked to leave by the Home Office . . . Mariella has grown up in an atmosphere of intrigue. She is very nervous. What my husband's secrets were I don't know – but we still get frightening echoes here in London . . .'

Novotny herself said her childhood was 'idyllic' until the communist takeover. 'I was never quite sure what my father did for a living,' she wrote later, 'but we were well off. What I am certain of is that almost alone of his family he was not a communist. He was, if you like, a political black sheep of the family. All I know is that my father was tipped off that the communists were about to seize power, and it would be best if he got out of the country . . .'

Novotny's mother, traced by us in 1985, refused to discuss her daughter. 'What does it matter?' she asked. 'They won't believe the truth.' The truth as to the whereabouts of Novotny's father, and, most important, his political loyalties, remains elusive. While it does, Mariella Novotny's role in the Profumo scandal remains especially intriguing. It began shortly before Christmas 1959, when she met Stephen Ward's friend, Hod Dibben.

FIVE

MARIELLA IN NEW YORK – THE KENNEDY CONNECTION

Dibben was playing nightclub boss again. With the take-over of Esmeralda's Barn by the notorious Kray twins, he opened a new club in Mayfair, called the Black Sheep. It would, he said, cater for 'black sheep from the titled families, because they are the rarest'. Dibben's customers included, among others, the Duke of Kent, Antony Armstrong-Jones and Douglas Fairbanks Jr. By the time Mariella came to the club, she was a teenage veteran of London nightlife. After training as a model, at her mother's suggestion, she had started as a hat-check girl at the Pigalle Club, then graduated to topless dancing. Now she wanted a job as a dancer at the Black Sheep, but settled for waitressing when told there were no vacancies. Novotny was probably introduced to Hod Dibben at the club by abortionist Teddy Sugden. He was fifty-four and she only eighteen, but they were to be married within the month.

It all came about, supposedly, as something of a joke. Novotny, though sensationally good-looking, was so short-sighted she could hardly see the customers she was serving in the gloom of the night-club. When one of the managers fired her she rushed up to Dibben in floods of tears, begging him to help. 'How about if I marry you?' he is said to have replied. Novotny stopped crying. 'I will,' she said.

Matt White, now Show Business Editor of the Sydney *Daily Mirror*, observed the touching scene. 'Hod, of course, was an antique compared to Mariella,' he remembers, 'but when he put a pair of black rimmed glasses on her she said, "I still love you. And I can't wait. Let's get married right away."' White sighs philosophically. 'God, knowing man's love for a puzzle, gave him woman . . . and Hod got Mariella.' Years later Novotny put it more prosaically: she did it to get away from her mother.

The couple married at Caxton Hall on 29 January 1960, with Dr Sugden as best man. So hilarious did they find the ceremony that the registrar threatened to stop the wedding. The large reception, at the Black Sheep, was photographed by David Bailey. It was on the honeymoon that Dibben discovered that his bride was terrified of sex – she said her fear was rooted in her childhood, when she witnessed rapes and public hangings during the chaos in Czechoslovakia and Austria at the end of the war. As we have seen, she says he did eventually take her to bed. Dibben, however, says that her marital 'first time' was a threesome: he watched while a male friend had sex with Novotny. If so, she started as she was to continue.

'Possibly my slow, late start as a promiscuous girl,' Novotny wrote later, 'urged me to taste more than most . . . Hod made it clear from the start I could be as permissive as I liked . . . The endless parties I went to were extravagant, and I met many famous names.' One of her first encounters on the London scene was with a friend of her husband who was going to become notorious, Stephen Ward.

Ward was at a party given by American millionaire Huntington Hartford, an occasion which Novotny called 'a turning-point'. Also, there was a forty-year-old show business whizz kid named Harry Towers, and he quickly showed interest in her. He telephoned after the party, inviting her to tea at Claridge's. Over the teacups, according to Novotny, 'Towers said he could make me into a television model for commercials in America.' Novotny already had a London modelling contract, but she decided to go to New York with her impresario.

Harry Towers, now a prosperous film producer working out of Hollywood and Toronto, rocketed to success after a wartime post as a programme director for British Forces radio. In the fifties he had been a leading figure in the founding of commercial television and become a senior executive of ATV. Later, however, one of his companies had gone into liquidation, with £48,000 owing to creditors.

Towers' secretary in 1960, Margaret Van Beers, thought him 'a genius in many ways' but 'a pig' in others. One of the things that offended her was Towers' sex life. She recalled, disgustedly, 'the times I left his flat and office and met some sleazy tart on the way up to him'.

According to Novotny, Towers invited her to his flat to meet his mother and a group of Americans, one of whom – having asked her into another room to speak privately – promptly stripped off his clothes. 'I was anxious to do well in New York,' she wrote, 'so I shrugged and decided to do whatever was necessary . . . Neither Towers nor his mother gave any indication of knowing what we had done on our return to the drawing-room . . .'

Towers, said Novotny, drew up a contract for her to work for him in the United States. Towers says he simply said, 'Do you want to come to New York and have a laugh?' Novotny agreed, and – since he was going on ahead – he bought her a plane ticket. 'The day before I flew to America,' Novotny said, 'Stephen Ward came to dinner and drew three sketches of me.'

Towers and Novotny offer diverging accounts of what happened in New York. She later told the FBI, 'Towers took me to the Great Northern Hotel . . . The following afternoon Towers brought a prostitution date to me, —————————,* who paid me $40 to commit a sexual act. Thereafter I entertained prostitution dates regularly and earned approximately $400 a week. I gave Towers about $300 of this money.' Later, Novotny told the FBI, 'Towers was present when prostitution acts were committed', at a Manhattan apartment. She provided detailed lists of madames and prostitutes who had arranged dates, or gone on threesomes with her – all, she claimed, introduced to her

*Name blanked out in FBI release.

by Towers. She named some of her customers who, she said, paid for a peculiarly British speciality. 'They desired to be whipped with cat-o'-nine-tails.'

Towers says today, 'I had an affair with her and didn't know she was a hooker. Our total involvement was that she joined me in New York and lived with me in a couple of hotels . . . I got into trouble through my own stupidity.' Towers dismisses Novotny's accounts as 'absolute fantasy'.

One thing that was brutal reality for both Towers and Novotny was the day in March 1961, three months after Novotny's arrival, when police of the 18th Precinct raided Towers' apartment. Assistant District Attorney William Reilly had received an anonymous call advising him that Novotny was plying her trade as a prostitute at that address. Patrolman Thomas Flood later told a court how he arrived in plain clothes, posing as a customer. Then, when Novotny was half-naked, he identified himself as a police officer.

Towers still shivers at the memory. 'I was in the other room writing a screenplay,' he says. 'She came rushing into the room – she wasn't living with me then, she'd asked if she could come up to meet somebody – I was busy working when she rushed in naked and said there was a policeman in the other room.' Novotny, in her memoir, remembered it differently: 'Towers was hiding in a walk-in cupboard. They hauled him out . . . He denied knowing me when asked about our relationship.'

The couple were arrested and charged, Towers for importing a woman for prostitution and maintaining a disorderly house, and Novotny as 'a wayward minor'. Bail for Towers was set at $10,000, bail for Novotny at $500.

The Assistant District Attorney prosecuting the case, Alfred Donati, remembers Novotny well. 'Confident, pretty, with a sense of humour . . . she looked like a model, not like a whore . . . she made no great denial of the charges.'

Two things about the Novotny case troubled Donati. Novotny had told him, and so had the FBI, that she was related to President Novotny of Czechoslovakia. Moreover, he says, 'It was not just a prostitution case for me. I knew it would be high profile. I thought celebrity names would be brought in.'

Weeks later, at a further court hearing, Donati demanded that Towers' passport be confiscated and a higher bail set. He now spoke of information that 'a large number of men and women of prominence and very substantial financial means were customers or otherwise involved in the defendant's procurement business. The trial, of necessity, would expose a number of people to a great deal of unwanted publicity, so that should some or all of them desire to make their resources available to the defendant to induce him to leave the country . . . there would be nothing to lose except the sum of $10,000 bail presently imposed.'

The Assistant DA's request was rejected by Judge Matzner, a recent federal appointee. He then asked the FBI to maintain surveillance on Towers and Novotny, but was told it was impossible. Donati was therefore not surprised, a week or so later, to receive a call from a reporter informing him that Harry Towers had flown the coop. He had left the country – destination unknown. Not long after, Mariella Novotny vanished too. On 31 May 1961, she sailed for London aboard the *Queen Mary*, under the name Mrs R. Tyson. She managed to board without a passport – probably as though she was seeing someone off – and was only discovered once the liner was at sea. When the ship arrived at Southampton, Novotny was allowed to enter the country without difficulty.

'One faction,' Novotny wrote later, 'sighed with relief when I left . . . I had become a political pawn . . . Three authorities, the State Police, the FBI and Immigration, were all claiming I came under their jurisdiction, but the most popular theory is that the CIA made my escape easy . . .'

Later, in London, Stephen Ward talked to Mandy Rice-Davies about Novotny's return from America. 'He said,' Rice-Davies says, 'that one night the CIA or something had picked her up, literally, from her apartment, and eventually put her on a boat, and that was that. Stephen said it in a matter-of-fact sort of way. This was years before she said so.'

Novotny was not alone in her theorising. At the time of the Profumo Affair, an FBI official stated flatly in a report, 'Marie [sic] Novotny was obviously aided by persons unknown to leave the US . . .' Who was behind the escape, and why did they want Novotny out of the country?

On her arrival in England, Novotny told her story to Peter Earle, senior crime reporter for the *News of the World*. It was published as a rambling tale that told much of her arrest and escape, but little of what she had actually been doing in New York. In fact, Earle now reveals, his newspaper refrained – for diplomatic reasons – from printing the story Mariella poured out: that Towers had successfully manoeuvred her into the bed of the man about to be inaugurated as President of the United States, and of his brother Robert, shortly to become Attorney-General. Earle, a veteran reporter, believed the story, and believes it still.

Shortly after her arrival in New York, Novotny said in her memoir, Towers introduced her to a man who 'went away highly impressed with the new import from "Swinging London"'. A round of hectic lunches and parties followed. The first lunch date was at Luchow's, and there I met Peter Lawford, one of the leaders of the Kennedy clan . . . Then I was shot into the whirl of parties and was introduced to JFK, the President-elect. I heard several stories of his escapades, and met some of the girls he had had affairs with . . . The first time I met JFK was at a large party held at the Hampshire House.* Vic Damone, the singer, was the host . . .'

'The suite contained a number of rooms,' according to Novotny. 'JFK was simply called the Senator and we were shown into an empty bedroom . . . it seemed quite natural to be taken aside for a quiet talk. He talked about England briefly, but locked the door and undressed as he chatted . . .' Novotny recalled a hurried sexual encounter,

*In New York.

followed by a discreet return to Vic Damone's party. It ended abruptly, she said, when Damone's Asian girlfriend locked herself into a bathroom and slashed her wrists. 'I have never known a party finish so quickly. JFK disappeared with a group of close associates – I was bustled out among a crowd of nervous guests . . .'

In a second document, apparently written after her first memoir, Novotny made a point of correcting an error. The first meeting with John Kennedy, she said, was actually at an apartment in New York's Gracie Square. It was the first sexual encounter, she explained, that took place at the Hampshire House, and it was this that was arranged by Peter Lawford.

Nobody today seriously denies that John Kennedy was a chronic philanderer. 'He had the most active libido of any man I have ever known,' said his close friend and confidant, Senator George Smathers. 'Travelling with him was like travelling with a bull,' said a fellow congressman.

Kennedy, forty-three when he allegedly bedded the nineteen-year-old Novotny, had no qualms about paying for his pleasure on occasion. One White House staffer recalls being stopped on his rounds by a Secret Service guard who explained, 'The President has got a hundred-dollar hooker with him right now.' (That was expensive in the early sixties.) One District Attorney's investigator, in Los Angeles, got used to requests from Secret Service colleagues to 'find a woman for the President'. Sometimes the order was for two girls at a time.

Peter Lawford, Novotny's first contact with the Kennedys, was married to Kennedy's sister, Patricia. With Frank Sinatra, he had been at the forefront of the Kennedy election propaganda campaign. He was a debauched figure, a devotee of group sex – and something of a masochist, a trait that may have made Mariella Novotny seem especially interesting. One former female associate recalls that, rather than making love, Lawford 'wanted me to bite his nipples till they bled'. 'I saw Peter,' says Dean Martin's former wife Jeanne, 'in the role of pimp for Jack Kennedy.'

Kennedy was elected President in November 1960 and

inaugurated on 20 January 1961. He stayed at his usual New York base, the Carlyle Hotel, during the first week of January. As is now well established, Kennedy had his own escape route from the hotel, a series of tunnels that connected the Carlyle with nearby apartment houses and hotels. Novotny had arrived in New York in December, and did not leave the country until the end of May.

According to Novotny, she also took part in a group sex game with Kennedy. The scenario played out involved two other prostitutes who pretended to be nurse and doctor to Kennedy as patient. Peter Lawford, Novotny claimed, recruited the prostitutes. They duly arrived, 'an attractive blonde with a stern face . . . and a younger girl with a kind, fresh look'. One of them had indeed studied medicine at the University of California. After a teasing session with the girls in hospital uniforms, they all had sex together. Later, said Novotny, she visited the President at a house in Washington and also had sex with the President's brother, Robert.

There is nothing especially implausible about this. John Kennedy had long been chronically ill with back and glandular problems, and almost certainly had Addison's Disease. He was no stranger to hospitals, and – if he was to have fetishes – a nursing scenario seems as likely as any. Anecdotes of his sex life, from women and from law enforcement sources, leave little doubt that he enjoyed group sex. It has emerged recently that Robert Kennedy, long regarded as a sexual puritan, also had extra-marital affairs.

Mariella Novotny gave the FBI an address book, listing names of her New York clients from the world of politics, law and business. According to the Bureau it has now been destroyed, as has the FBI's New York file on Towers and Novotny.

The Kennedy brothers, of course, are dead, as is Mariella Novotny. Following his escape from New York, Harry Towers was first reported to be in Copenhagen, and was then seen by a friend in Moscow. Today he says, 'I realised I had less to fear from the law than from the press

. . . The most inaccessible place I could think of was to do a tour of the USSR. It took an awful long time to live it down, and all I did was spend four or five months in the USSR, Czechoslovakia and Hungary . . . It was immediately assumed on top of everything else that I was a communist spy . . .'

Nearly twenty years later, Harry Towers pleaded guilty to the lesser charges of bail-jumping and contempt of court. He continued to deny the prostitution charges, and they were now dropped. He has resumed his business activities in the United States.

The man who originally handled Novotny, Alfred Donati, was asked in 1982 whether there had been an espionage connection in the case. He replied, 'I can't comment on that . . . Things get back to confidentiality between the District Attorney and the FBI.' Asked if the Novotny affair was just an open-and-shut vice matter, Donati replied, 'If it were just an open-and-shut case I could certainly comment on it. Right? You understand what I'm saying? I cannot be more specific . . .'

Mariella Novotny's New York activity in early 1961 may have been independent of Towers. He says, and Novotny in her memoir agrees, that he spent much of his time away in London. Meanwhile, Novotny's nominal husband – and Stephen Ward's friend – arrived on the scene. Hod Dibben confirms that he visited New York at that time, 'to see Mariella and to buy antiques at Parke Bernet'.

Dibben says he was at the Hampshire House party at which Novotny allegedly had her first sexual encounter with John Kennedy. He remembers the President-elect being bundled out of the building when it was discovered that a girl had slashed her wrists in the bathroom. Novotny told him about the Kennedy contacts, and he believed her. And there was something else.

'I received a special delivery letter from Douglas Fairbanks Jr,' Novotny writes in her memoir. 'Stephen Ward had told him to get in touch when he was in New York. Hod and I went to see him and were amused at his prominent display of photographs of the Royal Family. I found him almost a caricature of himself, but he was fun for a while . . .'

Dibben remembers going to see Fairbanks with Novotny, and recalls specific details of the Fairbanks' apartment. Fairbanks, for his part, told us in 1984, 'Although I am very interested in your letter, I am sorry I cannot help you, because I don't remember meeting or even knowing anyone by the name of Mariella Novotny . . . If I did meet Miss Novotny it must have been in a group . . .'

Fairbanks did know Stephen Ward and, as we saw earlier, two of Ward's girls claim to have gone to bed with him. He had also been a patron of Dibben's Black Sheep Club in London.

Mariella Novotny was back in England, after her curiously easy escape from the District Attorney in New York, by the beginning of June 1961. 'In London,' she wrote, 'Stephen Ward was the first to contact me . . .' Soon she was a visitor at the Cliveden cottage, preparing for a new career as London's premier orgy hostess. She was now to play a new role, in Operation Honeytrap. Back in Washington, Novotny's most famous sex partner was now President – with doomsday worries on his mind.

SIX

MI5 SETS THE TRAP

The President of the United States did not sleep easily in the summer of 1961. His friends and family noticed a change in him. The jaunty young man who had taken office just a few months earlier seemed suddenly worn, preoccupied, and would fall into deep thought in the middle of social occasions. One night, sitting up late at the White House, the President telephoned Paul Fay, Secretary of the Navy and an old wartime friend.

'Have you,' asked John Kennedy, 'got around to building that bomb shelter yet?'

'No,' laughed Fay, 'I built a swimming-pool instead.'

'You made a mistake,' said Kennedy quietly.

The Kennedy presidency had begun with a disastrous skirmish with communism, when an American-sponsored invasion of Cuba ended in humiliating defeat at the Bay of Pigs. Now a far greater confrontation was looming – with the larger and more dangerous adversary, the Soviet Union. Khrushchev, the Soviet leader, was trying to force the West to relinquish its occupation rights in West Berlin.

The giants were wrestling, in a bout that would not end till the Cuban Missile Crisis in late 1962, when the world trembled – more than ever before or since – in the shadow of nuclear war.

The political thunder the world hears comes from the bombast of politicians: Khrushchev banging his shoe on the desk at the United Nations, Kennedy's cry of 'Ich Bin Ein Berliner!' from atop the Berlin Wall. The real doomsday clock ticks down more quietly, in private places where diplomats talk alone, the Rose Garden of the White House, at Chequers, the British Prime Minister's country mansion, and at meetings rarely known to anyone but the participants – the secret assignations of spies. Huddled in hotel rooms and restaurants, at airports and border crossings, these men spin the thousand threads for the tapestry of information that makes more public men choose between peace or war. In 1961, Dr Stephen Ward became part of that tapestry, in a way that has been obscured for a quarter of a century.

In 1963, when the Profumo Affair was at its height, Prime Minister Macmillan asked Lord Denning, the senior judge of the Court of Appeal, to enquire into the security aspects of the scandal. His specific brief was to 'examine the operation of the Security Service . . . and to consider any evidence there may be for believing that national security has been, or may be, endangered'. What had British Intelligence been up to, and had there been a security leak? Those were the questions that mattered, the ones being asked in Parliament, and the ones that mattered far more than who had slept with whom.

Three months later Denning submitted his report. Its 343 numbered paragraphs somehow obscured the very issues it set out to investigate. The Report's conclusions, themselves almost lost in verbiage, were that British Intelligence had rightly decided that 'there was no security interest in the matter', and that there had been no security leak.

There was a very real security issue, and there were excellent reasons – from the point of view of the Government and of British Intelligence – for covering it up. The spy part of the story, as Lord Denning told it, began only because Stephen Ward – the dead man held responsible for everything – wanted to go to Moscow. Ward, according to the Denning version, was therefore introduced to Captain Ivanov, the Soviet Assistant Naval Attaché, by the obliging editor of a national newspaper. And so, according to

Denning, events tumbled one upon another, by chance
rather than design. Ward met Ivanov, who met Ward's girl,
Christine Keeler. Ivanov and Keeler both met Minister
Profumo at Lord Astor's swimming-pool. The Minister for
War went to bed with Keeler, and the seeds of scandal were
sown.

It was not like that at all. The evidence bears, rather, the
fingerprints of British Intelligence, manœuvring against
Soviet Intelligence, groping to please its counterparts at the
CIA. This is a story that takes place on the espionage
battlefield during the political drama that shook the world
in 1961 and 1962. It began, however, with a tiresome case of
lumbago.

The man with the bad back was Captain Colin Coote,
Managing Editor of the Conservative paper, the *Daily
Telegraph*. According to Coote, in his memoir, a friend had
suggested he visit Stephen Ward for treatment. It worked,
and a grateful Coote invited Ward to his home for bridge.
Ward played a 'quite passable' game, and the two men got
to know each other. It was Coote who brought Ward and
Captain Ivanov together.

In January 1961, Stephen Ward found himself hurrying
up the stairs of the Garrick Club, a few minutes late for the
lunch that would in the end lead to his downfall. Waiting for
him were Coote, David Floyd, the *Telegraph*'s specialist on
communist affairs, and the Soviet Assistant Naval Attaché.
'Sir Colin is a great gourmet,' said Ward in his memoir.
'The food and wine were excellent. So was the conversation, and I listened with fascination as Floyd and Eugene
Ivanov argued backwards and forwards on issues which I
had never heard discussed before in an intelligent and
informal manner.'

After lunch, Ward and the Russian went from the Garrick to Ward's consulting-rooms in Devonshire Street,
stopping on the way to visit the impresario Jack Hylton at
Savile Row. While Hylton played the piano, the osteopath
and the spy talked. 'I realised for the first time,' Ward
wrote, 'that this ought to happen more often – a frank

discussion of points of view between ordinary Russians and Englishmen. We arranged to meet again.'

The meetings that followed were to have momentous consequences. But why did Colin Coote introduce them in the first place? Coote said later that he had done so as a favour to Ward. He claimed that, knowing Ward's talent as an artist, he had hired him to go to Israel to draw scenes at the trial of the Nazi murderer Adolf Eichmann. Later, during further back treatment, Ward complained that he was having trouble getting a visa to travel to the Soviet Union, where he wanted to draw Khrushchev. It so happened, according to Coote, that he had met Ivanov a few days earlier during a visit to the *Telegraph* offices by a group of Soviet naval officers. He thought Ivanov might be useful in getting Ward a visa, and therefore set up the luncheon at the Garrick.

Denning would later deal with this entire episode, the beginning of the Profumo Affair, in just nine lines. Coote's version of the matter, published within two years of the Affair, is a jumble of inaccuracies. Ward indeed covered the Eichmann trial for the *Telegraph*, but not until months *after* Coote had introduced him to Ivanov. Stephen Ward himself, in his memoir, said flatly: 'There is no truth in the suggestion that I befriended Ivanov because I wanted to draw Khrushchev.' Colin Coote had simply suggested he join the lunch party to meet Ivanov, whom he thought Ward would find 'fascinating'.

David Floyd, the only man at the lunch still available for interview, says he was 'drawn into it by Colin Coote, who wanted someone to translate'. Yet there was no translating to do, for 'Ivanov spoke very good English'. Floyd says he attached little importance to the lunch at the time.

Coote, in his memoir, poured venom on the dead Ward. The osteopath's political views, he said, referring to Ward's interest in a continuing dialogue with Russia, 'would have seemed ludicrous to a mentally deficient child . . . I should doubt,' he went on, 'whether a more trivial person has ever seriously embarrassed a government.'

Yet Ward was a man whom Coote had chosen as bridge

partner and dining companion. And there was something else. Contrary to the impression Coote gave – that he had met Ward not long before the scandal – Ward himself referred to Coote as 'a friend of mine for many years . . . it was this friendship which led me into the limelight over the Profumo Affair.'

Coote seems to have been unnaturally keen to distance himself from Ward, to explain away the fact that his actions triggered the contacts between Ward and the Russian. He does not mention anywhere a second visit by Ivanov to the *Telegraph*, mentioned by Ward in his memoir. That perceptive observer of political affairs, Rebecca West, who studied the Profumo case at the time, was perplexed by the public explanation of the Garrick lunch. 'The story,' she mused, in her book *The Meaning of Treason*, 'is already odd.'

Odd it was. At the height of the affair, just before the Profumo debate in Parliament, Prime Minister Macmillan wrote a curiously careful letter to Coote:

Dear Colin,
I think I ought to let you know that in my speech . . . I shall refer to the fact that as it happened Captain Ivanov was first introduced to Mr Ward by you. I shall say expressly that there was nothing whatever *unusual or reprehensible** in this introduction. It is only that it forms part of my narrative.
Yours ever
Harold Macmillan

Coote and Macmillan were both Balliol men, as the saying goes in the language of Oxford snobbery. They were old friends from pre-war days, when both opposed appeasement policies in the Conservative Party. Macmillan's note seems more than a formality – it is almost as though the man known as the 'Old Actor-Manager' is making sure everybody gets the story straight, as though there is something

*Authors' italics.

unspoken between the two men. A hard look at Coote's background may provide a clue.

After distinguished service in World War I, Coote served as *The Times* correspondent in Rome in the twenties and thirties. During that period, though, he also had another role – as controller of an Intelligence network run by Desmond Morton, who had been the number three man in MI6 – the Secret Intelligence Service. In World War II Coote headed the Public Relations department at the War Office, and was involved in propaganda operations. In the years leading up to the Profumo Affair, Coote was a close friend and golfing partner of Roger Hollis, the Director-General of MI5. He was introduced to Ward by Sir Godfrey Nicholson, who recommended him to Coote as an osteopath. Nicholson, a Conservative MP, would later be involved, like Ward, in negotiations with the Soviets.

Although it may trouble some readers, none of this is very exceptional. British Intelligence has always used journalists, and there was a time when '*Times* correspondent' was almost synonymous with 'Intelligence agent'. As late as 1975, the *Washington Post* reported that all London dailies had some journalists who were in the pay of British Intelligence. The most famous reporter on the MI6 payroll was Kim Philby, the double-agent who used the *Observer* and the *Economist* as cover in the fifties. The Soviets later published a list of 'agent' journalists, probably supplied to them by Philby. It included the name of Michael Berry*, owner and editor-in-chief of the *Daily Telegraph* – the boss of the man who set up the meeting between Ward and Ivanov. Why would British Intelligence contrive such a meeting?

For many reasons, some justifiable and some less so, straightforward reporting about British Intelligence is notoriously difficult. Clearly, writers must decide carefully when to reveal the identity of agents who might be personally damaged by the disclosures. The present Government,

*Later Lord Hartwell.

at the other extreme, using the discredited Official Secrets Act, has gone to ludicrous lengths to prevent former Intelligence officials publishing memoirs, and to protect secrets that need no longer be secret. From this point on in this book, although sources will always be named if possible, a number must remain anonymous. We must ask the reader to bear with us as we investigate British Intelligence and its operations after Captain Ivanov arrived in Britain.

It was March 1960 when Ivanov took up his post as an Assistant Naval Attaché at the Soviet Embassy, ten months before the fateful introduction to Stephen Ward. He held the rank of captain, second rank, in the Soviet Navy, equivalent to a commander in the British service. He was thirty-seven years old, dark and tall, unusual in a man who claimed Mongol ancestry. Christine Keeler thought him a 'huggy-bear of a man'. Colin Coote found him 'an agreeable personality'. He was well-mannered and more sophisticated than most of the Soviet diplomats Moscow sent abroad in those days. He enjoyed socialising, and seemed free to meet foreigners – as at the Coote luncheon – without a Soviet colleague tagging along. There was something different about Ivanov, and MI5 noticed.

MI5's D branch, responsible for counter-espionage, quickly identified Ivanov as a Soviet Intelligence officer using diplomatic cover, a common practice worldwide. According to one source, part of Ivanov's mission may have been to supervise Soviet penetration of the Portland naval base in Dorset. Portland, the development base for several of Britain's most secret submarine and radar projects, was, in the late fifties, the specific target of Soviet spy Gordon Lonsdale, who in turn controlled Harry Houghton and his girlfriend Ethel Gee, who worked at the base. MI5's surveillance of the Portland spy ring continued for more than a year, until arrests were made in January 1961 – the month of Ward's introduction to Ivanov. With or without the Portland connection, MI5 had built up a dossier on Ivanov by early 1961.

In April 1961, three months after Coote's luncheon with Ivanov and Ward at the Garrick Club, one of the most important events in the history of modern espionage took place, at dead of night, at the Mount Royal Hotel in London. The chief delegate of a Soviet trade delegation quietly left his room and proceeded to a suite of rooms on the floor above. The suite had been specially prepared for a major intelligence debriefing. There were tape-recorders, encoding machines, radio equipment, and a special phone-link to the CIA in Arlington, Virginia. The team waiting for the Russian included two members of MI6, codenamed 'Grille' and 'Miles', and George Kisvalter of the CIA, nicknamed 'Teddy Bear'. The Russian traitor, now to be interrogated, was – for Allied Intelligence – the 'single most important spy' ever to bring his country's secrets to the West.*

The Russian was Oleg Penkovsky, nominally a senior civilian member of the State Committee for Coordination of Scientific Research, actually a Colonel in the GRU – Soviet Military Intelligence. Contrary to popular notions, it is the GRU rather than the internal security apparatus, the KGB, which has been responsible for most Soviet intelligence successes since the Revolution. The best evidence is that the GRU has considerable independence, and that GRU officers consider themselves the professional superiors to their KGB counterparts.

Colonel Penkovsky had fallen into the lap of MI6 in November 1960, after he approached an official at the Canadian Embassy in Moscow. The contacts matured on his London visit in spring 1961, when he sat in the Mount Royal Hotel pouring out a treasure trove of Soviet secrets. There was so much talking to cram into his night-time visits that MI6 kept a doctor on hand with drugs to keep Penkovsky awake. His nickname became 'Sleepless Nights' and the resulting material was code-named ALEXANDER.

The ALEXANDER dossier produced a wealth of information directly relevant to MI5's interest in Captain Ivanov. Penkovsky, using his access to GRU central registry and

*Some believe to this day he was a Soviet plant. We tend to the view that he was authentic, and the controversy has no place in these pages.

thus to the personal files of numerous GRU officers, was able to brief British Intelligence in great detail on GRU personnel at the Soviet Embassy in London. They included the GRU station chief Nicolai Karpekov – case officer for the homosexual Admiralty spy William Vassall – his deputy Anatolij Pavlov, and Assistant Naval Attaché Ivanov.

When a new Soviet diplomat arrived in town, Western Intelligence usually had little more to go on than a name, a rank, and another taciturn foreigner in an ill-cut suit. The rest was a blank that needed laborious filling in. From Penkovsky's information, passed on by MI6, and their other sources, MI5 could now put features on the Ivanov blank. He was, they learned, a son-in-law of the Chairman of the Soviet Supreme Court, Alexander Gorkin. Gorkin's other son-in-law, Igor Konstantinov, was married to Ivanov's sister-in-law. He was a drinker and womaniser, and Gorkin had once had to intercede to save him from dismissal.* The man who tried to fire him was the current head of the GRU, General Ivan Serov, a veteran of SMERSH and the KGB, of which he was head in the mid-fifties.

These and other details told MI5 a good deal about Ivanov. He was well-connected by marriage to a man high in the Moscow élite. Whatever his talents, he had risen through the bureaucracy thanks to family patronage. Ivanov, by now known in London diplomatic circles as 'Foxface', had brought his wife with him, a shy, petite former teacher. Yet, as MI5 had not failed to observe, she was regularly left to cool her heels at home. The attaché spent a good deal of time out alone, driving his black Austin A40. He drank a good deal, without being a soak, and he bought his clothes at John Barker's in Kensington.

Ivanov, especially by 1961 standards, was an interesting Russian. As the Coote lunch had shown, he was trusted to meet Westerners on his own. But, MI5 had to wonder, was he a dedicated GRU man doing his job, or was he – just

---

*In 1971, Konstantinov would be one of the 105 Soviet agents expelled from Britain.

maybe – vulnerable? The regime of Ivanov's boss, General Serov, was a time of unparalleled corruption, remarkable even in a system in which corruption is a way of life. Historically, it was also the one period when a number of GRU officers voluntarily made contact with Western services and provided valid information. Handled cleverly, would Ivanov prove a useful source? Was there even a possibility that, in intelligence parlance, he could be turned? Was he potentially the ultimate prize, a valuable defector?

The Denning report says that – at a much later date – 'a thought occurred to the Security Service that . . . it might be possible to get Ivanov to defect?'

Denning was in an unprecedented quandary. He had to go through the motions of showing he had investigated the performance of the security services, because that was his brief. The very notion, though, was a contradiction in terms. The Security Service in Britain was built on the principle that it must remain just that – secret. It is not recognised by law, and its existence is not even mentioned in the Official Secrets Act, the law governing national security. In 1963, an Establishment under attack had no interest in rocking the boat of the Security Service, a creature of the Establishment staffed by Establishment officers born and bred in the same mould as the Conservative Prime Minister and his ministers.

Denning was able to report that he made two visits to the headquarters of MI5, that he had interviewed its chief, Roger Hollis. MI5 even gave him some documents for publication, the first and only time such material had been provided by British Intelligence. Lord Denning said in 1986, 'I had complete access to their files, memoranda, correspondence.' A senior MI5 officer, however, speaking unattributably, said flatly, 'Denning had wool pulled over his eyes.'

The MI5 officer at the centre of the 1987 row over publication of his memoirs, Peter Wright, said of his own case, 'None of the files will be released. The Director has supreme power at the time . . . what they do is, they cook the files for an enquiry.'

Wright was speaking as if from experience, and he was with MI5 at the time of the Profumo Affair. We know that MI5 did not cooperate willingly with Denning – it was ordered to do so by the Prime Minister. It seems more than possible that Denning was shown files doctored, or sanitised, by high MI5 officials. At best, MI5 did not lie – it simply did not tell the whole truth, certainly not about its plans for Ivanov.

The thought of Ivanov's defection did not just 'occur' to MI5. The turning of an important defector is a matter as sensitive as the catching of a salmon on a difficult stretch of river. The right lure must be selected, the cast made well, the right moment chosen to strike. And if the lure is taken, the salmon must be played with skill – and often great patience – before it ends up in the landing net. One false move, and the prey is gone. So it is in intelligence. MI5 would happily devote months, even years, to the turning of an Ivanov.

Today's best guess is that Colin Coote's luncheon, in January 1961, was the moment the operation began. Stephen Ward, probably unwittingly at that point, was the lure. One MI5 source has said, unconvincingly, that British Intelligence only became interested in Ward months later, because of Ivanov's visits to his flat. The source claimed they discovered Ward's identity only by matching his name to his address – 17, Wimpole Mews – on the Electoral Roll. We found that Ward's name did not appear linked to that address in 1961, nor in any other year. The MI5 story collapses on scrutiny.

It is much more likely that British Intelligence was aware of Ward *before* the Ivanov operation was planned. A former MI6 source says his service was briefed on the plan, and that MI5 knew about Ward through his friend Lord Astor, himself a former Naval Intelligence officer with experience in turning enemy agents. The decision to bring Ivanov together with Ward was made after the attaché visited the *Daily Telegraph* as part of a Soviet naval group. Colin Coote, a personal friend of the head of MI5, could then invite Ivanov to lunch without it seeming too contrived.

Both Astor and Coote knew Ward well, and he fitted the bill as a lure excellently. Ward seemed soft on the Soviet Union – he was forever talking about dialogue between nations and seeing the good side of communism as well as the bad. He was a social gadfly, and nothing would delight him more than to roam London society with a real live Russian in tow.

Finally, and most importantly, Ward would give Ivanov a good time. As Astor had known for years – and as half the rich bachelors in London knew – Ward could always provide a 'popsy'.

All the elements were there for, at least, a harmless reconnaissance. Perhaps, just perhaps, there might be a successful Honeytrap.

The Soviets themselves have always been the principal exponents of the Honeytrap ploy, but – by the early sixties – Western intelligence services were interested in turning the trick back against the enemy. KGB and GRU officers were taught that girls in bars and nightclubs were likely to be in the pay of foreign intelligence. Sexual liaisons outside Soviet Embassy communities were forbidden. That aside, while Russians did not have the Western puritanism about sex, they were tied by the corset of convention.

This Russian, Ivanov, was married, and a trained agent. However, as Denning was to report when it was all over, he also 'drank a good deal, and was something of a ladies' man'. An introduction to Ward was a way of bringing him into the company of women who were not common prostitutes, and therefore more likely to catch him off his guard. A Honeytrap might work. In any case, an introduction to Ward was a way of bringing the Soviet attaché into the orbit of men who were simultaneously Ward's friends and friends of MI5 – in a way that would not scare him off. It might work.

And so it came to pass that Stephen Ward found himself walking through the streets of London with Eugene Ivanov after lunch at the Garrick Club, and inviting him to visit the cottage on Lord Astor's estate at Cliveden.

In his open social life at any rate, Ivanov was always careful to observe the Foreign Office rule that Soviet diplomats may not travel more than twenty-five miles outside London without special permission. Happily Cliveden was just inside the red circle on the map the Russian kept in his car. That very weekend, he drove down to the cottage.

Ward was to write, 'We all chip in there with the work, chopping wood, washing up, cooking and cleaning. He joined in with gusto . . .' Soon Ivanov was a regular guest. 'We used to ramble in the lovely woodland, and picnic on the lawn,' said Ward. 'He used to heave rocks about as I built my rock garden, and we constructed a flight of steps which we christened the Steppes of Russia.'

Back in London, Ivanov began spending a good deal of time at the Wimpole Mews flat in Marylebone. He and Ward played bridge, a game Ward loved and Ivanov knew a little. Ivanov's bridge improved, and he began to meet Ward's friends. 'He used to come round at any time,' Ward recalled, 'usually bearing vodka or some rare and undrinkable liqueur from some remote part of Russia.'

There were discussions about politics. 'Many were the arguments and discussions we had, some heated, always ending in a draw,' Ward said later. New acquaintances soon got over their misgivings about hobnobbing with a Russian. People discovered, Ward thought, 'that Russians could be very human, and that it was possible that there was another side of the question. I seldom saw disapproval . . . there was curiosity and interest.'

There were two other things. Ivanov was 'obviously fascinated' by the idea of visiting the big house at Cliveden, Lord Astor's mansion, half a mile from Ward's cottage. The Russian was convinced that the aristocracy still played a key role in Britain, and in 1963 – though Ward argued the point – he may not have been entirely wrong. Meanwhile, in London, Ivanov rarely brought his wife with him when he came to see Stephen Ward. And on the visits to Wimpole Mews Ivanov encountered several of Ward's girls. One of them was Christine Keeler.

As winter turned to spring, Stephen Ward the artist was busier and more successful than he had ever been. In January 1961, the month he had met Ivanov, his work had been exhibited at Leggatt's of St James, the fine art gallery. It was an honour, the first time the gallery had shown the works of a living artist since its foundation in 1820. The editor of the *Illustrated London News*, Sir Bruce Ingram, was so impressed that he offered Ward a commission to do a series of sketches of the Royal Family.

Ingram had been a close friend of the Queen's grandfather, King George V, and that oiled the approach to Buckingham Palace. Between March and July, Ward sketched eight members of the Royal Family. They were Princess Margaret and Antony Armstrong-Jones, the Duke and Duchess of Gloucester, the Duke and Duchess of Kent, Princess Marina and Prince Philip. Ward drew the Prince at Buckingham Palace. The Queen's husband was, Ward thought, 'a wonderful sitter, still as a rock, but relaxed'.

As the sitting began, Prince Philip exclaimed, 'By Jove, you're the osteopath. I never connected you with this appointment.' He had not realised that the artist Stephen Ward was one and the same as the Stephen Ward whom he had met back in the late forties. Before he left the Palace, Ward recalled before he died, he and the Duke 'discussed the old days'.

'The old days' – the years of the Milford Haven debauches – were not a topic the Duke would relish becoming a public talking-point, and he would not have been so relaxed had he had an inkling of the scandal that was to break around Ward. The intriguing fate of Ward's royal portraits will be revealed later in this book.

In April 1961, Ward went to Israel on an assignment for the *Daily Telegraph*, to cover the Eichmann war crimes trial. His companion on the trip was the Earl of Birkenhead, brother-in-law of the *Telegraph*'s editor-in-chief, an author and veteran of political intelligence work at the Foreign Office. The Earl's account of the trial accompanied Ward's sketches.

In little more than a year, Ward had drawn – apart from the Royal Family – Prime Minister Harold Macmillan, Sir Winston Churchill, Home Secretary R. A. Butler, Harry Hylton-Foster, the Speaker; Foreign Secretary Selwyn Lloyd; the Chancellor of the Exchequer, Derick Heathcoat Amory; Hugh Gaitskell, Leader of the Opposition; Canadian Prime Minister John Diefenbaker; Archbishop Makarios, the Cypriot leader; a man he already knew well socially, filmstar Douglas Fairbanks Jr; and numerous others.

Selwyn Lloyd sat for Ward twice, on the second occasion as Chancellor of the Exchequer. Ward, irritated about the Government's 'Pay Pause', added a little joke, a minute hammer and sickle behind the Chancellor's ear.

Meanwhile, as he scurried from sitting to sitting, Dr Ward the osteopath continued to see his full complement of distinguished patients, and, especially at weekends, the Soviet Assistant Naval Attaché. It was a fascinating period for Ward, doubtless for Ivanov too, and a worrying time for the world.

SEVEN

RECRUITING DR WARD

On Sunday, 4 June 1961, at the start of a broiling summer, President Kennedy flew into London. Accompanied by Prime Minister Macmillan, he drove through the streets of London in an open car, cheered by enthusiastic crowds.

Kennedy knew England well. He had spent time here as a young man, when his father was ambassador, on the eve of World War II. Then, and on subsequent visits, he had enjoyed himself amongst the élite of British society. He met the Astors and the aristocratic Cliveden set, who became controversial for their efforts to keep Britain out of the war. The President was even linked to Harold Macmillan by marriage – Macmillan had married the daughter of the ninth Duke of Devonshire, and Kennedy's sister Kathleen had married the son of the tenth Duke.

On this London visit, the President was staying near Buckingham Palace, at the Georgian townhouse of his sister-in-law, Princess Lee Radziwill, whose daughter's christening he was to attend at Westminster Cathedral. Kennedy's chronic bad back, recently wrenched during a tree-planting ceremony, was giving him great pain. The President was also weighed down with worry about a grave international crisis.

Kennedy had flown to London from a gruelling Summit meeting with Khrushchev. The Soviet leader had taken the two great powers a step closer to military confrontation over Berlin. He claimed that, sixteen years after the war, it was intolerable that West Berlin should retain its separate status as an island in East Germany, accessible to Allied troops. The East German state and its borders remained unrecognised, and that, too, was intolerable. Khrushchev told the President he intended to sign a treaty with East Germany, within months, which would cancel all Allied occupation rights. The Soviet leader meant to force the withdrawal of Allied troops from West Berlin, and introduce Soviet forces.

Khrushchev said these changes would bring peace. Kennedy – rightly – saw it as an ultimatum. What Khrushchev wanted would disrupt NATO, give Moscow the ideological initiative in Europe, and demoralise the West German government. The West would be humiliated, the balance of power shifted. Existing plans for trouble over Berlin assumed a US military response, and the real likelihood of World War III – Nuclear War.

In London, smarting from Khrushchev's belligerence, the President consulted Harold Macmillan. Already France, under Charles de Gaulle, and West Germany's Chancellor Adenauer, had urged the United States to make a show of strength. Now, over drinks at Downing Street, Macmillan told the young President not to make Khrushchev feel trapped. Driven into a corner, the Soviet leader might resort to violence. The President listened, then flew home. His wife stayed on, to dine next evening with an old admirer, Jakie Astor, brother of Stephen Ward's friend Lord Astor.

Immediately after the President's departure, American ambassador David Bruce got a letter from Sir Bruce Ingram, the editor of the *Illustrated London News*, asking him to sit for a portrait by Ward. When the portrait was done, a few weeks later, Bruce and the artist–osteopath got on well with each other.

Home in the United States, President Kennedy took his damaged back to Florida for a few days' rest – on crutches. He had seen specialists and received pain-killing injections during the European trip. According to one source, one of the specialists may have been Dr Stephen Ward. Bizarre though that sounds in the light of the ensuing scandal, the consultation may have happened. Averell Harriman, who accompanied the President to Europe as a senior adviser, had been one of Ward's first famous patients when he was ambassador in London after the war. Another, more recently, had been President Eisenhower. When another President arrived, suffering agonies from back pain, Ward would have been a natural choice.

During the President's visit to Europe, Ward had a prophetic conversation with Eugene Ivanov:

'What would happen to a Russian in Moscow who had an Englishman for a friend?' Ward asked the Russian.

'Oh,' replied Ivanov, 'he'd be visited pretty soon by the Secret Service, just like you will be here.'

'Nonsense,' Ward replied, but Ivanov said firmly, 'Oh yes you will.'

The Soviet attaché was right. Within a week, on 8 June, Ward received a telephone call from the War Office, asking the osteopath if he would mind meeting 'our Mr Woods' for 'a little chat'.

'Woods', we now know, was Keith Wagstaffe, an MI5 officer working for DI(a) Operations, a section of the Counter-Intelligence branch. The address he gave Ward, Room 393 at the War Office, was MI5's front address. Intrigued, Ward met Wagstaffe for lunch in Marylebone High Street, and found him 'charming, well-dressed, obviously an army officer in plain clothes'.

We have two accounts of the meeting: Ward's memoir and Wagstaffe's report, as supplied by MI5 to Lord Denning. Wagstaffe, Ward said, was straightforward about his affiliation to MI5. He said his people had 'noticed' Ward's friendship with Ivanov. When Ward asked whether they had any objection, Wagstaffe replied, according to Ward, 'None at all. In fact, we like the Russians to meet ordinary people in this country.'

Wagstaffe asked what sort of questions the Soviet attaché had been asking, Ward recalled. 'I put his mind at rest at once. Ivanov had never sought any guarded information.' Wagstaffe told him, 'If anything should happen that you feel we should know about, I want you to contact me immediately.'

As reproduced in the Denning Report, Wagstaffe's contact report read:

> Ward, who has an attractive personality and who talks well, was completely open about his association with Ivanov . . . Ward asked whether it was all right for him to continue to see Ivanov. I replied there was no reason why he should not. He then said that, if there was any way in which he could help, he would be very ready to do so. I thanked him for his offer and asked him to get in touch with me should Ivanov at any time in the future make any propositions to him.

The MI5 officer also said of Ward, according to the Denning excerpt: 'Despite the fact that some of his political ideas are certainly peculiar and are exploitable by the Russians, I do not think that he is of security interest, but [authors' italics] *he is obviously not a person we can make any use of.*' Is this sentence credible, or was it deliberately inserted – in MI5 material doctored for publication in the Denning Report? We suspect Wagstaffe's report was indeed doctored, to distance MI5 as much as possible from Ward.

Colin Coote's introduction, and information from Intelligence sources, indicate that Ward was deliberately brought together with the Soviet Assistant Naval Attaché. Now MI5 was risking a direct approach to Ward, not least because it would seem the natural development, the one Ivanov had in fact predicted. *Not* to contact Ward at this point would, indeed, have been a suspicious omission.

Ward saw Ivanov within days of the meeting with Wagstaffe, and asked him whether he could arrange a portrait sitting by the Soviet Minister of Culture, Mme Furtseva, who was about to visit London. Ivanov did arrange it, and the portrait duly appeared in the *Daily Telegraph*. Surprisingly, the *Telegraph* acquiesced to a Soviet plea that Ward's account of his talk with the Minister should not be published. Furtseva was a powerful figure in the Soviet Union, of whom it was said, 'What Furtseva thinks,

Khrushchev says . . .' Furtseva's daughter was married to a Deputy Prime Minister, Koslov, who was regarded as a possible successor to Khrushchev.

Furtseva's talk with Ward covered a wide range of political topics, and in some depth. Published or not, it may have been passed to Colin Coote's friends in Intelligence. Why, though, was Ward given this unusual opportunity to talk privately with the Minister? As MI5 watched Ivanov, and as the Berlin Crisis developed, what was Soviet Intelligence up to? It seems evident that this was the year of the Honeytrap, and that both sides knew it.

A week earlier, the *Daily Express* carried a story about Soviet tricks for the sexual entrapment and blackmail of foreigners. It appeared thanks to an approach to the writer of the report, Chapman Pincher, by an MI5 officer identified by Pincher today only as 'Michael M'. Michael M had told Pincher that British Intelligence was concerned about the risks to British nationals attending the forthcoming Electronics Trade Fair in Moscow. An article on past cases, the MI5 officer suggested, would serve as a timely warning to our businessmen not to fall for sexual approaches while in the Soviet Union.

If that was the hope, it failed. It was while attending the Electronics Fair that Commander Anthony Courtney, a Conservative MP, walked into a Soviet trap. The Commander, who had been campaigning in Parliament for a reduction in Soviet embassy personnel in London, succumbed to seduction by an Intourist guide, in reality a 'swallow', a female KGB agent with special training. The Soviets then used photographs of the Commander and the girl, in various states of undress, to cause his disgrace at home. Courtney duly lost his seat at the next election.

Also in Moscow in April, on a vital mission, was Greville Wynne, an MI6 agent posing as a businessman. His task was to renew contact with Colonel Penkovsky, the Soviet who had passed on so much information, including details on Ivanov, during his recent visit to London. This time, as a double-blind, Wynne was to pass low-grade technical data to Penkovsky, so that Penkovsky could claim – as cover – that *he* had recruited Wynne. During this visit, Wynne was to report, a Soviet 'swallow' tried to get him into bed. But the Englishman was a trained agent, and the attempt failed.

Meanwhile, in London, the *Daily Express* writer Pincher had an eventful luncheon at Rules Restaurant with the Soviet Press Attaché, Anatolij Strelnikov. Strelnikov ranted on at Pincher for publishing the story about sexual entrapment, then made a blatant attempt to bribe the journalist to reveal his sources. Pincher duly reported the episode to his contact in MI5.

Stephen Ward has never been linked to any Soviet official except Assistant Naval Attaché Ivanov. Today, though, we can reveal that Ward was in contact with at least two other Soviet officials.

Following Ward's death, in 1963, a calling-card was found in his pocket. It bore the name of Evgenij Beliakov, a First Secretary at the Soviet Embassy. Ward had presumably met Beliakov much earlier, for he had left Britain by mid-1962. Also amongst Ward's possessions were ten 35mm colour transparencies, taken by Ivanov outside the Cliveden cottage and at the Soviet Embassy. Details in the pictures suggest they were taken in the summers of 1961 and 1962, and two of them show Press Attaché Strelnikov – the Soviet who tried to recruit Chapman Pincher.

What are we to make of these additional Soviet contacts with Ward? And why, at his death in summer 1963, was he carrying the card of a Russian who had left the country at least a year earlier? Did he simply meet the two diplomats socially in the course of his acquaintance with Ivanov, or was there more to it? Was Beliakov's calling-card planted on Ward's body to tar him as a communist? Why is there no mention of this evidence in the Denning Report, which was set up specifically to examine the security angle?

We may never know now who was playing what game. The Soviets, suspicious of Coote's introduction of Ivanov to Ward – and perhaps knowing of Coote's connections –

may have sought to turn the situation in their own favour. MI5, on the other hand, had been hoping to obtain evidence of subversion that would get Strelnikov expelled from the country. They would have had it, after Strelnikov tried to bribe the *Daily Express* journalist, but the newspaper's editor, Arthur Christiansen, refused to make a formal complaint to the Foreign Office for fear of endangering his new correspondent in Moscow. Did MI5 hope that, through his Ward connection, Strelnikov would compromise himself again? We cannot tell what the game was, only that there certainly was a game.

One report by Ward's MI5 contact, Wagstaffe, contains a significant aside. 'More than once,' it reads, 'Ward assured me that if Ivanov . . . showed any inclination to defect, he would get in touch with me immediately.'

It must be stressed again that this is Wagstaffe's report as published by Denning. And, once again, it is odd. Since Ward had no reason to imagine that Ivanov would consider defection – the osteopath's memoir shows that the Soviet attaché struck him as a dedicated communist – it seems highly unlikely that *Ward* brought up the possibility of defection. The evidence, though, indicates that during June, immediately after the Wagstaffe meeting, Ward began setting a Honeytrap for Ivanov.

He started by trying to capitalise on the return from New York of Mariella Novotny, fresh from the brush with the law that had followed her encounters with John F. Kennedy. According to Novotny, he got in touch within days of her arrival at Southampton on 4 June. 'He pestered me almost daily,' she wrote in her memoir, 'to meet Eugene Ivanov.'

If Novotny's version is truthful, she proved an unwilling candidate for seductress of a Soviet diplomat. One can understand why: 'After my strange experience in the States, I vowed to avoid politicians of either side. I had been warned by a responsible lawyer that I should be careful who I mixed with in the political scene. I appreciated this sound advice . . . [Ward's] most pressing invitations to attend Soviet Embassy parties etc. were all rejected

. . . But Ward was not to be put off, he pressured me to have lunch one Sunday at Cliveden . . . he gave me his assurance Ivanov would not be present . . .'

That weekend, Novotny left her husband Hod Dibben in London and drove down to Cliveden alone, in the Mercedes sports car she had acquired. Ward had told her to come well before other lunch guests arrived so he could show her Lord Astor's famous gardens. 'He took me straight into the cottage,' she said. 'A man stood with his back to us, looking from the window onto the river . . . It was Ivanov – Ward introduced us quickly and rushed from the room . . . Ivanov talked well, and said that he was aware I had avoided meeting him . . . His manner was so nice it was difficult to fault . . . Ward brought drinks in, explained he had had no idea Ivanov was coming, and left us alone.'

According to Novotny, Ivanov tried to play on her missing Czech father, hinting that he could assist in arranging a visa to Prague – a trip that, Novotny had always assumed, would normally be fraught with problems because of her father's affiliation to the anti-communist underground. 'The temptation was great, exactly what I had hoped for one day,' she wrote. She was suspicious and afraid, though, and cut him short 'before he could tell me what was expected on my part.'

'I left him alone,' she claimed, 'and joined the other people arriving for lunch.' Hob Dibben remembers this episode: 'She realised she was being set up.'

'My controversial American involvement was of special interest, I was later informed,' Novotny said years later, referring to her relations with John Kennedy. She did not say who told her this was Ivanov's interest, but clearly the details would have been of great interest to a Soviet agent. Ward, she said, had been describing her to all and sundry as 'the girl who made such an impact in America with the Kennedy clan'.

Novotny had no doubt the meeting with Ivanov had been deliberately orchestrated. She also felt 'that Bill Astor had a hand in the matter. From evidence I later saw, it was obvious Astor gave Ward his orders and controlled him to a great extent . . .'

Ward's role of procurer for his wealthy friends was continuing, in dangerous parallel to his efforts on behalf of MI5. Soon, Novotny noticed, Ward was trying to pair her off with John Profumo, the Minister for War. 'His tireless endeavours to introduce me succeeded after dozens of refusals from me . . . Profumo was another friend of Ward's I did not take to . . .' True or not – it was surely uncharacteristic of Novotny to be so choosy – Ward was now busily putting the finishing touches to a girl in his own stable.

That summer Novotny learned from Hod Dibben about an odd evening spent at Ward's flat in Wimpole Mews. 'Hod watched Christine serve dinner. Ward had finished training her, but to test her ability instructed her to cook, lay the table correctly, and eat with them. Hod related to me her lapses, and how Ward told her not to sprinkle salt on her food. She obediently poured a small amount on the side of her plate. Several such mistakes were criticised by Ward – he wanted to impress Hod with his teaching technique.'

Was this Pygmalion's refresher course, and – if so – with what in mind?

Stephen Ward and MI5 officer Keith Wagstaffe had not parted immediately after their first meeting, the lunch in early June 1961. Instead, the doctor led the MI5 man, with his pinstripes, bowler hat and briefcase, back to Wimpole Mews. There, according to Wagstaffe's report as published by Denning, 'he introduced me to a young girl, whose name I did not catch, who was obviously sharing the house with him. She was heavily painted and considerably overdressed, and I wonder whether this is corroborating evidence that he has been involved in the call-girl racket.'

Subsequently, Wagstaffe has vouchsafed that he thought that the young woman, who served tea, was the loveliest girl he had ever seen. The girl was Christine Keeler, who recalls chuckling about Wagstaffe with Ward once he had

departed. If MI5 was hoping to set a Honeytrap for Ivanov,
Keeler evidently filled the bill as the honey.

Exactly a month later, two bees would be buzzing about
the honey. One would be Ivanov. The other, and the most
persistent, would be the British Minister for War. That,
most surely, was not part of the MI5 operational plan.

EIGHT

THE MINISTER FOR WAR: A SCREW OF CONVENIENCE

'The first time I met Jack Profumo he was in a dinner jacket and I was clutching a towel around me. My hair was hanging in strings, water was pouring off me – and I was acutely embarrassed.'

Two years later, less than acutely embarrassed by a massive fee from the *News of the World*, thus did Christine Keeler describe her fateful encounter with the Minister for War at Lord Astor's swimming-pool, in July 1961.

The high summer that year had brought little relaxation for world leaders. Now, in the United States, President Kennedy was advising a friend that – instead of a swimming-pool – he should be building a bomb shelter. As the Berlin Crisis rumbled on, British Prime Minister Macmillan was trying to unite the European allies. 'It is quite clear that we cannot countenance interference with Allied rights in Berlin,' he declared. 'This is an issue on which the peoples of the Western World are resolute. It is a principle which they will defend.'

This was a time of pressure for John Profumo. It was his task to honour promises that Britain would increase its forces in Germany, and that was virtually impossible. There were simply not enough soldiers, and Profumo was responsible for recruitment. There were serious problems, too, with a current operation in the Middle East. Six thousand troops had been sent to shore up the beleaguered oil emirate of Kuwait, under military threat by neighbouring Iraq. The rescue force, unprepared for conditions in the Persian Gulf, was not performing well, and War Minister Profumo had to take the blame.

On Saturday, 8 July, as the Kennedy White House worried about the Berlin Crisis, Britain's War Minister took a weekend off. Accompanied by Valerie, his actress wife, he headed for Cliveden, where Lord and Lady Astor were playing host to some thirty guests.

Astor's house party included Lord and Lady Dalkeith, several Tory MPs, the Profumos, and, as the principal guest, the President of Pakistan, Field Marshal Ayub Khan. Khan was on his way to Washington to discuss Berlin, and the role of the non-aligned nations, with President Kennedy.

For a bizarre reason, Khan's presence at Cliveden would cause a separate and special frisson of panic when the Profumo scandal broke two years later. Khan was a close friend of the former British High Commissioner in Pakistan, Sir Gilbert Laithwaite. Laithwaite, as we have seen, was a homosexual close to Lord Astor's stepbrother, Bobbie Shaw. He had homosexual connections with numerous Foreign Office officials now scattered around the world as senior diplomats. Both Laithwaite and Shaw were indebted to Stephen Ward for introductions to homosexual partners, and both had visited him at his Cliveden cottage. When the Profumo Affair occurred, according to their friend, writer Robert Harbinson, they rushed to consult Lord Astor.

Although it has been described many times, and has become a familiar scene in the national memory, we may not have been told the whole truth about what happened that weekend. Very possibly, the facts were bent somewhat to protect the Astors and their distinguished guests. Drawing on all the sources, what follows is the best reconstruction now possible.

Ward was at his Cliveden cottage that weekend, and he had several visitors. There was Paul Mann, a bridge-playing friend, Gerry Wheatman, who rented the garage at Wimpole Mews, a girl who had been brought along by

Christine Keeler, and Keeler herself. It was hot, about seventy degrees, and Ward had a standing invitation from Lord Astor to use the swimming-pool.

According to Keeler and others, including Lady Astor, Ward and his party went straight to the pool from the cottage. It was now between ten and eleven o'clock. Up at the mansion, dinner was finishing. The guests, some of the men in evening dress, some of the women actually wearing tiaras, were talking. For the gentlemen, it was time for brandy and cigars.

This is not quite the way the episode was remembered by a member of the Astor staff. 'The one thing they never told straight,' she insisted, 'was that Dr Ward and Miss Keeler were up at the house already. Then people set off for the pool together.' If this version is the right one, it suggests the story was adjusted later to dissociate the Astor party from the Ward group, to cover the fact that Ward and Keeler were already actively socialising with the VIPs present.

Whatever the sequence of events, Keeler ended up in the pool. According to her, she first picked out one of the swimming-costumes provided by Lord Astor for his guests. It was not very comfortable, and – Keeler says – Ward laughingly suggested that she take it off. A moment later she was naked, and diving in. She still remembers how grand it felt, plunging nude through the dark water.

According to the traditional account, the sound of splashing and laughter drifted up from the pool, and some of the guests decided to wander down and take a look. Two of the men, the host and the Minister, walked ahead of the others. By now, Ward had turned a spotlight on Keeler.

'Suddenly,' according to Keeler, 'in came two figures in dinner jackets. One was Bill [Lord] Astor, and the other Jack Profumo. I'd met Bill before of course. I didn't even know who the other fellow was at that moment. All I knew was that I was naked as the day I was born – and I swam into the far end of the pool. It was then that Stephen played another of his little jokes. Laughing his head off he tossed my costume clean into the bushes . . . "Now you're for it, little baby," he chuckled. I jumped out, and grabbed a towel.'

As Keeler stood there dripping, Lord Astor said, 'Christine, I'd like you to meet Jack.' A moment later the rest of the guests arrived. Ironically, it was Mrs Profumo who offered Keeler a swimsuit. 'So,' as Keeler put it, 'the first time I met her husband I also took her bathing-costume.'

'It was totally innocent high jinks,' says Lady Astor today. 'You couldn't see that the girl had nothing on. Besides which I was expecting my first baby, and I went early to bed.' While Lady Astor slumbered, the high jinks continued. Ward and his companions were invited up to the house, and Profumo and Keeler paired off – on the excuse of a guided tour of the vast mansion.

Profumo, Keeler recalled, was 'a type I find it hard to say no to . . . I didn't terribly mind being alone with him . . . There were some suits of armour in one room and, on a dare, I let my companion dress me up in one. He paraded me in front of the others. Everybody laughed like hell. I am quite certain that the guests forgot their problems for a few hours that evening. Lord Astor invited us to return the next day for an afternoon swim.'

Sunday dawned fine and even hotter than the previous day. Christine Keeler, who had returned to London over-night, set out for Cliveden once again, accompanied by two more girls – and Eugene Ivanov. They made straight for the pool, and there the working-girl from Staines had some fun with the rich, the powerful, and the Soviet spy.

'Ivanov and JP had a race down the pool,' Ward remembered. 'We started it off with a countdown, "Three, two, one, fire!" in Ivanov's honour. And although no legs were to be used, John Profumo shot ahead – using his legs.' 'That'll teach you to trust the Government!' joked Profumo, having won the race by cheating. Everyone, including Ivanov, then went up to the house.

The Soviet diplomat was, to put it mildly, happy. 'There it all was,' wrote Ward, 'all his dreams come true. There was the Minister, the President of Pakistan, the Pakistan

High Commissioner, duchesses, peers, and even officials of oil companies. Well, of course it was difficult to explain that this was not the hatching of any dreadful plot concerning oil, the Far East, and all points west . . . I could see the sort of report that was going back to the Embassy.'

Christine Keeler did not have international relations on her mind: 'I liked Ivanov. He was a *man*. He was rugged with a hairy chest, strong and agile. But somehow when we decided to have a water piggy-back fight, it was Jack Profumo's shoulders I climbed on . . .'

'Once or twice,' Keeler has said, 'I caught sight of Stephen's wicked, twinkly grin as he noted Jack and Ivanov vying for my attention: Ivanov certainly saw Jack's hand accidentally brush against my calf . . . I was lying by the side of the pool when, with Jack's back turned for a moment, he came up to me and touched me . . . It was all very pleasant.'

Both the Englishman and the Russian made their play for Christine Keeler that weekend. Profumo surreptitiously asked her for her telephone number. She told him to ask Stephen Ward. That evening she drove back to London alone with Ivanov. The Russian had known her for some time, apparently without making any advances. What happened now remains the subject of controversy.

According to Keeler, in her first public account, 'He had a bottle of vodka with him. We sat on the green divan at Stephen's Wimpole Mews flat. I knew that if he came for me I wasn't going to resist overmuch . . . Suddenly he was kissing me, rolling his dark curls into my neck . . . I dropped my glass . . . I was as surprised as I was pleased. Gosh. I'd always wanted him, why shouldn't I admit it? He came at me again. I half rose, and the obvious happened. We fell clean off the divan. There was a wild thrashing about, a real Russian romp! We crashed across the room. A little table went flying. He pinioned me in a corner by the door. I relaxed. Because he was just kissing me with all the power of a man in a frenzy of passion . . . Our very impetus carried us through the door, and we half fell into my bedroom. From that second I threw all reserve to the winds

. . . we had been together, Russian man and English girl . . .'

True, or false? Keeler said she told Stephen Ward next morning, and they joked about it. Ward, on the other hand, wrote in his memoir, 'She said she would *like* to have intercourse with him. I have always believed myself she never did. I think, like a lot of people, she tells a story often enough and comes to believe it and does tell lies.' Mandy Rice-Davies, who was very close to Keeler at the time and often saw Keeler and Ivanov together at Ward's flat, says she knew of no affair with the Russian. 'She didn't tell me at the time, and Stephen never mentioned it. Something always puzzled me about this. The first time I heard about it was in the *News of the World*.'

Lord Denning, who interviewed Christine Keeler twice, said he was not sure. If there was sexual intercourse with the Russian, the judge thought it was a solitary incident, never to be repeated. Yet, in her first account, for the *Sunday Pictorial* – a version that was never published – Keeler spoke of 'having an affair' with Ivanov. Perhaps that was a newspaper euphemism for 'having it away' just once, as Keeler usually describes sex. Certainly, she swore that she had bedded him, on oath at Ward's trial.

Today Keeler remains adamant she did sleep with the Russian. It does not really matter, though, whether Keeler fooled around with him, went to bed with him once, or had a full-blown affair. What matters is that she saw the Soviet spy very frequently, that he was a regular visitor at the Ward flat, at a time she was sleeping with the British Secretary of State for War. And that affair is not in doubt.

Two years later, when he owned up to his famous lie in the House of Commons, John Profumo merely admitted that there had been 'impropriety' with Christine Keeler. The Denning report covered the matter in two paragraphs, merely confirming that there was an affair. Profumo did not respond to an interview request for this book, and so we must rely mainly on Christine Keeler's account.

Clearly fired by the meeting at Cliveden, the War Minister did not waste time. Although he knew Ward, he quickly used Lord Astor to pass on word that he 'had been much taken with Miss Keeler, and would like to meet her again'. Then a tryst was arranged, by telephone – almost certainly on the Tuesday after the weekend encounter.

According to Keeler, 'I got a phone-call from Jack. He said, "What about a drive?" I replied "Hi! Nice to hear from you again." The upshot was that he came round to the flat while Stephen was out. We drank, chatted, and mucked about in general. I didn't think he was handsome, but his ways appealed to me . . . But then, as was so often to happen in our future meetings at the flat, I had to say, "Stephen will be back very soon", and, as always when Stephen's name was mentioned, Jack got up and said that he had better be going.'

'Jack Profumo and I became lovers,' according to Keeler, 'the third time that he came around . . . We started laughing and talking as usual, and then suddenly we both stopped. There was one of those electric, potent silences and then without a word we were embracing, and he was kissing me, and I was returning his kisses with everything that I suddenly felt for him. That was how it all started.'

Lord Denning interviewed Profumo twice, and his Report confirms that the Minister had sex with Keeler at the Wimpole Mews flat. If others were there, Denning noted, 'he would take her for a drive until the coast was clear'. 'Our meetings were very discreet,' said Keeler. 'Jack drove a red Mini car. We never once dined out, or had a drink in a pub, or went anywhere . . . He was worried about the press finding out about us. And above all he was worried about Valerie.'

Keeler seems to have exaggerated Profumo's worry about his wife, in her public statements. Once he took his mistress to his home, a grand Nash house in Regent's Park. 'It was late,' said Keeler. 'The butler and the rest of the staff were in bed, and Jack let us in with his own key. We crept round the lovely rooms. And then we got to *their* bedroom . . .'

In a police statement, part of which was made public,

Keeler described Profumo's house in detail that leaves no doubt she had actually been there. 'I went up some steps,' she told the police, 'into a square hall where there are two large ornamental animals . . . The stairs bend to the left and on the wall is a picture, of all the things that Valerie likes and dislikes, including pigeons and jewellery. From the top of the stairs is Jack's office, with a drinks cabinet inside. I noticed a strange telephone and he said it was a scrambler. Next door is the Profumos' bedroom with an adjoining bathroom . . .'

The couple had sex, said Keeler, on the marital bed. Profumo exuded power. It was, she reflected later, the way other women might feel about 'fucking Marlon Brando'.

The night of the adventure at Profumo's home, according to Keeler, they drove to Chelsea to see Profumo's friend and former Secretary of State for Air, George Ward. Viscount Ward was a wealthy brother of the then Earl of Dudley, the friend of Stephen Ward who had recently proposed to Mandy Rice-Davies. In 1986 he told us, 'I never met Stephen Ward.'

On one occasion, said Keeler, Profumo borrowed a 'big black car. It had a silver hare on the bonnet as a mascot.' It was a Bentley, and belonged to Profumo's friend John Hare, Minister for Labour. Hare, who later became Viscount Blakenham, would later deny lending the car to his colleague, and then – under pressure – recovered his memory.

John Profumo took extraordinary risks. At Ward's trial on prostitution charges, in 1963, a Major James Eynon admitted he had intercourse with Christine Keeler on several occasions, and paid for it. Once, he told the court, he called at Wimpole Mews only to discover that another man was already there. Keeler recalled that Jim Eynon 'arrived at the door . . . I had to let him in, and introduce him to the War Minister . . . Jim obviously recognised him, but behaved in true Army fashion; no names . . . Jack nearly died.'

The husband of another of Ward's girlfriends, Mariella

Novotny, had a similar experience. Hod Dibben says of Profumo, 'Oh yes. I remember seeing him then. I was at Stephen's flat when he came to pick her up one night. He didn't come in. He waited at the door.'

Sometimes, Keeler told the reporter in charge of the *News of the World* team, Peter Earle, she and Profumo made love in his car. Once they did it in the open air, in Regent's Park, near his home. He gave her some presents, including a Flaminaire cigarette lighter and, on at least one occasion, money. 'She said her parents were badly off,' Denning noted, 'and he gave her twenty pounds for them, realising this was a polite way on her part of asking for money for her services.'

Later Keeler summed up the relationship. 'It was,' she said, 'a very, very well-mannered screw of convenience; only in other people's minds, much later, was it "An Affair".' We too shall refer to the relationship as an 'affair' – it is the only convenient euphemism available.

How long the affair was to last and what it meant in terms of national security, hung on two factors not yet considered – the role of Stephen Ward, and the continuing role of MI5.

On the morning after the night before, Monday, 10 July 1961, Stephen Ward and Christine Keeler had discussed the eventful weekend. Keeler told Ward she had been to bed with Ivanov. Knowing that Profumo was keen to see her, he exclaimed, 'My goodness! What with Eugene on one hand and your new friend on the other, we could start a war . . .'

Ward joked, but he was also worried. In private Keeler later spoke of having had 'an argument with Stephen', a row so fierce that she stormed out of the flat.

Playing with human beings had finally backfired on the great manipulator. Ward had every reason to be troubled. He was an intelligent man, and a Profumo–Keeler–Ivanov triangle would obviously be dynamite. Ward must have seen at once how dangerous it was, how easily it could go way out of his control, out of anyone's control. To boost that fear, there was something Ivanov had asked Ward, something that made the sexual imbroglio even more worrying. Also on that Monday, Ward called his MI5 contact, Keith Wagstaffe. They met on Wednesday.

According to the Denning Report, Ward told Wagstaffe that Profumo, Ivanov, and Keeler had all been present at the Cliveden house party. He noted that Ivanov was attracted to Keeler, and that the couple had drunk two bottles of spirits between them at Ward's flat on the Sunday evening. Ward said Profumo was a fairly close friend, and sometimes visited Wimpole Mews. He did not, on this occasion, say Keeler was having an affair with the Minister – for the excellent reason that it had not started yet. His main worry, though, was this, as reported by Denning: 'Ivanov had asked him to find out when the Americans were going to arm West Germany with atomic weapons.'

Ivanov's question, as we shall see, was highly relevant in July 1961. By reporting it, Ward was doing exactly what MI5 man Wagstaffe had asked him to do, to get in touch 'should Ivanov make any propositions'. Yet, in public at any rate, Ward was to get no thanks for doing the right thing. If anything, he was to be smeared as a suspected traitor.

In 1963, as the scandal began to break, Christine Keeler told the police that, 'on one occasion when she was going to meet Mr Profumo, *Ward* [authors' italics] had asked her to discover from him the date on which certain atomic secrets were to be handed to West Germany by the Americans.' Keeler said much the same thing to *Sunday Pictorial* reporters. Then in the *News of the World*, she said: 'One night a friend asked me directly to find out from Jack when Germany was going to be armed with atomic weapons, but I refused. I felt instinctively and deep down that this was spying. I also knew that even if I were capable, which I wasn't, I couldn't do it. Jack and I were just not that way. He never talked to me about business and affairs of state. How could I possibly ask him such a thing when all he wanted with me was to relax?'

Several years later Keeler told the story a little differently. She recalled a night when she slept with Stephen Ward, one of the nights they shared a bed for companionship's sake. While they were lying in bed, she said, 'Stephen asked me if anyone had mentioned to me anything about the bomb . . . What bomb? At the time I was totally innocent of world affairs, since I never read the papers or watched the news.' Ward replied, 'The bomb America is giving to Germany . . . you could easily find out about it if you tried.'

Keeler was baffled, and said, 'But no one would discuss anything like that with me.' Ward then laughed, and said, 'I was only joking.' She replied uneasily, 'It all seems so funny to me, you and the other two . . .' The other two were Ivanov and Profumo, and Keeler was worried. But Ward changed the subject, and they went to sleep.

Was this the fiction of a young girl, being paid too much money for her memoirs? Apparently not. In 1985, in an interview for this book, Mandy Rice-Davies recalled visiting London Zoo with Keeler in 1961. They walked between the cages, chatting about their relationships with men, and Keeler talked about her affair with Profumo. Then she said, as Rice-Davies remembers it, 'I've got to tell you something. Stephen has asked me to ask Profumo about "bomb-heads", or "missile-heads", for West Germany.'

Not sure whether her friend was serious or not, the astonished Rice-Davies asked, 'What are you going to do?' Christine replied, with all gravity, 'I would never betray my country . . .'

On the face of it, there is a massive contradiction here, one that has barely been noted, let alone resolved. On the one hand, as recorded in the Denning Report, we have Ward – asked a question on a sensitive matter by a Russian spy – promptly informing his MI5 contact, as requested. On the other hand, we have a believable report that Ward deliberately tried to get Keeler to worm the answer out of Profumo. Was Ward a loyal citizen, or would-be traitor? Or was he trying to serve two masters?

Lord Denning and Ward were, for once, at one in the way they explained away Keeler's allegations. In his memoir, Ward made the whole thing sound lighthearted. He claimed that, when Ivanov asked him to get information on nuclear warheads, he said he might if Ivanov responded by arranging a visa for Ward to go to Moscow to draw Khrushchev's portrait. Not very convincing.

As for the sinister-sounding request to Keeler, Ward had a way to pass it off. 'I did joke with Keeler at the time of her affair with Profumo,' he said. 'I cannot remember my exact form of words. But it concealed my genuine anxiety. It was something like this: "All it needs now is for me to get the information that Ivanov wants, and we would have a real setup here."'

Lord Denning accepted the 'joke' version. He thought there had been 'a good deal of talk in [Keeler's] presence between Stephen Ward and Captain Ivanov about getting this information. And Stephen Ward may well have turned to her and said, "You ought to ask Jack about it." But I do not think it was said as seriously as it has since been reported.'

Clearly Christine Keeler took it seriously, and for a long time afterwards. In 1963, while making a tape-recording of her experiences for Robin Drury, her business affairs manager during the scandal, she baulked when it came to discussing the 'bomb-heads' issue. 'Christine asked me to turn off the tape-recorder,' said Drury, 'because what she had to tell me was too dangerous . . . it was the touchiest item in the whole scandal . . .'

Today Keeler still remembers the incident, and says that Ward was deadly serious, and looked worried. The public only heard Denning's remarks on the subject, and, as so often when he dealt with a knotty problem, they were diffused through different sections of the Report. If he had heard Christine Keeler's clear recollections, or Mandy Rice-Davies' corroboration, he did not say so. Yet there is no dodging Keeler's account. It is too specific to have been fabricated, let alone by a teenager – she was only nineteen at the time the incident occurred – and entirely ignorant of politics. Stephen Ward clearly did ask her to pump Profumo. But why?

On the face of it, it made no sense for Ward to ask Keeler to question Profumo, *after* warning British Intelligence that Ivanov wanted the information. Even if he fancied himself as a double-agent, that would have been inviting trouble, almost suicidal. The answer to the conundrum lies in the scheming of British Intelligence, in the question itself, and above all in its timing. MI5 probably instructed Ward to ask the 'bomb-heads' question.

In early July 1961, as the Berlin Crisis deepened, the Soviet traitor Oleg Penkovsky was back in London, again pouring out information of immediate relevance. At Coleherne Court, on the Old Brompton Road, Western intelligence officers milked the Russian for information on the Soviet rocket programme. Penkovsky had arrived in London carrying two rolls of microfilm, containing data about troop movements and Khrushchev's plans for the East German treaty designed to alter the status of Berlin. Khrushchev, Penkovsky learned, had personally ordered the Soviet ambassador in London to study the likely response of the British Government to a confrontation over Berlin.

As vaguely presented in the Denning Report, Ivanov had asked Ward 'when the Americans were going to arm West Germany with atomic weapons'. Elsewhere, this becomes 'American intentions to provide the West Germans with the Bomb'. Put that way, the request was almost laughable. There never was any question of giving West Germany the nuclear bomb – to this day they do not have it.

In fact, as Keeler told a friend in 1962, the question as passed on to her was about something much more specific, '*nuclear warheads*'.

Even today Mandy Rice-Davies, an intelligent woman with excellent recall, remembers Keeler telling her – in their talk at the Zoo that year – about a request regarding 'bomb-heads' or 'missile-heads'. Whichever it was, the *heads* part stuck in Rice-Davies' mind. As a subject of Soviet interest in 1961, that makes much more sense.

Just a week before the Cliveden party there were press reports that the United States were planning increased

fire-power for West German ground forces. The Bundeswehr might shortly be receiving a jeep-mounted artillery
missile, the Davy Crockett rocket, and a medium-range
ballistic missile known as the Sergeant.

The Davy Crockett was a small weapon. It could be
deployed on the battlefield with a three-man crew, which in
German hands would mean difficulties in ensuring absolute
American control. Both the Crockett and the Sergeant were,
according to *Jane's Weapons Systems*, 'capable of carrying
either a nuclear or a high-explosive warhead'. Ivanov's
interest now starts to make sense.

It is almost impossible, living in the West and in 1987, to
comprehend the scale of the gravity with which the Soviet
Union regarded German re-armament. Even today, Moscow's propaganda voice talks as though Germany might
again become an aggressor. In 1961, Russia's political and
military leaders were men who remembered both world
wars, wars in which the Soviet Union – with nearly twenty-
nine million casualties – suffered incalculably more than
any other nation. This is the Soviet psychology that demands that Germany remain divided, and that no German
finger should ever rest on a nuclear trigger. In 1961,
Khrushchev's concern was not all neurosis.

In 1960, members of the US Congressional Committee
on Atomic Energy, on a European inspection tour, had
observed US fighter aircraft 'loaded with nuclear bombs
sitting on the edge of runways with German pilots inside the
cockpits and starter plugs inserted'. The only indication of
American control was 'an American officer somewhere in
the vicinity with a revolver'. The American congressmen
were appalled. Thanks to Soviet Intelligence, Khrushchev,
too, must have been aware that some control of nuclear
weapons was beginning to pass to the Germans.

In 1961, the West German Defence Minister was the
pugnacious rightwinger Franz Josef Strauss. In early
summer he made public demands for 'atomic armament for
the Bundeswehr'. He claimed that any delay in delivery of
tactical nuclear weapons to West Germany would have
disastrous consequences for Army morale and for the

Christine Keeler — aged 12, now, and as she burst upon the public in the *News of the World* series that broke her story of sex with a Minister and a spy.

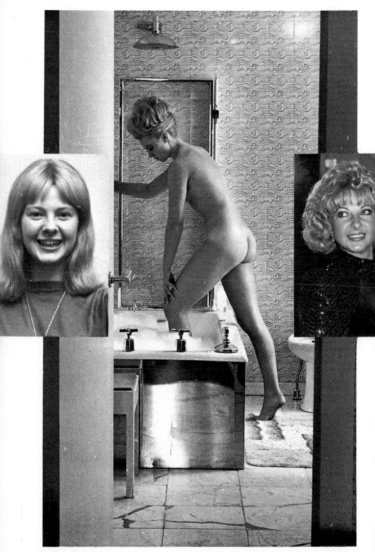

The survivor. Mandy Rice-Davies, as a schoolgirl in Solihull, in the days she dreamed of being a modern Lady Hamilton, and in 1986 at the premiere of *Absolute Beginners*, in which she acted. She is also a successful author.

Evidence of suicide — this letter was addressed to Noel Howard-Jones, Ward's host on the night of the barbiturate overdose. There were several such letters.

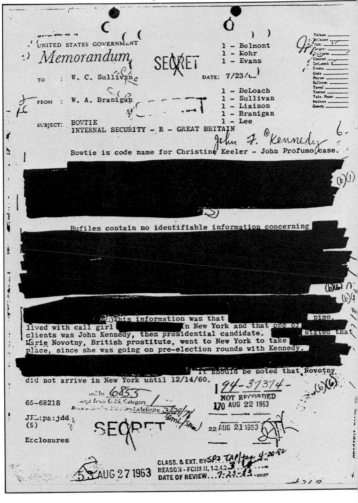

UNITED STATES GOVERNMENT

Memorandum

TO : W. C. Sullivan

FROM : W. A. Branigan

SUBJECT: BOWTIE
INTERNAL SECURITY - R - GREAT BRITAIN

DATE: 7/23/~

1 - Belmont
1 - Mohr
1 - Evans

1 - DeLoach
1 - Sullivan
1 - Liaison
1 - Branigan
1 - Lee

John F. Kennedy 6.

Bowtie is code name for Christine Keeler - John Profumo case.

Bufiles contain no identifiable information concerning

This information was that   piDD
lived with call girl   in New York and that one of
clients was John Kennedy, then presidential candidate. Stated that
Marie Novotny, British prostitute, went to New York to take
place, since she was going on pre-election rounds with Kennedy.

It should be noted that Novotny
did not arrive in New York until 12/14/60.

65-68218

JFL:pa:jdd
(5)

SECRET

Enclosures

94-37374-
NOT RECORDED
170 AUG 22 1963

22 AUG 21 1963

CLASS. & EXT. BY SP2 TAP/fay 4-20-82
REASON - FCIM II, 1.2.4.2
DATE OF REVIEW...7-23-13

55 AUG 27 1963

The American Connection — from the FBI's BOWTIE dossier on
the Profumo case. It informs William Sullivan, Hoover's
Assistant Director in charge of Counter-Intelligence, about
allegations that — before he became President — John F.
Kennedy slept with two women linked to Stephen Ward.

Evgenij I. Beliakov,
First Secretary.

London.   *Embassy of the U.S.S.R.*

TEL. DAY 6451

Commander E. M. Ivanov,
ASSISTANT·NAVAL ATTACHÉ

Embassy of the U.S.S.R.
16. Kensington Palace Gardens.
W.8.

A second mysterious contact — the calling card of Evgenij
Beliakov, allegedly found in Ward's pocket after his death.
Beliakov was a First Secretary at the Soviet Embassy. Ivanov's
card was also found on the body.

QUEEN

Sentences I'd Like To Hear The End Of...

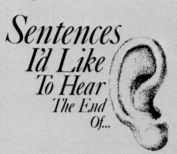

BY ROBIN DOUGLAS-HOME

"...and I'd just ordered her a stiff Martini when who should walk in with my wife but her husband wearing a false...."

"...introduced to a charming young man in a frightfully smart uniform called Colin Jordan, who seemed a bit shy, so I asked him what regiment he'd been with during the war, and he......................"

"...never told me there were two Ted Heaths, so when I asked him if he'd brought his trombone with him, he......."

"...overheard David explaining that he still thought Michael Frayn funny because...................."

"...then, just as Selwyn was demonstrating to Alec how to twist, the door opened and Harold..................."

"...called in MI5 because every time the chauffeur-driven Zis drew up at her front door, out of the back door into a chauffeur-driven Humber slipped...................."

"...gave his name as just Cronin, but Jackie didn't twig till one day she picked up a copy of Playboy, and there on the centre ...."

"...she said next on Charlie's take-over list is..........."

The first public hint of scandal, 31 July 1962.

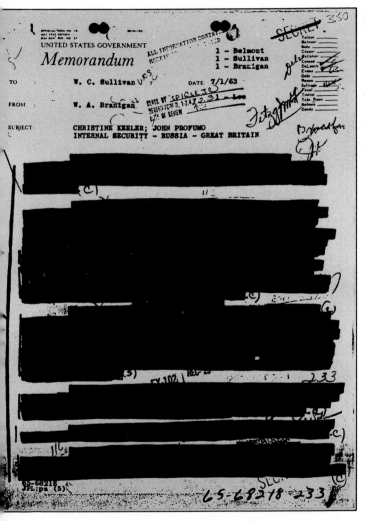

Dear Pelham,

Thank you for everything. There will probably be some money over. Give some to Julie & distribute the rest as you all see fit. — including yourself?

Yrs Ever

Steph

(give 500 to Tom for (Ronna)

Give 150 to Sylvia Parker. the v.n good

Addressed to journalist Pelham Pound, this letter shows that Ward went to his death thinking of his girls. He asked for money to be given to Ronna Riccardo, the prostitute who admitted her testimony against Ward was false, and to two women who stood by him, Sylvia Parker and Julie Gulliver.

political fortunes of the Adenauer Government. 'There can be no second-class allies,' Strauss was to say, where defence was concerned.

Strauss' strident demands were eventually to lead to a full-blown political upheaval in West Germany. In 1962, the issue would lead to Strauss' resignation. In summer 1961, though, he was very much in power, and demanding that West Germany be supplied with both Crockett and Sergeant missiles, with *nuclear warheads*.

The Soviets, with the Berlin Crisis under way, urgently needed to know whether Strauss would get what he wanted. Would the United States be sending the weapons to West Germany, and would German troops be permitted to use them? If so, when were they due to arrive, and, above all, would they carry conventional or nuclear warheads? Against that scenario, Ivanov's question to Ward fits into place.

In 1963, many scoffed at the notion that Christine Keeler could possibly be used as a Mata Hari, and doubted whether John Profumo would know the answer anyway. On the first point, we must look at the question, and what we know of the way Ward put it to Keeler. The question itself was simple enough, and the issue had been in the newspapers. It would not have been impossible for Keeler to put the question, perhaps in a conversation in which the young mistress – blatantly ignorant on current affairs – asked her eminent lover to explain the current crisis.

'What atomic secrets,' asked former Prime Minister Macmillan as late as 1980, 'could Jack Profumo possibly have known?' The War Minister was not privy to all 'secret' material, but he did have access to a great deal of classified information. Profumo was on the Defence Committee, and the British Rhine Army was a major part of his brief. There was close cooperation between the American, West German and British Forces, and the Secretary of State for War certainly knew whether battlefield weapons were to be conventional or nuclear. It is now a documented fact that, some time later, he almost resigned during a Government debate over the Blue Water missile, a weapon capable of carrying a nuclear warhead. Just three days before the Cliveden weekend, Profumo had been asked about nuclear weapons policy in Parliament. He had declined to reply, in order not to 'disclose information which might be useful to a potential enemy'. Ivanov had every reason to ask his warhead question, and every reason to believe Profumo would know the answer. And, as we shall soon see, there was a way MI5, briefed on the question in advance by Ward, could turn it to their advantage.

Probably that same month, troubled by Ivanov's persistent talk about the Americans re-arming West Germany, Ward, according to his memoir, decided to bring the Russian to see the man who had originally brought them together, *Daily Telegraph* editor Colin Coote. Soviet Intelligence, Ivanov told Coote over lunch, thought the decision to supply Bonn with the controversial weapons systems had already been taken. Neither Denning, nor Coote in his memoir, admits that this lunch even took place.

Two days after Cliveden, Soviet cosmonaut Yuri Gagarin, the first man in space, arrived in London. His visit coincided with the Soviet Trade Fair at Earls Court, and a Sputnik was on display suitably sanitised of secret equipment. Among the visitors was a young woman called Christine Keeler, and the Russian showing her the exhibits was Eugene Ivanov.

Throughout the week after Cliveden, as Gagarin made his triumphal way from ministerial reception to Buckingham Palace luncheon, the Berlin Crisis continued to deepen. Khrushchev fulminated about nuclear war, and refugees rushed to freedom in West Berlin, rightly afraid it might be their last chance. The Soviets moved more troops into East Germany.

NINE

AN OPERATION BOTCHED

Six days after Cliveden, Gagarin was star attraction at a glittering reception at the Soviet Embassy. Stephen Ward was there, monkeying around in the reception line to get his picture taken with Gagarin. 'I passed on into the reception room,' Ward wrote in his memoir, 'and ran at once into John Profumo and Valerie, his wife. And at that moment up came Ivanov, splendid in a gold and beaded uniform with several medals. We chatted for a moment, and he went off to get vodka for Valerie.' It was the second time in a week that the Minister for War and the Russian spy had met. In the space of those few days Ivanov had spent a boozy night with Christine Keeler, and Profumo had begun his seduction routine.

According to Keeler, Stephen Ward was on his way out when Profumo arrived at the Wimpole Mews flat for their first date. The Minister and the osteopath waved to each other. Later Profumo took Keeler off in his 'long, shiny black car' on a drive to the War Office and Downing Street. When he dropped her back at Wimpole Mews, Ward was there, 'lolling about awaiting my return', with a raised eyebrow, a languid 'Well?' and a request for a full account of the afternoon.

On Wednesday, as the Denning Report tells us, Ward was closeted with Keith Wagstaffe, his MI5 contact, whom he had first contacted on Monday, the day after Cliveden. It was now that MI5 learned that Keeler, Profumo and Ivanov had all met at Cliveden, and that Keeler had spent the evening getting drunk with Ivanov.

According to the Denning account, there was no reference at this meeting to any intimacy between Keeler and Profumo – indeed, Denning claimed, MI5 would know nothing of that until January 1963, when the Profumo scandal began to break. If that is what MI5 told Denning, it was not true.

'It seemed to me that Jack was behaving foolishly,' Ward told Warwick Charlton shortly before he died, 'so I reported the matter to Mr Woods [codename of Ward's contact, Wagstaffe] of MI5. He told me he would deal with the matter . . .'

Ward's memoir makes it clear that – not least because of Ivanov's persistent conversation about German rearmament – he felt he had to tell MI5 what was now going on. 'This was in the summer of 61,' he wrote. 'It was around this time that JP met Keeler – you can possibly now understand my anxiety about this relationship . . . I felt that I must inform the Security people of the friendship which had developed . . . I sought to be as practical as possible as I broached the delicate subject . . . I had got it off my chest.'

The Denning Report says that MI5 asked the Metropolitan Police Special Branch, at the end of July, to 'get more information about Ward's establishment and about Christine'. Two sources indicate there was surveillance of Ward's flat in July 1961. Robin Drury, Keeler's business adviser in 1963, said, quoting his client, that 'MI5 took a picture of a man leaving the flat. They thought it was Ivanov, but when it was developed it turned out to be Profumo.' According to a second account, the surveillance was bungled.

At the height of the scandal, the *Daily Telegraph* reported a farcical episode. 'Mr Profumo was followed by security men,' wrote reporter Barry O'Brien, 'when he met Miss Keeler at Dr Ward's London home . . . Captain Ivanov was being watched by security men at the same time, and I understand that one night security men watching Mr Profumo had an encounter in Wimpole Mews with security men watching Mr Ivanov.' The source of the story, according to O'Brien, was Ward himself – who presumably either witnessed the confrontation personally or learned about it from his MI5 contact. Almost certainly, the mix-up resulted from a communications failure between MI5 and the police Special Branch, with whom MI5 liaise.

British Intelligence, according to the *Telegraph* article, 'had a record' of Profumo's meetings with Christine Keeler. In his memoir, written months before publication of the Denning Report, Stephen Ward said that Profumo visited Keeler at his flat five times, while he was away at the Cliveden cottage. 'Christine has told me of those visits,' Ward said. 'Intercourse took place on each occasion – Christine has told me intimate details that leave no doubt in my mind that this is so.'

At once, Ward recalled, he took action: 'When I realised what was happening, I contacted Mr Woods [Wagstaffe] of MI5 . . . I also mentioned to Woods at this time that she was in some relationship with Ivanov. I used these words: "Please do not make an official report on this matter. I have no wish to damage Mr Profumo, but you will see that I am in a very invidious position here."'

Ward's memoir says he then gave the MI5 man a second look at Christine Keeler, and she corroborates this. During her affair with Profumo, she has said, 'Stephen had a visit from MI5 . . . I remember the man coming. I opened the door to him . . . I don't know what he said to Stephen as I didn't stick around. They didn't seem to want me to.'

Keeler is quite clear that this MI5 visit was after she had started meeting Profumo, and that Ward did tell Wagstaffe about her and Profumo.

'Afterwards,' Keeler said, 'Stephen told me that it was perfectly all right. It was just that they were checking up on who I was, because Ivanov was also a frequent visitor to our flat. After that, Stephen and I used to get up to jokes on the telephone. We suspected our line was being tapped. So we would ring one another up and say curt things like, "Is it all right? Have you got the plans? Right!"'

People who think their phone is tapped are usually indulging their fancies. In this case, Ward and Keeler were almost certainly right. If surveillance men were watching the flat and taking photographs, they were most likely bugging the phone as well. There would have been little difficulty in obtaining the necessary warrant – not that we need believe that warrants are always obtained.

On 31 July, just three weeks after the Cliveden weekend, the head of MI5, Roger – by now Sir Roger – Hollis, spoke to the Cabinet Secretary, Sir Norman Brook. Brook was one of the most powerful men in Britain, an *éminence grise* in the true sense of that phrase. From 1947, for fifteen years, he attended all Cabinet meetings and was the confidant of four Prime Ministers. Anthony Sampson, author of *Anatomy of Britain*, describes him as 'caught up in an intricate, secret world . . . the central cog in the British Government . . . When, in fifty years' time, the official secrets are revealed, the name of Brook will certainly feature a good deal in the making of decisions.' Of all the Prime Ministers he served, Brook was closest to Harold Macmillan. He had long experience of liaison with MI5.

The head of MI5 contacted Brook, according to Denning, with two things in mind. He wanted to warn Profumo to be careful what he said to Ward – Ward was a chatterbox, sometimes indiscreet, and might pass on to Ivanov snippets of information dropped in casual conversation.

Hollis's second point was central to MI5's real purpose. He suggested, Denning reported, 'that perhaps with Mr Profumo's help, it might be possible to get Ivanov to defect. Mr Profumo might be a "lead-in" to Ivanov.' Hollis wanted Profumo to become part of the Honeytrap.

Sir Norman Brook saw John Profumo just over a week later, on 9 August, and passed on MI5's messages. Brook, the older man, concealing a first-class mind behind a languid manner, had quite a conversation with the urbane Profumo. It was an odd exchange, no doubt conducted in that understated fashion in which one British gentleman discusses a sensitive matter with another.

Profumo, whose stomach must have filled with a thousand butterflies, thanked Brook for warning him to be careful around Ward. Privately, as well he might, he assumed that MI5 had found out all about his affair with Keeler. He assumed that Brook's visit was a polite way of telling him to stop seeing her.

Then, very delicately, the Cabinet Secretary moved on to MI5's request for assistance. 'Was it possible,' Brook asked, for Profumo 'to do anything to persuade Ivanov to help us?'

Clearly, there was more to the proposal MI5 made to Profumo. MI5 now knew, from Ward and its follow-up surveillance, that Christine Keeler was intimate with both the Minister and the Soviet spy. Profumo's amorous adventure had not been in the MI5 plan to entrap Ivanov. It now threatened to wreck the operation at a crucial stage – unless Profumo either disengaged altogether or agreed to become a co-conspirator. It was a pivotal moment for all concerned.

British Intelligence must have decided, before the Brook –Profumo meeting, just what it was they wanted Profumo to do for them. Today, we can hazard a guess as to what it was. If we are right, it makes sense at last of Ward asking Keeler to get information out of Profumo on missiles in Germany. With the Berlin Crisis at its height, British Intelligence may have hoped to pull one of the most effective and time-honoured tricks in the Intelligence book: to mislead the Soviets with false information. Specific disinformation, swallowed whole by the enemy, can change the course of history. At very least, it sows confusion, and that itself is a worthwhile goal.

Profumo's sudden interruption of the Honeytrap operation could perhaps be turned to advantage. If Ward could manipulate Keeler into asking Ivanov's question, and if Profumo was primed into giving her the answer – a phoney one – on cue, the Russians might be successfully fooled. It was a matter of stage-management.

According to the Denning Report, Profumo turned down MI5's request. He 'thought he ought to keep well away from it'. Convinced that he had been caught out in his sexual folly, his mind must have been filled with foreboding of disaster – ruined career, marital misery, the whole catastrophe that would eventually be his lot. Helping MI5 with its scheme was a complication Profumo could well do without.

The War Minister plumped for self-preservation, and help for colleagues who might end up in the same boat. He told the Cabinet Secretary that a number of other men in Ward's circle should also be warned, including another minister. The second minister, who was cautioned, has never been publicly identified.

That same day, within hours of seeing the Cabinet Secretary, Profumo sat down to write to Christine Keeler – on War Office notepaper. Because she kept the letter, we know that it read:

9/8/61

Darling,
  In great haste and because I can get no reply from your phone – Alas something's blown up tomorrow night and I can't therefore make it. I'm terribly sorry especially as I leave the next day for various trips and then a holiday so won't be able to see you again until some time in September. Blast it. Please take great care of yourself and don't run away.

Love J.

  PS I'm writing this 'cos I know you're off for the day tomorrow and I want you to know before you go if I still can't reach you by phone.

Profumo spent most of the parliamentary summer recess with his family in the tiny village of Bembridge on the Isle of Wight. In London, his ambiguous letter to Keeler lay in a drawer in her bedroom, a paper time-bomb.

Did the affair with Keeler end with that letter, and did Profumo stick to his refusal to help MI5? Profumo eventually told Denning he stopped seeing Keeler in August. Earlier, though, in Parliament, he said he saw her as late as December. Keeler herself said they last met in December.

The Denning Report noted that she 'adopted this date, evidently following him'.

There is no special reason to accept the December date – the statement in which Profumo offered it was the one in which he lied to Parliament and said there had been no affair. Two witnesses told Denning that the affair continued into 1962. One was Keeler's subsequent lover, Lucky Gordon. The other, never properly identified by Denning, was 'a man called Hogan', who claimed he had taken the couple tea in bed together at the Dolphin Square flat Keeler used in 1962. Today there is fresh evidence on this, which we shall report later.

It seems extraordinary that Profumo would even consider seeing Keeler again after the frightening encounter with the Cabinet Secretary. Yet the letter of 9 August merely postpones their next meeting. It seems, too, that there were more letters. Keeler has referred to a total of three, and a meeting with Profumo which she placed firmly after the August postponement.

There came a day, according to Keeler, when Profumo suggested providing her with a flat, and maintaining her as his mistress. She says she declined the offer, telling him she was content with her present situation. 'But darling,' Keeler quotes Profumo as replying, 'I won't be able to go on seeing you while you live here with Stephen . . .' Profumo was pressing. Keeler has repeatedly quoted him as saying he could continue seeing her only if she ceased living at Ward's flat in Wimpole Mews. Keeler suspected that Profumo's plan was to turn her into a call girl – on permanent call to his friends in Government. It is a fact that, in December 1961, Keeler moved to new accommodation in Dolphin Square.

The date and contents of Profumo's second letter are not known, but Keeler has referred to the last one. In it, she said, Profumo told her 'that if I wanted to see him again, I could get in touch with him'. She never did reply, she said, and that marked the end of the affair.

If Profumo did continue to see Keeler after the warning, was it the ultimate in foolhardiness? Or did he, perhaps, do so under pressure to help MI5 after all, as British Intelligence forged ahead with its efforts to make Ivanov defect? The one sure thing is that the War Minister was now highly vulnerable to pressure from anyone with knowledge of his affair with Keeler.

'What is certain,' wrote former Labour minister Lord Kennet, 'is that the triangle Profumo–Keeler–Ivanov laid Profumo wide open to blackmail. The scandal which broke when it was finally discovered, and the degree of ruin which overtook him personally, can hardly have surprised Profumo. The extent to which he expected them is the measure of his vulnerability to blackmail. In the market of these things, big scandal equals big hush payment, and big hush payment may be made in big secrets. We should probably know if Profumo had been unsuccessfully blackmailed by the Russian Intelligence Service; he would probably tell us about it if he had stood up to them. But we do not know, and we shall never know, whether he was successfully blackmailed in the nineteen months between August 1961 and March 1963; we only know that the Russians had good leverage on him . . . It cannot be assumed that a man who has lied to conceal adultery from the House of Commons will not lie in order to conceal a breach of security from Lord Denning, any more than it can be assumed that he will . . . when you have a real hold over a man there is no longer any reason to complicate the channel with cut-outs, whether conscious or unconscious . . . the risk was high.'

Labour leader Harold Wilson, speaking in Parliament in 1963, was to say, 'Let us be clear on this: whether there was a breach of security at any time, whether there was a leak of information, is something we shall never know . . . There is no means now of finding out . . .'

For two years, until his resignation, Profumo was indeed open to manipulation – not only by the Soviets, but also by anyone with knowledge of the extent to which he was compromised. British Intelligence had that knowledge and, not least because it would not clash with his patriotic instincts, John Profumo may have decided to help MI5 after all. Ivanov was to remain a target for Honeytrap for another eighteen months – until January 1963, when he left London.

Stephen Ward remained the tool of MI5. In 1982, the Government sought an injunction against a publication of a book on MI5 by Nigel West, an author with excellent intelligence sources. His book, eventually published with deletions, contained sensational insights into the Profumo Affair. *The Sunday Times* reporters, Barrie Penrose and Simon Freeman, following up West's information, succeeded in extracting interviews from several former MI5 officers, what they had to say amounted to the rehabilitation of Stephen Ward.

Senior MI5 officers, speaking anonymously, said Ward's call-girl contacts were 'the very qualities MI5 thought valuable.' Ward was approached in 1961, *The Sunday Times* reported, because British Intelligence had earmarked Ivanov as a potential target for entrapment. Ward was told it would be 'helpful' if Ivanov became friendly with Ward's girlfriends. This would allow MI5 to exert pressure on him. Christine Keeler, interviewed in 1982, admitted that 'it was Stephen Ward who encouraged me, nudged me, towards Ivanov.'

One of the MI5 officers was asked whether Ward was encouraged to see himself as a patriot spying for his country. 'Exactly. That is so,' the officer replied. 'He was a very nice, very pleasant chap,' said one officer. 'He did his very best for us,' said another.

'Nowhere in the Denning Report,' said a former senior official, 'does it say that Ward was acting under our instructions. That is very unfortunate.' Lord Denning, asked to comment, said only, 'I would prefer to stay out of this.'

British Intelligence did not merely use Ward for a few weeks in the summer of 1961, in the weeks after the weekend at Cliveden. They continued to use him, according to MI5 sources, for long months afterwards, until the scandal broke in 1963. Operation Honeytrap was not abandoned.

Even in his memoir, compiled when he was being made a scapegoat, Ward did not finger his masters in British Intelligence. Perhaps he was afraid to – they, after all, had a great deal on him. Perhaps he was simply loyal. Ward did hint at the Honeytrap operation, saying of Ivanov, 'There can be no doubt that he was marked. I was, of course, the means by which this was done. Did I do wrong? . . . I personally think that it is tragic that such portentous matters should have been dealt with in this amateur fashion . . .'

For many months to come, whenever it was convenient to either side, the pawn called Stephen Ward was pushed around the London square of the political chessboard. He revelled in it.

TEN

THE LOYAL ENGLISHMAN, AND THE MAN IN THE MASK

On 3 August 1961, as tension built between Moscow and Washington, Stephen Ward the artist got some publicity in the London *Evening Standard*. The reason for the interview was his sketching of famous subjects, and his hope of going to Moscow for the *Daily Telegraph*, to draw Khrushchev. The article went unnoticed at the time of the Profumo Affair, and turned up by chance during research for this book – but there is a revealing postscript.

'Dr Ward became nervous,' the *Standard* reporter wrote, 'when he talked to me about Berlin. He has friends in the Soviet Embassy. One of them has warned him to watch out for "big trouble" in the autumn. Said Dr Ward, "He said he thought America would give West Germany the bomb, and if they did China would have the bomb within five minutes.*"' Dr Ward was, the reporter noted, 'frankly worried by the situation'.

Everyone had reason to worry. Ten days later, before dawn on 13 August, East German troops began erecting barbed-wire barriers between East and West Berlin. Five days later it had become an obscene cinder-block divide – the Berlin Wall was in place. President Kennedy, alerted by a military aide as he climbed into his golf-cart at Hyannis Port, was at

---

*The rift between China and the Soviet Union did not become serious until the next year, 1962.

first furious. Later that month, American and Soviet tanks faced each other 'eyeball to eyeball' across the Berlin boundary. Kennedy, however, resisted calls for actual military action.

Odious though the Wall was, there were those in the West who welcomed its appearance. It discredited communism by its very existence, while simultaneously allowing Khrushchev to cut off the embarrassing haemorrhage of refugees daily streaming to the West. The Soviet leader, meanwhile, withdrew his six-month deadline for enforcing new border arrangements. The crisis between the superpowers eased, but only momentarily. It was to begin building again, month by perilous month, towards the most dangerous moment of all, the Cuban Missile Crisis of 1962. For the moment, though, the Soviet tone softened. In London, Assistant Soviet Naval Attaché Ivanov asked a willing Stephen Ward to carry messages to the British Government, behind the scenes. Ward jumped to oblige.

On 2 September, Lord Astor wrote to the Foreign Office, suggesting that his friend Dr Ward might act as intermediary between the Government and the Soviet Embassy. Ward was interviewed at the Foreign Office a fortnight later. Then he turned to a man he had known for twenty years – his good friend and patient, Conservative MP Sir Godfrey Nicholson. Nicholson, aged sixty, was Chairman of the Parliamentary Estimates Committee, and thus privy to a great deal of sensitive information. He not only carried Ivanov's messages to the Foreign Office but saw the Foreign Secretary, Lord Home, in person.

Nicholson then wrote three letters to Ivanov, each of them approved by the Foreign Office. He entrusted their safe delivery to Stephen Ward, perhaps because Lord Home had warned him to avoid personal contact with Ivanov.

Ward recalled in his memoir: 'A series of suggestions were made through me which had the sanction of the FO and had been passed by security. These I gave to Ivanov, except the last and probably most important, which I delivered myself to the Soviet Embassy, since Ivanov was temporarily back in Russia for a holiday.'

The letters, it seems, may have been delivered by an unlikely courier. On three occasions, Keeler has written in her autobiography, Ward sent her off to the Soviet Embassy carrying letters for Ivanov. He told her they were invitations to play bridge, or apologies for missing one of the Russian's social occasions. Much later, Keeler says, she remembered how bulky the envelopes had been – too bulky to have been mere notes. Keeler made her deliveries accompanied by a Persian boyfriend called Manu.

Ward's role as an intermediary – then and later, during the Cuban Missile Crisis – has been used to suggest he was a Soviet agent of influence, or at least a fellow-traveller. He certainly gave that impression to a number of people. One of his patients, whose husband moved in Ward's circle, told the writer Rebecca West she thought he 'had been a convinced communist for about seven years, from about 1955 or 1956 . . .' The entertainer Michael Bentine, who had known Ward for years, thought him 'extremely left-wing', and so did sports broadcaster Max Robertson, who got to know the osteopath after receiving treatment for a tennis injury. Lord Denning called him 'without a doubt a Communist sympathiser . . . a potential danger'.

Ward had his own answer to this. 'I believe,' he wrote, 'and I will bring a shower of wrath about my head, that the real sin in the world is failure to try to understand the views of others, and to respect them when genuine, however different from our own. The culmination of our present way is to try to destroy an idea with a bomb.' Many would dismiss such talk as naïve pacifism. Others – not least in 1987 – see continuing dialogue as essential to our survival.

Sir Godfrey Nicholson, who was as much a part of the London approaches as Ward, is no leftwinger. Lord Denning called him 'a most loyal Englishman'. Out of party loyalty – he was an MP for thirty years – Nicholson has declined to discuss the detail of his role in the back-door diplomacy of 1961 and 1962. He has written to us, however, in staunch defence of Ward: 'The side I saw was generous and compassionate, and I liked it . . . He was, I am quite certain, a patriotic British citizen, and he would, I am sure, never have done anything harmful to this country.'

Perhaps, though we do not know this, Nicholson acted in 1961 and 1962 with the knowledge we have only now, that Ward had long been acting on the behalf of British Intelligence. If, as MI5 officials now say, he cultivated Ivanov at their request, it would certainly have been necessary for him to express open sympathy for the Soviet point of view. On occasion, however, he was not afraid to argue with Ivanov.

On 15 September, during the Ward–Nicholson diplomacy, a military clash over Berlin seemed a distinct possibility. In the disputed air corridor over Germany, Soviet MIGs buzzed US civilian airliners. At the end of the month, at the United Nations for high-level talks on the crisis, Lord Home said, 'One false step, one failure in communication, even one failure in comprehension, might mean war.'

Ward took Ivanov to task over the Soviet provocations. 'Why,' he asked the Russian, 'when you talk of a gesture, do you do this?' Ivanov had no answer – his Ambassador was away. 'It brought home rather vividly,' Ward went on, 'that none of them would express an opinion unless they had been briefed.'

As the global crisis stuttered on, Ward celebrated his forty-ninth birthday. When his ego was not being pumped by contacts with the high and mighty, what was left for him? 'The trouble with Stephen,' a female friend was to say, 'is that he has a Peter Pan complex.' Ward's charm was still there, but the fabric of life was threadbare. The parties, though, went on.

One night in December 1961, Keeler and Rice-Davies were sitting around at home when the telephone rang. It was Ward. 'There's a party over at Mariella's,' Keeler told Rice-Davies. 'He wants us to go over.' They went. Soon the two girls were ringing the doorbell at the flat in Hyde Park Square shared by Mariella Novotny and her husband Hod

Dibben. They were just in time to join a party that has kept the rumour-mill going for twenty-five years, the Man In The Mask Party.

'I was determined to be the best hostess of my age,' wrote Mariella Novotny years later, reminiscing about her antics in the early sixties. On her return from America, she 'started to give lavish dinner parties in London, and weekend parties in Hampshire. Since my name was linked with extremely erotic activities, I decided to entertain on a large scale . . . I chose to concentrate on exotic food and fascinating personalities. This combination stunned my friends when my sexual games completed the dinner parties. Within weeks my parties became the subject of gossip among the élite in London . . .'

Some of Novotny's entertaining was entirely innocent. 'I normally arranged for twenty-four to dine, and served about seven or eight courses . . . The sort of friends I invited were not dumb. Among them were Walter Flack, Charles Clore's partner,* Bill Astor, Sir William Emrys-Williams, Chikie Moss, Sheila Scott, Count Manfred Czernin, Beecher and Bobbie Moore, Eustace Chesser, Douglas Fairbanks Jr, Felix Topolski, Lord Belper, Lord Spencer, and many others.'

Some on this guest list are already well-known characters in the story. Sir William Emrys-Williams was Secretary of the Arts Council and a Trustee of the National Gallery. Chikie Moss was the step-daughter of the golfer, Henry Cotton. Sheila Scott, of course, was the flying ace. Beecher Moore was the wealthy American expatriate, whose collection of pornography was later donated to the British Museum. The then Lord Spencer was a member of the Advisory Council of the Victoria and Albert Museum. He was the grandfather of today's Princess of Wales. Those on this list from the art world were presumably invited to Hyde Park Square because of Hod Dibben's work as an antique

---

*As we have seen, both Flack and Clore knew Ward's girls, Flack wined and dined Mandy Rice-Davies and Clore had sex with Keeler.

dealer. There was no question of any impropriety. Others had more exotic evenings at the Dibbens'.

'Eustace Chesser, the sex expert,' Novotny recalled, 'I amazed him with my games!' Some of her guests, said Novotny, attended 'both kinds of parties,' but others took no part in her 'games'.

When she did hold orgies, 'some strange incidents developed'. It was something of an understatement. 'The bizarre became normal for me,' she wrote later. 'Nothing surprised me at my parties . . . My sadistic nature was no secret. I became humorously known as the Government Chief Whip.'

Stephen Ward was a frequent guest at the parties. 'He had a strong fetish for shoes with high stiletto heels,' Novotny noted. 'These he pressed over his nose and mouth without any physical sexual activity.'

It was Lord Denning who was to call Novotny's December 1961 orgy the Man In The Mask Party. Those who claim to know all about it call it the Feast of the Peacocks. According to Novotny, it was one of a kind.

When Rice-Davies and Keeler got to Hyde Park Square, the party was virtually over – though it still managed to shock Rice-Davies: 'Stephen met us at the door, wearing nothing but a sock. I thought it was a joke. Everyone was in déshabille, and Mariella was there wearing a kind of black corset, and carrying a whip. Naked people were everywhere, draped over chairs, or standing around laughing and joking. But the real orgy had finished, nothing was going on – everybody was weary if not fainting . . .' Things were not entirely over. Keeler observed Novotny on a bed, entertaining six men at once.

Rice-Davies and Keeler did not stay long. 'I didn't know where to look,' Rice-Davies says. 'After all, I *was* only seventeen, even if I had been around. I remember spotting this plate of tangerines – they were a rarity in winter in those days – and I attacked those tangerines and some chocolates until I felt sick. We must have spent about twenty minutes there. Then we left, with Stephen . . .'

Only one person has offered a detailed account of what happened earlier that evening, and she should have known the facts best of all – the hostess, Mariella Novotny. In her manuscript, she devoted several pages to the Man In The Mask orgy. 'The man,' she wrote, 'was strapped between wood pillars. A flail or whip was in front of his naked figure. As each guest arrived they gave him one stroke, then left the man to join the party. When he was released before dining, he was ordered to remain beneath the long table, out of sight . . .'

'I cooked a pair of young peacocks for the main dish,' Novotny goes on, 'skewered their necks and heads in position, and added the colourful tail feathers of older birds. When they were carried to the table, a girl became hysterical and screamed that they signified death. She created havoc and had to be sent home, before she ruined the party . . . Badgers were another unusual animal I cooked.'

'I object to my parties being called vile and revolting,' Novotny protested. 'Had they been unpleasant, the clamour to be invited would not have been so enormous.'

'The man in the mask was a masochist and asked me to treat him as my "slave". I willingly agreed, and caused him mental and physical pain. This was what he wanted – I did nothing against his wishes. The humiliation he underwent was extreme, but was the dream of his life. Under the table he obeyed any order I gave him to please my guests . . . Everyone went home well satisfied.'

What people wanted to know eighteen months later, of course, when the Profumo scandal broke, was just who Novotny's satisfied guests had been. Rice-Davies noticed 'some well-known actors and a politician . . . There was one well-known barrister . . .' Novotny, in her manuscript, identified only one participant, Conservative MP ————————.*

Who, though, was the Man In The Mask himself? According to Rice-Davies and Keeler, Ward gave them

*Name deleted for legal reasons.

the impression it was the Minister of Transport, Ernest Marples. Ward, testifying to Lord Denning, denied ever saying this, and thought the girls must have picked on something said later in jest.

'There is no question about who it was,' says Roy East, former Chief Crime Reporter on the *People*, who got to know Ward well, and gave evidence to the police and to Lord Denning. According to East, 'Stephen didn't know who it was. It was a poor little businessman from Sheffield who used to come to Mariella's parties . . .'

The two people best qualified to say who the masked man was, of course, were the host and hostess, Hod Dibben and Mariella Novotny. Lord Denning interviewed them both, in the presence of an unnamed solicitor. Denning reported that the guests 'did not include any Minister or any person prominent in public life', and that the host and hostess told him the identity of the masked man. The man later gave evidence and, according to Denning, was 'grievously ashamed of what he did'.

Who was he? With Novotny dead, perhaps only Hod Dibben knows for sure. In his own way, he is a man of honour: 'I promised the person in question I would never reveal his name and I never will, even though the man is dead.' Dibben has, however, been prepared to say who the man was *not*, and that helps considerably.

'There is absolutely no truth,' Dibben says flatly, 'in the idea that it was Ernest Marples.' That canard out of the way, we turned to what survives of Mariella Novotny's statements. 'I lied to Lord Denning,' Novotny wrote in her memoir, 'but not about a politician – my lies were to protect someone from ruin and a criminal charge . . .' Elsewhere, in brief notes written later – probably in the mid-sixties – Novotny revealed, 'he himself was not a politician. He was a peer of the realm . . . it was Lord Asquith.'

At first this seemed a bizarre calumny. Properly speaking, 'Lord Asquith' in 1961 was Julian, Second Earl of Oxford and Asquith, and grandson of the Liberal Prime Minister. In 1961 that Asquith, a diplomat, was appointed Governor of the Seychelles, following a three-year posting

to the Caribbean. There is no reason whatsoever for thinking that the second earl was at the Feast of the Peacocks, or
that he ever attended sex orgies, in London or anywhere
else. He was thousands of miles away from the Man In The
Mask party. In any case, Hod Dibben dismissed the suggestion that he was the masked man.

There was another Asquith, coincidentally *known* as
'Lord', who is a likely candidate for the role of the Man In
The Mask. This was the Honourable Anthony Asquith,
youngest son of the Prime Minister, the First Earl of
Oxford and Asquith – by his second marriage – and one of
Britain's most successful film directors. After education at
Winchester and Balliol College, Oxford, Asquith went on
to direct a string of films including *Pygmalion*, *French
Without Tears*, *The Winslow Boy*, *The Millionairess*, *The
VIPs*, and *The Yellow Rolls-Royce*. In 1961 he was fifty-
nine, and President of the Association of Cinematograph,
Television and Allied Technicians. Before his death, in
1968, he was to become a Fellow of the British Academy
and Governor of the British Film Institute.

Anthony Asquith, affectionately nicknamed 'Puffin' by
his friends, was dubbed 'Lord' by his film technicians. He
was a man of great talent, but he did not find happiness.
Asquith was dominated by his mother in childhood, and
never married. Some thought him homosexual. At
weekends the earl's son could sometimes be found serving
in a lorry driver's café near Catterick, in Yorkshire. The
actors Michael Denison and Dirk Bogarde, who were both
involved in his films, drew a parallel between Asquith and
Lawrence of Arabia, whose life Asquith once hoped to
bring to the screen. 'His recurrent trips to Joe's Café at
Catterick,' said Denison, 'seem to me very like T. E.
Lawrence's escape into anonymity.' Lawrence, of course,
was a masochist.

'Puffin was born to be a mind,' another friend, Pierre
Rouvé, said of Asquith. 'The body was there as an appen-
dage, which he dragged behind that mind all his life.
Consequently everything that was a concern of the body, a
pleasure of the body, seemed alien to him . . . Such vio-

lence as he depicted on the screen always seemed to me to be an attack by him on that enemy of his, the body, to prevent it taking possession of the mind and destroying the mind.'

Was Anthony Asquith the man in the rubber mask, strapped between the wooden pillars at Hyde Park Square in December 1961, gratefully accepting the lash from arriving guests, grovelling under the table while the guests scoffed peacock on the table above? Ward's friend Warwick Charlton says Anthony did attend Novotny's parties. Asked whether Anthony Asquith attended Novotny's parties, Hod Dibben said 'Yes,' and smiled secretively. Asked straight out whether Asquith was the Man In The Mask, Dibben refused to comment at all. He did not deny it, as he had the names of all other possible candidates.

While Dibben stands by his vow of silence, the matter must rest there – with the high probability that the Honourable Anthony Asquith, son of a Prime Minister, was indeed the Man In The Mask. We strongly emphasise that there was no link whatsoever between Novotny, or anyone involved in this story, and any other member of the Asquith family, alive or dead.

In 1963, Lord Denning succeeded only in dispelling the notion that the Man In The Mask had been a Conservative minister. He could not alter the wholly accurate impression that people in high society, including prominent members of his own élite, led private lives that made a mockery of their public role as defenders of respectability and the public good. 'It is a fond illusion,' said Labour MP Sydney Silverman in the House of Commons in 1963, 'that Lord Denning's Report established the falsity of the rumours. It did nothing of the kind – it established their accuracy . . . He established the truth of every one of them. Do not let us fool ourselves.'

Things Fall Apart

Some would say Ward's life had always been sleazy, but in 1961 it took a definite downward turn. 'He started to look scruffier and more down at heel,' says Lord Dudley. 'There was a deterioration in his lifestyle. I think that's when he was getting involved with sort of, rather sleazy people . . .'

Lord Dudley had a point. The best and most beautiful girls were behind Ward now. To keep his rich friends happy, Ward was prepared to lower his sights. One night in 1961, a prostitute called Adrienne left her flat in Curzon Street, Mayfair. Adrienne was a drug addict, on her way to the chemist's shop round the corner. As she walked, a white Jaguar pulled alongside, and the driver struck up a conversation. It was Ward, and he offered to find her clients.

Today Adrienne – this is not her real name – has retired from the prostitution game. Now nearly sixty, but still showing traces of the looks that attracted Ward, she lives in a basement flat in West London with her addict husband. Ironically, Adrienne was not called as a witness at the Ward trial. She thought Ward 'kind and honourable,' so she said 'No' when a policeman asked her whether she knew him. Had she not done so, the prosecution case against Ward would have been stronger.

Adrienne still remembers the clients Ward sent her – 'some peers and MPs, and plenty of Americans.' She had given Ward a handful of her business cards, and the men he sent all brought one with them. One, she says, was the then Duke of Marlborough, whose wife had died in summer 1961. He annoyed her by sending his chauffeur round on a reconnaissance, but then he became a regular customer. Another aristocratic client, Lord ———,* is still very much alive. He was a close friend of Ward, and, to Adrienne, 'a rather sinister bisexual'. He used to make her sign a written contract before each sex act.

Adrienne is still a heroin addict – one of the rare long-

*Name deleted for legal reasons.

term survivors. She has been for forty years, since society doctor Lady Isabella Frankau began giving her a liberal supply of drugs. Frankau, who prescribed in the mistaken belief that she spared junkies the black market, operated from a surgery in Wimpole Street, just round the corner from Stephen Ward's flat.

In the two years before the Profumo Affair, the drug disaster was beginning in England. Though the full idiocy had not yet happened – it was still a matter of 'reefer parties' and marijuana supplied by West Indian immigrants – the evil of drugs was beginning to gain ground. It affected those around Stephen Ward. John Hamilton-Marshall, a close associate of Ward through his sister Paula, was an addict. In 1963, Ward would insist that he had done all he could to protect his girls from drugs. He was tolerant, though, when Christine Keeler became interested in marijuana. It was a mistaken indulgence, for the drug connection was to play a crucial role in the breaking of the Profumo Affair.

In December 1961, on the night of the Man In The Mask Party, Mandy Rice-Davies arrived at Peter Rachman's place smelling of marijuana. Rachman, her patron and lover, angrily accused her of smoking dope herself. Today, she remembers the cause of the problem – marijuana smoke had adhered to her clothes during the drive home with Keeler in Ward's Jaguar.

Keeler had been interested in marijuana for several months, certainly since the night in October when she, Ward, and the portrait artist Vasco Lazzolo, visited the El Rio Café in Notting Hill. Ward and Lazzolo liked the raffish atmosphere of the place – it was a West Indian hang-out, a haunt for the young black men of the immigrant wave, and a place where drug deals were made.

Lazzolo wanted some marijuana, but was leery of buying any. Keeler thought he and Ward looked like plain-clothes policemen, and told them to wait outside in the car while she tried to buy some herself. She made for the back of the premises, where the toilets were, and there she came across a West Indian, clearly loitering. The man sold Keeler ten shillings' worth of dope, then kept her talking. He assumed she was a prostitute. Keeler, knowing Ward liked black girls, told him they might be able to get together again, if he could supply 'a sister for my brother'. The man said he had plenty of sisters, and Keeler gave him the telephone number of the flat at Wimpole Mews.

It was a fateful meeting. The black man was Aloysius 'Lucky' Gordon, and his encounter with Keeler was very unlucky for many people. Gordon, thirty-one, had arrived in Britain from the West Indies thirteen years earlier. During his National Service he had been discharged from the Army for threatening an officer, then jailed and deported from Denmark for another assault. According to Keeler, in her autobiography, another offence was for 'sticking a knife up a girl's vagina'.

Two days after the meeting at the El Rio, Gordon called to invite Keeler and Ward to a party. The combination of drink and drugs made Keeler ill, and Ward had to take her home. Gordon kept on calling, and said he wanted help in fencing some jewellery. According to Keeler, she and Ward had previously been to a club frequented by criminals. She knew that stolen goods were handled by the clientele, so she thought she might be able to help Gordon.

Keeler accompanied Gordon to a house, to see the alleged jewellery. There, according to her, he held her at knifepoint for many hours, raping her time and again. The only way she could escape, said Keeler, was to promise to see Gordon again. The West Indian was endlessly persistent – and nobody could have guessed the sort of fuss his attentions would cause in the end.

Soon Gordon was at Wimpole Mews, accompanied by a drug dealer, asking to see Keeler in private – to apologise. In her bedroom, he turned violent, and Ward called the police. Keeler bore no obvious injury, so the police decided not to bring charges. According to Ward, he then did all he could to woo Keeler away from the world of drugs. They went together, he said, to see a Drugs Squad inspector at Scotland Yard. Keeler denies this, but Dr Ellis Stungo,

Ward's psychiatrist friend, remembers the osteopath sending Keeler to him out of concern that she was smoking marijuana and seeing black men.

In early 1962, Christine Keeler was living with a friend in Dolphin Square, not far from the House of Commons. Like Mandy Rice-Davies, she rarely stayed in one place for more than a few months during this period. Sometimes she moved on after a few weeks. At this point, according to Keeler, she was using marijuana regularly. She and her friends had become the vanguard of the Swinging Sixties, smoking dope and making the bars and nightspots of London their playground. At home, she said, they 'thought nothing of wandering around or answering the door entirely in the nude.' One of the people on the doorstep was Lucky Gordon. According to Keeler, he rampaged through the flat for the next forty-eight hours, threatening her and her friend with an axe. Again the police were called, and Gordon was charged – only to have the charges dropped when Gordon's brother persuaded Keeler that she would never be bothered again.

Gordon could not leave Keeler alone – and, in spite of everything – she went on seeing him. In summer 1962, he was sleeping on the fire escape of the flat at Dolphin Square. Very briefly, Keeler actually shared a room with Gordon at the home of his brother. It did not last, and she returned to an old lover, Michael Lambton. Then, when Rice-Davies had a chance to go to the United States, Keeler rushed to join her. Peter Rachman and Lambton paid their expenses.

On the liner to the United States, Rice-Davies told us, 'Christine took a fifteen-year-old's virginity in a ship's lifeboat, slept with the first officer and the captain, all in five days.' The trip to America was a disaster. Both girls suffered severe sunburn on a trip to Fire Island, a well-known homosexual resort. Then after sending home for extra money, they flew back to London seven days after their arrival in New York. Lucky Gordon was waiting – and now Keeler was frightened. She turned for help to another West Indian, John Edgecombe.

'I was going about my business one day,' says fifty-five-year-old Edgecombe, in his first interview since 1963. 'Christine, whom I didn't know, and Paula Hamilton-Marshall were in a taxi going the other way. They stopped it and called me . . . and Paula opened the taxi door . . .'

Paula Hamilton-Marshall, an actress's daughter, had a police record as a prostitute, and that was how Edgecombe knew her. When she and Keeler picked him up, the three of them went back to Hamilton-Marshall's flat in Devonshire Street, near Ward's consulting room. 'When we got there,' says Edgecombe, 'there was a guy in the doorway with his hat down, and Christine fell on the floor of the taxi and started saying "That's him!" Eventually we went upstairs, and every time the doorbell went, Christine hid in case it was Lucky . . .'

Edgecombe, who also became Keeler's lover, quickly concluded that he had been recruited to protect her from Lucky Gordon. He tried, but Keeler seemed unable to keep her distance from her persecutor. Once he beat her up she says, in the street. Keeler was in the fast lane, mesmerised by the drugs scene, by black men, and by Gordon in particular. Her relations with the West Indians soon brought a different sort of danger. Both men found out about the affair with the Minister for War, John Profumo – an affair that had supposedly ended, according to the Denning Report, in late 1961.

In summer 1962, Gordon told a detective a year later, Keeler tried to get rid of him by volunteering that 'she had friends in high places, including a Cabinet Minister, and that – if he didn't stop pestering her – she would have him dealt with by the Minister.' One evening, Gordon told his interviewer, he saw a man enter Christine's flat, then leave after about an hour. Though he didn't really believe her at the time, Keeler told him the visitor was John Profumo. A few days later, Gordon saw John Profumo's photograph in a newspaper, and thought he recognised him as the mysterious visitor.

John Edgecombe also learned about Profumo. 'This chick,' he recalls today, 'looked as if she had some class, and I asked her what she was doing running round with a cat like Gordon . . . To turn it around she told me about Profumo. I took it all with a pinch of salt – I mean, I didn't know who the fuck Profumo was anyway . . .'

Edgecombe soon heard a good deal more about the Minister. 'If she needed some bread,' he says, 'she could always ring up and arrange to see Jack. She would go off and see him, and he'd give her some money. I don't think it was a lot, fifteen or twenty pounds, maybe. Yes, she was sleeping with him – she wouldn't see the guy for anything else. I don't know how many times she rung him . . .'

As Keeler's rackety life began to threaten John Profumo, Stephen Ward walked the social tightrope. He joined Keeler in West Indian dives one day, hobnobbed with the aristocracy the next. He was also still cultivating Eugene Ivanov. The mix was ever more dangerous.

In the third week of June 1962, Ward took the Soviet diplomat to an Ascot Week house party thrown by Lord Harrington. 'There were so many guests,' Ward wrote, 'that a large marquee had been put up in the garden, and was known as the House of Lords. Hence, until we came, the inhabitants were all peers of the realm.' Before Ascot was over, Ward took Ivanov to Guildford, in Surrey, to the home of millionaire Paul Getty. The osteopath had been there once before, when he landed on the lawn in a plane piloted by his cousin, an RAF wing-commander. The company this time included Getty's son, a Russian lady aristocrat, a Czech-born girlfriend of Ward's and two other women.

The Czech girlfriend was not Mariella Novotny, but a twenty-one-year-old naturalised Austrian called Ilya Suschenek. She had met Ward through Ivanov, with whom she used to play poker, and had visited Lord Astor's estate at Cliveden. The visit to the Getty residence ended in chaos for her, Ward, and everyone involved.

'Of course,' Ward said in his memoir, 'when Russians get together . . . vodka and more vodka, toasts to this and that, and then song, it went on the whole afternoon. When we left most of us were in a sorry state. We loaded Paul's guests into a car and sent them home and set off back to Lord Harrington's. Ivanov, when asked whether he could drive, said, "I am a Captain in the Russian Navy, and I can navigate anywhere." So he did, and we found ourselves in the middle of the rifle ranges, hopelessly lost. At that moment a head popped over the back seat, and there was one of Paul's guests who had stowed away without our knowledge, very much under the weather . . . We decided to send her back the thirty miles to Paul Getty, COD. From then on we had a series of horrifying bulletins of her progress across the countryside. As each one was brought in by the butler we laughed louder and louder – and eventually, to cap it all, a message from Mr Getty that he would not pay the taxi, and that it was all the fault of the Russian Captain . . .'

While Ward cavorted with Ivanov in high society, Christine Keeler's black odyssey continued. By now she really wanted to shake off Lucky Gordon. She could not, and she was frightened. As 1962 dwindled down, she decided to buy a gun. She gave 'a very respectable bloke' twenty-five pounds for a German gun and ammunition. Then she went into the countryside near her parents' home, and practised firing the gun. 'It worked,' Keeler said later. '. . . If Lucky Gordon came at me again I was going to kill him . . .'

Christine Keeler never did use her weapon on Lucky Gordon – John Edgecombe took it away from her. The shots he would fire would ruin the British Minister for War, and destroy Ward. Before that happened, though, the world came close to a nuclear holocaust.

ELEVEN

NOT THE END OF THE WORLD

On a bitterly cold evening in autumn 1962, a man stood on the runway of the American airbase at Greenham Common, in Berkshire. He too had a gun, a service revolver, nestling in his pocket. At the same time, another man sat hunched in his Jaguar car, heading for London up the A4. The first man was already caught up in the most serious international crisis of all time, the second soon would be.

Sunday 21 October marked the start of the Cuban Missile Crisis, a drama so far hidden from all but a trusted few. The man on the way to London was Stephen Ward, on his way back to Wimpole Mews after a damp weekend at Cliveden. The man with the revolver at Greenham Common was David Bruce, the American ambassador to London, and so far he had no idea why he had been summoned to the airbase, armed, under cover of night. Above in the dark, aboard a US Air Force Boeing, was the elderly man who would shortly explain all, former Secretary of State Dean Acheson and accompanying Acheson were three CIA agents, three armed guards and a briefcase. This was a most secret mission.

For a moment, when the ambassador welcomed the statesman on the tarmac, there was laughter. Bruce proffered a bottle of whisky, then told an astonished Acheson to feel the gun in his pocket. 'I was told by the Department of State to carry this when I met you,' said Bruce. 'There was nothing said about shooting me, was there?' Acheson responded. Then, without delay, the men got down to business.

Acheson had flown to England, on the orders of President Kennedy, carrying air surveillance photographs of Soviet missile sites under construction on the island of Cuba. For weeks, in an extraordinary series of contacts between a senior GRU agent and the President's brother Robert, Khrushchev had been assuring Kennedy that Soviet aid to Cuba would not include offensive missiles. The agent was a specialist in deception, and the assurance was a lie. At breakfast on 16 October, still in his dressing-gown, Kennedy was shown photographs proving conclusively that missile sites were under construction, missile erectors deployed, and a storage site for nuclear warheads in position. Some actual missiles might already be on the island, and more Soviet freighters were on their way. The launch sites were for medium-range ballistic missiles, capable of hitting American cities with great accuracy, and – once operational – they would irrevocably alter the nuclear status quo. The United States could not tolerate them. The Cuban Missile Crisis had begun.

The British Government, and British Intelligence, were factors in the crisis from the start. The GRU traitor, Oleg Penkovsky, who was being handled by MI6, had provided information that, according to the defence expert Anthony Verrier, 'allowed the CIA to follow the progress of Soviet missile emplacement in Cuba by the hour'. Just as important, Penkovsky had demolished the myth, energetically propagated by Khrushchev, that the Soviets had more intercontinental ballistic missiles than the United States, and that these were capable of precision attacks. Penkovsky said the Soviet ICBMs 'couldn't hit a bull in the backside with a balalaika.' Just as important, his assessment was that the Soviet Union had no real intention of going to war. The plan to place missiles in Cuba was part of a gamble designed to give Khrushchev greater leverage on the United States, and to test Kennedy's resolve.

In the weeks leading up to the crisis the MI6 Station Chief in Washington, Maurice Oldfield – later to become head of MI6 – laboured to convince the President and other key Americans that Penkovsky was a genuine source rather than a Soviet plant. Kennedy's people were finally persuaded on the eve of the crisis, when surveillance pictures were compared with a missile manual provided by Penkovsky. The match was exact. With this and other intelligence, the President was ready to call Khrushchev's bluff.

By Sunday 21 October, American officials were working night and day – soon they would be moving camp beds into their offices. Even so, the President made time that day to have David Ormsby-Gore, the British Ambassador, to lunch at the White House. Ormsby-Gore, later Lord Harlech, had been a personal friend since Kennedy's days in London at the start of World War II. Now, in the shadow of nuclear war, he was the only foreign diplomat promised a place in the presidential fall-out shelter. He was a trusted confidant of both Kennedy and British Prime Minister Macmillan, and the families of all three were linked by marriage.

The President was worried about how Britain, and Prime Minister Macmillan specifically, would react in the crisis. Earlier, during the Berlin Crisis, Macmillan had counselled great prudence in dealing with Khrushchev. Many in Britain were nervous about the American attitude to the Soviet Union. Now, as the President prepared for a military showdown with Khrushchev, there was a risk that the older man's caution would look like vacillation. Would Macmillan try to play the statesman, to mediate in some way, a move the Soviets might interpret as a sign that the Western Alliance was shaky?

In Washington, Ormsby-Gore quietly supported the President's plan to take a tough stance. To convince Macmillan of the urgency of the matter, he suggested Kennedy send him the missile photographs. So it was that Dean Acheson flew into Greenham Common on his secret mission, and that – on the morning of Monday 22 October – the British Prime Minister sat examining them at Number 10 Downing Street. Late that night London time, as England slept, President Kennedy went on television to announce a naval blockade of Cuba, and to warn that the United States would retaliate in kind if attacked.

The evening of the next day, Tuesday, was a crucial moment in the crisis, but behind the scenes. MI6 learned that Penkovsky's luck had run out. He had been arrested in Moscow, doomed to face trial and a death sentence.

Khrushchev at once asked for a damage assessment of Penkovsky's treachery, and – after a briefing by the Soviet Embassy in London – he knew how serious the leak had been. For him, Penkovsky's arrest was more a presage of defeat than a cause for celebration. Khrushchev had to assume, now, that Kennedy had sufficient knowledge of Soviet intentions to call his bluff. He now desperately needed a way to climb down without publicly losing face. Until that way was found, the Soviet leader remained unpredictable and dangerous.

Next day, Wednesday 24 October, the Missile Crisis came to Wimpole Mews. Captain Eugene Ivanov, at the Soviet Embassy, placed a call to Stephen Ward. 'Ivanov wanted,' said Ward in his memoir, 'to get a message behind the scenes to the Government. He came armed with full authority, he said, to speak for the Soviet Government in this matter, and replies could be obtained from Moscow in a matter of hours direct from the Kremlin. There is no doubt at all that this was so. No one from the Soviet Embassy would dare to speak in this way were it not so.'

Ivanov's call triggered several days of contacts with the British Government, with Ward acting as go-between. Ivanov first came to Ward's Devonshire Street consulting-rooms for a meeting with the osteopath and Sir Godfrey Nicholson, the Conservative MP who had contacted the Foreign Office on Ivanov's behalf a year earlier during the Berlin Crisis.

'We listened to Ivanov with growing amazement,' Ward wrote, 'as he unfolded his suggestion, no less than the calling of a Summit Conference in London . . . On this offer being accepted the Russians would agree to reverse the course of their ships, at that moment sailing on a collision course with the American Navy . . . On the subject of rockets in Cuba he told me that discussions on a quid pro quo basis would be started at once.'

British officials later tried to play down the role played by Ivanov and Ward during the Missile Crisis, and the Denning Report would call Ward's activities 'misconceived and ill-directed'. Ward himself had no doubt he had become the hinge on which the fate of humanity would turn. One day that week, Mandy Rice-Davies remembers him saying portentously, 'Pray for me, Mandy, if I fail to bring about the meeting I've planned it could mean the end of the world.'

It was characteristic of Ward to inflate his own role, but anyone old enough to remember the Missile Crisis will recall that everything seemed out of proportion that week. It did seem that humanity was about to destroy itself. Ward, moreover, had every reason to believe Ivanov's approach was serious. As he rightly pointed out in his memoir, no Soviet diplomat would take such an initiative without authorisation.

It was also reasonable for Ward to assume that the British would treat the Soviet approach seriously. The previous year, when Nicholson was acting as intermediary, the Foreign Office had approved Nicholson's written communications with Ivanov. Ward, in that knowledge, had arranged their delivery to the Soviet Embassy. There is nothing improbable about the Soviets using lowly intermediaries to carry momentous messages. As we shall see, the use of such a messenger in Washington played a major role in the resolution of the Missile Crisis. In London, the messenger was to be Stephen Ward.

The Soviets were snatching at any straw of hope that Britain would offer to mediate between Moscow and Washington, a move that would delay matters, and perhaps help Khrushchev save face. 'The Prime Minister and myself,' the British Foreign Secretary had said, 'will, once we have checked the present fever, play our full part in an attempt to end the Cold War.' Home had said this the day before Ivanov's call to Ward, perhaps giving the Soviets the impression that Britain might intervene in the crisis, as 'an honest broker'.

British Intelligence, drawing either on phone-taps or an agent inside the Soviet Embassy, learned at this time of an embassy message to Moscow reporting, in summary, that 'the British Government is not happy about developments'. At all events, Ivanov's message to Ward and Sir Godfrey Nicholson was that, in the view of the Soviet Government, Britain offered the only hope of mediation in the Cuban Crisis.

Ward and Nicholson both followed up that same day. Ward telephoned the Foreign Office and left a message with the resident clerk for the Permanent Under-Secretary of State, Sir Harold – now Lord – Caccia. Lord Astor, said Ward, had suggested he call personally to put himself forward as an intermediary. Ward and Caccia knew each other already – they had lunched together, along with Sir Godfrey Nicholson, following the earlier attempt by Ivanov at back-door diplomacy.

Nicholson, meanwhile, went personally to the Foreign Office, then reported back to Ward that he had delivered the Soviet proposal for a Summit to Sir Harold Caccia. The Head of the Joint Intelligence Committee, Sir Hugh Stephenson – a contemporary of Nicholson's from Oxford days – was also briefed.

As the Englishmen began their lobbying, Ivanov was nervy. While his official message was about peace talks, the Soviet attaché was openly aggressive about the alternatives. That Wednesday, at a coffee-bar near Ward's consulting rooms, the solicitor Michael Eddowes came across Ivanov and the osteopath in deep conversation. Eddowes had known Ward for many years and had recently been to him for treatment, so he joined them at table. The solicitor asked Ivanov what he thought would happen if the US Navy forcibly prevented the Soviet ships from reaching Cuba. Ivanov's reply, according to Eddowes, was vehement. 'We will blockade Norway [the site of American missiles],' blustered the Russian, 'or we will drop a bomb in the sea a mile off New York, creating a tidal wave, or we will destroy England [also the site of US missiles] in seven minutes.'

Events next morning, Thursday 25 October, at first seemed to augur well for the Soviet approaches. Nicholson's confirmation that he had passed on Ivanov's message was followed by news that the Soviet Chargé d'Affaires, Vitalij Loginov, had called on Lord Home. Ivanov soon learned, however, that the meeting had been unproductive. It had been a sticky session, he told Ward, with a shorthand writer recording a catalogue of recriminations for past events. As we now know, Home had decided on a tough stance. He told Loginov that Britain 'had no intention of seeking to mediate'.

Macmillan would remember the Soviet overtures as an effort 'to drive a wedge between ourselves and the United States . . . a natural part of the Soviet attempt to weaken our resolution'. Ivanov, at the time, justified the need for Britain to mediate with a burst of rhetoric. 'It's like a motor accident,' he told Ward, 'where two drivers are arguing while a victim, which in this case is humanity, bleeds to death.'

The Soviets did not give up easily. In Britain, as in other European capitals, Russian officials continued to work behind the scenes. Mandy Rice-Davies, then staying at Wimpole Mews, remembers returning there one afternoon – almost certainly on the Thursday – to find Ivanov and Ward in a huddle with a new arrival, Lord Astor. 'There was much talk about offensive and defensive missiles,' says Rice-Davies today, 'but I was very young, and it didn't make much sense to me.'

One day that week, Ward drove Rice-Davies to Whitehall and gave her some pro-Soviet leaflets to distribute. She giggles now at the memory. 'I just walked into the Foreign Office. Nobody stopped me, and I left them all over the place. Stephen waited for me round the corner in the car . . .' Ward's purpose, perhaps, was to reinforce Ivanov's impression that Ward was firmly on his side, and to be trusted.

Ivanov confided to Ward and Lord Astor that he was

working on direct orders from Moscow, and without the knowledge of the Soviet ambassador. He favoured an informal gathering of interested parties, Members of Parliament and diplomats, at Cliveden. He was still, it seems, convinced of the influence of the British aristocracy, and inspired by the history of the Cliveden Set, the group of British aristocrats who, under the patronage of Lord Astor's parents, are said to have plotted to keep Britain out of World War II.

'Ivanov's judgement,' one observer has commented, 'appears to have been on a level with that of the Nazi leader Rudolph Hess who flew to Scotland in 1940, thinking that if only he could have a word with the Duke of Hamilton he could stop the war.' If so, Ivanov may not have been so far off the mark as one might think. Recent research on the Hess affair indicates that the Nazi's trip was more rational, and his choice of contacts more pertinent, than has ever been conceded by British officialdom.

Ivanov thought the mere fact of being a lord meant a man was able to influence events in Britain. That was clearly an exaggeration, but Ivanov's basic theory was by no means foolish in 1963. The Macmillan years did see great power placed in the hands of a small set of wealthy, aristocratic families. One could be forgiven for thinking that the Devonshires, the Stuarts, the Ormsby-Gores and the Salisburys really did run the country. At the centre of this powerful élite, a commoner married into the Devonshire family, was Prime Minister Macmillan himself. Ivanov's desire was to bypass Lord Home, an 'Ivan the Terrible' of the Foreign Office who, he thought, would only obstruct his efforts. Ivanov now wanted to be sure his message was getting to the very top.

'This time,' Stephen Ward said in his memoir, 'we aimed at the Prime Minister himself . . . I rang Lord Astor and through him arranged to take the Soviet offer to Lord Arran, and thence to the PM . . . It may seem a strange way, but so long as it worked it would serve.'

In the midst of the Missile Crisis, London social life continued – the bizarre fringe included. Mariella Novotny held court that week with her husband Hod at their home. 'Standing against the fireplace surrounded by discarded clothes,' Novotny later wrote in an unpublished memoir, 'was ——— ———, a Conservative MP.* He was addressing a small group as if in the House or in a courtroom, while a very pretty girl knelt on the carpet in front of him having sex with him orally. He appeared disinterested in her ardent attention, preferring the sound of his own pompous voice deliberating on the Cuban crisis. His orgasm caused him only to pause briefly, and call for his glass to be refilled.' Hod Dibben says this incident did take place, and remembers that Stephen Ward, too, found time to be at the party.

Friday 26 October, found Ward busily playing the messenger boy again. He once more contacted the Foreign Office on Ivanov's behalf, and had an afternoon meeting with Sir Harold Caccia's private secretary. Within hours, in the United States, another Soviet Intelligence officer tried another behind-the-scenes approach, through an American private citizen.

Just before lunch, Washington time, the telephone rang on the desk of ABC's diplomatic correspondent, John Scali. The caller was Aleksander Fomin, officially a counsellor at the Soviet Embassy but actually the KGB colonel in charge of the KGB office in Washington. Fomin, who knew Scali from previous encounters, asked if they could meet immediately.

Over lunch at the Occidental, Fomin behaved much as one gathers Ivanov did to Ward. 'Perhaps,' he whispered across the table, 'a way can be found to solve this crisis . . .' He said Moscow would dismantle its Cuban missile bases and pledge never to install offensive weapons on Cuba if the United States would agree not to invade Cuba. Within an hour, Scali was presenting a typed memorandum of the

*MP identified but name omitted for legal reasons.

conversation to the Director of Intelligence at the State Department, Roger Hilsman.

That same afternoon, a rambling message came in from Khrushchev himself. It was similar to the KGB communications, and fairly conciliatory. If the US Government would promise never to invade Cuba, said Khrushchev, 'this would immediately change everything . . .' That evening, at the White House, President Kennedy told newsman John Scali that the proposals made through Counsellor Fomin were an acceptable basis for a settlement. Scali was empowered to see his Soviet contact again, with a message for Moscow. At last, it seemed, both sides were edging towards a peaceful solution.

Across the Atlantic, in London, the Ivanov initiative had continued. On Friday afternoon Stephen Ward telephoned the man whom Lord Astor had suggested as a conduit to the Prime Minister, Lord Arran. The late Lord Arran, 'Boofy' to his friends, was an eccentric peer, best known for peculiar speeches in the Lords and a colourful column in the *Evening News*. He was, nevertheless, a good contact man.

'Life,' said Lord Samuel, 'is one Balliol man after another.' Lord Arran had been to Eton and Balliol College, Oxford, as had Harold Macmillan, and by 1962 many of his contemporaries were in the upper reaches of the Foreign Office. He was first cousin to David Ormsby-Gore, the British ambassador to Washington with the ear of President Kennedy. He had worked in the diplomatic service and at the Ministry of Information during the war, and the Soviets believed he worked for British Intelligence until much later.

Lord Arran responded to Ward's call by inviting him and Ivanov to Saturday-morning drinks at Pimlico House, his home in Hertfordshire. 'We drove out,' Ward wrote. 'Lord Arran greeted us in the drive, and we sat down to talk – with some excellent rosé for myself and vodka for Ivanov.' During the two-hour meeting almost a whole bottle of vodka was consumed, though Ivanov, according to Lord Arran, remained 'reasonably sober'. The Russian, Arran noted, 'made himself most agreeable. It became immediately clear that Commander Ivanov's mission was to get a message to the British Government by indirect means, asking them to call a Summit meeting in London forthwith. Such an invitation, said the Commander, would be accepted by Mr Khrushchev with alacrity.'

'We went back to London,' Ward continued, 'feeling that it was up to fate from now on. We stopped at the Shack Bar in Swiss Cottage, had lunch and drank to success.'

Lord Arran, meanwhile, acted quickly. The Soviet proposals were in the Prime Minister's office within hours. As Macmillan later revealed in his memoirs, he was also briefed by Ward's MP friend, Sir Godfrey Nicholson. The Ivanov initiative had gone as far as it could.

Macmillan and his Foreign Secretary, Lord Home, had not closed their minds to intervening in the crisis. Macmillan, the advocate of restraint in the recent Berlin Crisis, was shaken by the rush of events. Lord Home revealed at the end of the week that, if deadlock continued, he had definite proposals to put forward. On Saturday morning, though, even as Ivanov and Ward were about to see Lord Arran, Home again rebuffed the official Soviet embassy emissary, Loginov. Britain would stand by the United States.

In Washington, Saturday proved to be the worst and best day of a frightening week. Optimism was replaced by alarm and confusion. In the morning, news came that a US surveillance aircraft had been shot down in Cuban air space. Another US spy plane, straying across the Soviet border, was chased by Soviet fighters. A second message came in from Khrushchev, much colder than its predecessor. Now the Soviet leader was demanding withdrawal of US missiles from Turkey in exchange for dismantling the Soviet sites in Cuba. The missiles were obsolete and scheduled for removal anyway, but Kennedy could not be seen publicly to be bowing to pressure from Khrushchev.

At the Sheraton Hotel that afternoon, ABC newsman Scali took a grim message to his Soviet contact. 'If you think the United States is bluffing,' he said, 'you are part of the most colossal misjudgement of American intentions in history. We are absolutely determined to get those missiles out of there. An invasion of Cuba is only hours away.' That night, Attorney-General Robert Kennedy told the Soviet Ambassador much the same thing, while quietly promising that the US missiles in Turkey would shortly be removed.

At 1 p.m. on Sunday, London time, news reached London that the Soviet freighters had turned away from Cuba. 'We had been on the brink, almost over it,' Macmillan remembered later, 'yet the world had been providentially saved at the last moment from the final plunge.'

Stephen Ward had spent that morning digging his garden at Cliveden. Then, with his weekend guest Ivanov, he went up to Lord Astor's mansion for lunch. With Lord Astor, Lord Arran, and Lord Pakenham – now Lord Longford – they gathered in the long drawing-room to watch the news on television. 'Only vision came, no sound,' Ward recalled. 'To our bafflement and dismay we only saw Khrushchev's face and Kennedy's, and until we got the news a bit later we did not know an epic settlement had been reached. Ivanov looked stunned – "A mistake," he said.'

The Soviet attaché was seething. 'He kept on saying he couldn't believe it,' Lord Arran wrote later. 'He was sure Mr Khrushchev had some counter-demand to make on the Americans. We all felt almost embarrassed by the man's humiliation.' In a real sense, Ivanov was right. The United States removed its missiles from Turkey within three months. Most important, US covert operations against Castro were drastically scaled down.

In the immediate aftermath of the crisis, Ivanov was still fuming, as William Shepherd, Conservative MP for Cheadle, observed when he visited Wimpole Mews on 31 October. Shepherd had met Ward the previous week, at the height of the crisis, during a heated conversation at the Kenya Coffee House in Marylebone High Street. Shepherd's curiosity had been aroused by Ward's comments, and the osteopath had suggested a meeting with his friend Ivanov. Now, at Wimpole Mews, Shepherd found himself in strange company, listening to Ivanov's polemics.

The meeting broke up when Ward announced with a flourish that he and Ivanov were on their way to see Iain Macleod. Macleod was Leader of the House of Commons and Chairman of the Conservative Party.

Shepherd, puzzled and somewhat alarmed, later saw Macleod in Parliament, and told him, 'You'd better be careful, dining with a man I assume to be a Soviet spy.' Macleod denied knowing Ward, and claimed Ward and Ivanov had merely dropped in on his daughter's birthday party while he was out. He then went to great lengths to put this on record. According to the Denning Report, he spoke to Lord Home about the episode, and later repeated himself in a formal letter. Home, of course, by now knew a good deal about Ward.

Today, Shepherd still thinks Macleod's reaction was a little odd. 'It seemed to be taking a lot of immediate precaution,' he says. 'I mean, I wouldn't have bothered to do this the same day. But apparently he was concerned about this, and might have known more about Ward than I thought he knew.' Ward, in his memoir, was at pains to explain that he and Ivanov had gone to the Macleod party at the suggestion of a friend who was invited. In the event they stayed only a short while because the friend had already left. Ward wondered what all the fuss was about.

Macleod, a former member of the Thursday Club, may have known Ward better than he allowed. Mandy Rice-Davies remembers, too, the strange behaviour of David Davis, a friend of the Macleods whom Ward met at the party. He later 'hung around', apparently wanting to learn all he could about Ward's movements. 'I had the feeling,' says Rice-Davies, 'that he'd been sent to spy out the land.' Ward, for his part, gave Ivanov a present, a book called *Bridge Made Easy* by Iain Macleod. Later, in 1963, Macleod was a leading defender of John Profumo.

Stephen Ward, characteristically, made no attempt to hide his role during the Missile Crisis. He wrote to Harold Wilson, the Leader of the Opposition, describing the Soviet attempt to set up a Summit conference, and his own role as an intermediary. On 5 November, the crisis barely over, he was talking about it openly at a dinner attended by the Executive Assistant to the American Ambassador, Alfred Wells. Wells, now retired in France, says the events surrounding the Profumo Affair are today 'just a foggy memory'. At the time, though, as FBI files reveal, he hastened to report the Guy Fawkes dinner conversation to the ambassador, David Bruce.

In a memorandum the next day, Wells noted that Ward had 'made loud statements that he had been the principal liaison between the Soviets and the British Government during the Cuban crisis . . .' Wells further reported that another dinner guest had described Ward as an osteopath who 'procured girls for wealthy clients'.

The Profumo Affair was starting to blow. Security officers at the US State Department apparently learned the basic facts as early as October, the month of the Missile Crisis, long before Government officials in Britain had an inkling of what had been going on. According to the veteran Washington writer on intelligence affairs, Andrew Tully, the information came from the jilted American mistress of a Second Secretary at the Soviet Embassy in Washington. The diplomat,* said the woman, had openly boasted that the British Minister for War had been sharing a girlfriend with one of his colleagues in London. Within weeks, says Tully, the CIA confirmed the truth of the story, and British Intelligence was informed.

American officials received no response from London, according to Tully, and that is not surprising. British Intelligence had been playing Ivanov for the best part of a year, and John Profumo's amours had vastly complicated a most sensitive case. It was time, perhaps, to keep the powder dry. Time, though, was running out fast.

On the night of Saturday 27 October, at the climax of the Missile Crisis, Christine Keeler had been involved in a fracas at the All-Nighters Club in Soho. Her West Indian

---

*Probably Ivan Azarov, a KGB officer, who left Washington that October. He was expelled from Great Britain in 1971.

protector, John Edgecombe, chased the troublesome Lucky Gordon into a corner. A knife flashed and blood flowed. Gordon sustained a long, cruel cut to the face, requiring seventeen stitches.* Amidst bedlam at the Club, and while Edgecombe called a taxi, Keeler called Stephen Ward. She said she was going into hiding for fear of Gordon's revenge. 'I'll call you when it's safe,' she told Ward.

But soon there would be no more safety, and no more hiding, for Christine Keeler, or Stephen Ward – or for the Minister for War. The long party was over. The skeleton in Profumo's cupboard had started to rattle in public.

---

*Charges against Edgecombe in connection with this matter were later dropped.

TWELVE

DISASTER LOOMS

It was the smart set, suitably enough, who got the first public whiff of scandal. In the summer of 1962, readers of *Queen* magazine – required reading in those days for those with an antique coffee-table to put it on – had been offered a tantalising titbit of information. On 31 July, in a section of the magazine devoted to rumour and gossip, there appeared one sly sentence. Or rather part of a sentence. It looked like this:

"*. . . called in MI5 because every time the chauffeur-driven Zis drew up at her* front *door, out of the* back *door into a chauffeur-driven Humber slipped . . .*"

It had happened that way, of course, give or take a couple of details. Eugene Ivanov did not usually have a chauffeur, and John Profumo more often arrived alone in a Mini than a Humber. But, as Lord Denning was to note dryly in his Report, there were indeed occasions when only moments separated the departure of the Soviet spy and the arrival of the War Minister at Wimpole Mews.

Who fed this juicy item to the magazine? Its author was *Queen*'s Associate Editor Robin Douglas-Home, a nephew of the Foreign Secretary, and a socialite of long-standing whose name was linked romantically with that of Princess Margaret. In 1962 he was a member of the Chelsea Set, the latest label applied by the London press to the fashionable nightclub crowd.

Douglas-Home committed suicide in the mid-sixties, so

we cannot ask who passed him the most devastatingly accurate piece of scandal in the history of gossip columns. Some have guessed that the columnist got his information from Stephen Ward himself. If he did, then it was surely because Ward was loose-lipped, not because he wanted to see it in print. Later, Ward would be appalled when the newspapers got hold of the story, and he strove valiantly to protect Profumo from exposure in the press. In fact, with Wimpole Mews a crossroads for promiscuous chatterboxes, the story was bound to reach a journalist in the end, especially one like Douglas-Home, with his pedigree ears firmly pressed to the rich ground of the cocktail circuit.

It was now, on the very day the *Queen* article appeared, that John Profumo was thinking of resigning over a quite different matter. He strongly disagreed with his superior, the Minister of Defence, who wanted to scrap the Blue Water missile project. Profumo met privately with Prime Minister Macmillan before the decision was taken, but the cancellation went ahead. 'The poor boy,' Macmillan later told his press secretary, 'was nearly in tears.'

Profumo decided not to resign, but may that week have had a premonition of his eventual resignation and ruin. If *Queen* magazine landed on the Belgravia coffee-table of Mr and Mrs Profumo, and if he read the Douglas-Home piece, the Minister must have shaken in his shoes. It was a year now since the Cabinet Secretary had warned him against mixing with Stephen Ward, because of the osteopath's friendship with Ivanov. Profumo must have felt safe enough, perhaps so safe – if we are to believe what Lucky Gordon and John Edgecombe learned from Christine Keeler – that he still occasionally risked seeing Keeler away from Wimpole Mews. Whether he did or not. Profumo's folly was a fact that had spilled across the city. It was now congealing, slowly but surely, into his fate.

In early November, as people breathed easy in the realisation that the Missile Crisis had not brought the world to an end, two men went to an Armistice Day service at Stourbridge, in Worcestershire. Colonel George Wigg was spending the day with his local party agent, Tommy Friend. When they got back from church, Wigg was surprised to hear that someone had telephoned while he was out. He was puzzled, for nobody but his wife Minnie knew his whereabouts. When he called Mrs Wigg, and when she told him nobody had called her, Wigg was even more perplexed. Then the telephone rang again. The caller did not identify himself, and his message was brief. 'Forget about the Vassall case,' he told Wigg. 'You want to look at Profumo . . .'

Three weeks earlier, at the Old Bailey, William Vassall, an Admiralty clerk, had been sentenced to eighteen years in prison for giving secrets to the Russians. He was a homosexual, and had fallen for a Soviet Honeytrap. The British press, suspecting there had been a cover-up, was doing battle with the Macmillan Government, which saw the newspaper reporting as a witch-hunt. Wigg, as the Labour Party's expert on intelligence, was preoccupied with the case in late 1962. The Prime Minister was to set up an enquiry just two days after the anonymous caller told Wigg to forget Vassall and investigate Profumo.

Wigg could not forget Vassall for the time being, but he was intrigued. 'Driving back to London,' he said later, 'the nagging question kept recurring: how did the unknown caller know where I was, and how did he get my number?' And what did the message mean, and why had the call been carefully directed at Wigg, with his keen interest in military affairs and espionage, and his reputation for tireless investigation? George Wigg wondered about this for days. It was therefore all the more unfortunate – for the War Minister – that, less than a fortnight after the mysterious telephone call, Profumo crossed Wigg in Parliament.

Colonel Wigg, who had served in the Army for eighteen years, and came from a soldiering family, had served as Parliamentary Private Secretary to a Labour Minister for War, and was known as the Army's watchdog in the Commons. For a year now he had been collating information on the British military operation in 1961 to protect the emirate of Kuwait. Wigg's information was that British troops had been ill-prepared for desert warfare, and would have been decimated had there been any actual combat. He and Profumo then struck a deal on the way Wigg's questions could be handled in the House without party political rancour, and to the practical benefit of the Army in future operations. In the event, Profumo spiked Wigg's guns in Parliament, in a series of moves which Wigg regarded as dishonourable and deceitful.

George Wigg, the man who had watched six War Ministers come and go, had until now been quite impressed with Profumo. After this personal humiliation, he changed his mind. In the months to come, when the scandal broke, Profumo could expect no quarter from Wigg.

Meanwhile, away from the parliamentary chamber that would soon be ringing with their names, the seamy life continued for the men and women around Dr Stephen Ward – except for Mandy Rice-Davies' lover, Peter Rachman. His life came to an abrupt end. Rice-Davies, in Paris in late November with Senta Hitchcock – a member of the wealthy American Mellon dynasty – got no reply when she tried to telephone Rachman. She flew home, and hurried round to see Stephen Ward. 'I've got bad news for you, little baby,' Ward told her. Peter Rachman was dead, at the age of forty-two, of a massive heart attack, according to the death certificate.

The slum landlord, legendary for his wealth, left a mere £72,800 in traceable assets, a sum more than cancelled out by tax and liabilities. On his wrist when he died, however, was a gold bracelet engraved with serial numbers. The real fortune probably had been salted away in foreign bank accounts. Months later, before his trial, Stephen Ward would ask a friend, Pelham Pound, to clear up pornography he had left at a flat he used that had belonged to Rachman. Pound found few dirty pictures – someone had already removed most of them – but he did find a bag of jewellery that had been Rachman's.

Mandy Rice-Davies, distraught over Rachman's death, took shelter at Wimpole Mews for a while. Then, one night when Ward was out to dinner, she took an overdose of barbiturates. She drifted into a coma reading *Gone With The Wind*, thinking it was a shame she would never know the ending. Christine Keeler arrived at the flat, and called an ambulance. She saved Rice-Davies' life.

Christine Keeler had her own problems during those weeks – Lucky Gordon still refused to go away. A few days before Rice-Davies' suicide attempt, the spurned lover had turned up at Wimpole Mews asking for Keeler. Rice-Davies told him Keeler was not in – she was staying elsewhere, specifically to avoid Gordon. 'Give her these, with my love,' the West Indian growled, and thrust some tiny black objects into Rice-Davies' hand. She shrieked when she realised what they were – the seventeen stitches that had been sewn into Gordon's face a month earlier, after the knifing in the All-Nighters Club.

Undeterred by his injuries, Gordon continued his pursuit of Keeler. So did Edgecombe, who had gone to ground in Brentford, hoping to escape arrest in connection with the knife attack. Then, tiring of life in hiding, he asked Keeler to help him find a solicitor, one who would arrange his surrender to the police. Keeler, jealous because of Edgecombe's relationship with another woman, refused. Indeed, she now told her sometime protector, she planned to testify against him when he came to trial. This defiance had results that nobody could have foreseen.

Ten days before Christmas, on 14 December 1962, Edgecombe telephoned Wimpole Mews. Keeler was then visiting Rice-Davies and she spoke with him briefly. 'Look, Johnny,' she told him, 'you know how difficult everything is. I told you not to phone . . .' When Edgecombe persisted, Keeler slammed down the telephone. Frantic, Edgecombe slipped into his pocket the gun he had taken away from Keeler – the one she had acquired to protect herself from Lucky Gordon. It was loaded. Edgecombe called a minicab, and headed for Wimpole Mews.

It was about 1 p.m., and Stephen Ward was at his consulting rooms in Devonshire Street, treating a patient. 'The telephone rang,' he wrote, 'and I heard a girl saying someone was shooting at the door. I immediately rang Scotland Yard, and went on treating my rather surprised patient. Little did I know at the time that this was the start of a series of shattering events that would become known all over the world . . .' The girl on the telephone was Mandy Rice-Davies, announcing that mayhem had broken out in Wimpole Mews. Edgecombe had arrived in his minicab and started banging on the door of Ward's flat. 'Mandy came to the window,' Edgecombe remembers today, 'and said, "Christine's not here." I said, "Don't give me that bullshit!" and then Christine came to the window. I said, "I'm no fucking salesman, standing here shouting in the street. Come down to the door!" I said, "Man, this taxi's costing money." So at that she threw a pound out of the window, and that really did it. It really grated. I tried to break the door down, but I kept bouncing off. So I started blazing away at the lock, but that didn't work either. That's when she came to the window, and the gun went off again. I didn't mean to shoot her . . .'

Edgecombe had not injured anyone, but he realised at once how foolish he had been: 'I had to get rid of the gun, so I ran round the back of the house and stashed it. Then I got in the taxi, because I had another clip of ammunition in Brentford and I wanted to get rid of it before the police came.' The taxi driver was a helpful character. 'Hey, man,' Edgecombe asked him, 'do you think I made too much noise?' 'No,' replied the driver. 'I've been revving the engine . . .'

The shooting caused a positive explosion of events. The police, alerted by Ward, Rice-Davies and one of the neighbours, arrested Edgecombe at his home after a short siege. He was to be charged with shooting with intent to kill, possession of a gun, and with the earlier wounding of Lucky Gordon in the All-Nighters Club.

At Wimpole Mews, Keeler and Rice-Davies, as witnesses to the shooting, were asked to come to the police station for questioning. The press, meanwhile, had arrived on the scene even before the police – for reasons yet to be explained. Conceivably, Fleet Street was tipped off by the patient Ward had been treating when Rice-Davies called during the shooting, the wife of a deputy editor of the *Daily Mirror*. The *Mirror*'s headline next day shouted, 'GIRL IN SHOTS DRAMA'. This was a story with all the ingredients: two young girls attacked at the home of a respected osteopath, a West Indian on the rampage, and the use of a gun – a rare event in the London of those days. Stephen Ward asked the girls to stay away until it all blew over, and hoped things would quieten down. They went off to a flat in Great Cumberland Place, near Marble Arch, with Kim Proctor, a photographer at the Stork Club. Keeler had been using it for some time, as a place to hide from Gordon. Within hours, she lit a hydra-headed fuse.

At 7 p.m. that evening, Keeler made a phone call. According to her, she needed someone to talk to, someone responsible, and the man she picked was Ward's acquaintance and former patient Michael Eddowes. According to Eddowes, Keeler sounded agitated on the telephone, so he went round to see her at once.

Eddowes, who was fifty-nine in 1962, is a larger than life figure. In the fifties, after running a law practice specialising in divorce work, he had gone into business. He succeeded, with a property company, a copying machine company and a chain of restaurants called Bistro Vino. He is best known to the public for his penetrating investigation of the murders at 10 Rillington Place. Eddowes showed, and an official enquiry later accepted, that Timothy Evans was wrongly hanged for the murder of a child at that address – the crime was actually committed by Reginald Christie, who had slaughtered seven people and hidden their bodies in the house. For the past quarter-century, with less success, Eddowes has busied himself with research into the assassination of President Kennedy, on the premise – against all the evidence – that the alleged killer, Lee Harvey Oswald, was actually a Soviet impostor.

Rarely seen in anything but pinstripes, Eddowes is an old-fashioned gentleman. He is also rich, and fiercely anti-communist. These characteristics combined to make

him a dangerous new player on the stage of the Profumo
Affair.

Eddowes responded with alacrity when Keeler called
him after the shooting at Wimpole Mews. As we have seen,
he had come across Ward meeting Eugene Ivanov in a

coffee-bar at the height of the Cuban Missile Crisis. If that were not enough to pique his interest, something he claims Ward told him later certainly did. He confided, according to Eddowes, 'that both War Minister John Profumo and a Soviet Naval attaché, Captain Ivanov, were Christine's lovers.'

On the evening of the day of the shooting, sitting in the third-floor flat at Great Cumberland Place, Eddowes and Keeler watched the news on the television. Keeler got excited when she saw coverage of the shooting incident, complete with bullet holes. 'I thought it was a good opportunity,' Eddowes said later, 'to put my questions to her about the possibility of espionage. I asked her if Ivanov and Profumo were friends of hers. She said they were, and that one used to go out of one door, and the other come in the other. I judged the moment propitious to ask her if Ivanov tried to get her to get information out of Profumo. She said, "Yes." I said, "Anything in particular?" She said, "The date of the nuclear warheads to Germany." I cannot discuss whether she tried to get the information.* I was very shocked. I am convinced that Miss Keeler was telling the truth.'

Eddowes did nothing publicly after hearing Keeler's sensational story. Instead he hired a private detective, former policeman Michael Marler, to make further enquiries. Eddowes did nothing else, he said later, 'because I had good reason to believe the authorities were aware of what was going on . . . I had been informed by Dr Ward that the three people were being watched by the security people, and "It was none of my business."' Ward, who had duly reported to MI5 many months earlier, when Profumo's affair with Keeler started, may have said this to Eddowes. At all events, Eddowes kept quiet for the time being. Meanwhile, another fuse had been lit.

---

*By all other accounts it was Ward, as recounted earlier, who asked Keeler to get the information, not Ivanov. Eddowes, said Keeler, 'got it mixed up'.

'As we left the police station after making our statements after the shooting,' Mandy Rice-Davies recalls, 'a reporter came up to Christine. He was from the *Sunday Pictorial*. He told her his paper knew "the lot". They were interested in buying the letters Profumo had written her. He offered £2,000. We were both horrified . . . this seemed like very deep water.'

It was deep water indeed. But how did a major newspaper know such details, at this time? There was a spy in the Keeler camp, one of the immediate circle of friends she allowed into the flat at Great Cumberland Place. This was Nina Gadd, née Gorchekov, who had met Keeler at least a year earlier. Unknown to Keeler, Gadd was working as a freelance for the *Sunday Pictorial*, as a source of information. She had good credentials – she too had lived at Wimpole Mews for a couple of weeks in 1962.

'I met Keeler and Mandy through a hairdresser,' Gadd says today. 'Mandy was more intelligent and knew what was going on. She realised what my game was, whereas Keeler never really cottoned on. I had Keeler marked down as someone to watch. She was talking to everyone . . .'

From now on, Gadd was employed by the *Pictorial*, then one of the most powerful of the popular Sunday newspapers, to milk Keeler for information. She infiltrated a reporter, posing as a boyfriend, into the flat at Great Cumberland Place, and in the weeks to come, the *Pictorial* would be the first newspaper to get Keeler's account of the Profumo–Ivanov affair. Too nervous to publish, its editors were eventually to lose the story to the *News of the World*. For a while, though, the prospect of libel actions was to hold the newspapers back. But from now on, the reporters were on the trail.

Christine Keeler, simultaneously running from Lucky Gordon and the press, had the locks changed at the flat in Great Cumberland Place. Amongst those allowed entry, along with Nina Gadd, was an old friend called Paul Mann. Mann, a keen bridge player who regularly played at clubs like the Connaught, had long since struck up a friendship with Stephen Ward, who was also a bridge enthusiast. In 1961 he had made frequent visits to Ward's Cliveden cottage. Mann had met Ivanov, and was at Cliveden the weekend of the meeting between Profumo and Keeler. Now, in late 1962, he was staying at Wimpole Mews and making regular visits to Great Cumberland Place.

On Christmas Eve 1962, Mann took Keeler to what has been described as a party 'for old friends from the Cabaret Club'. As a result she met a man who had been waiting more than ten years for the opportunity to destroy Stephen Ward. Now he had it, and it did not matter who else got hurt in the attempt. And all the time, British Intelligence had been watching.

The Man With the Grudge

John Lewis, like Ward, had just turned fifty. He had made a fortune years earlier, largely from inventions connected with the industrial use of rubber. After the war he had become Labour MP for Bolton, and was at first well regarded, becoming Parliamentary Private Secretary to the Postmaster-General. Then, when he lost his seat in 1951, the Labour national executive refused to endorse him as a candidate for the next election. No reason was given, but a document in Labour Party files, released to us in 1987, states, 'The final refusal to endorse . . . has resulted in a spate of rumours that John Lewis is not a fit and proper person to represent the Party in Parliament, because of some lack of personal or business honesty or integrity on his part.'

During his time in Parliament, Lewis had clashed violently with both the then Labour leader, Clement Attlee, and the Party Secretary, Morgan Phillips. Publicly and privately, he was an embarrassment. The Party got unwelcome publicity when he ended up in court accused of bumping into a police car on the way to a parliamentary debate – not once but three times. He was thought to have obtained his post of Parliamentary Private Secretary cor-

ruptly, and that was consistent with his business reputation.
A veteran City analyst, Roger Whipp, recalls Lewis as 'a
nasty piece of work . . . I remember him making optimistic
reports about his own companies, when in fact they were
losing money.'

Lewis regularly resorted to law to silence those who
found him out. In 1961 he won enormous sums in damages
against the *Daily Telegraph* and the *Daily Mail* over stories
reporting that the Fraud Squad was investigating his affairs.
The police had indeed been on Lewis' trail, and an Appeal
Court judge later called the damages 'wholly unreason-
able', and ordered a new trial. Things were not put right,
though, until 1964, and Fleet Street was understandably
gun-shy when Lewis turned out to have a role in the
Profumo case. Had the press not been so frightened of
lawsuits, it might have turned a jaundiced eye on his role as
one of the main sources of information on the scandal – a
source intent on smearing Stephen Ward.

'John Lewis,' says former Conservative MP William
Shepherd, 'was one of the lowest forms of human existence
I've ever met. He was loathsome in every sense. I think no
one loathed him more than the Labour Party . . .' We have
failed to find anyone who had a good word for Lewis, who
died in 1969, with the exception of Christine Keeler, and
her case is special. He was apparently capable of veno-
mous, implacable hatred, a hatred directed above all at
Stephen Ward. Sex, as so often in this story, was at the
heart of the matter.

Three years after the war, Lewis married a beautiful model
called Joy Fletcher. It was a disaster, not least because of
Lewis' philandering and his alleged interest in bizarre sex.
According to the family physician, Dr David Minton, who
testified at the 1954 divorce hearing, Mrs Lewis brought her
troubles to him. 'Find yourself a lover,' was the doctor's
advice. 'Find yourself a man with whom you can commit
adultery.' The man she looked to for suggestions was Dr
Stephen Ward. Ward introduced her to the reporter, and
later successful novelist, Frederic Mullally.

Mullally had known Ward for years. Side by side, Mullally remembers, they had wined and dined at London's best watering-holes alongside the exotic cast of characters who have adorned this story: David, Marquess of Milford Haven, the Indian Maharajahs, the film stars, photographers Baron and Beauchamp, 'Dandy Kim' Caborn-Waterfield and John Profumo. For Mullally, it was a happy hunting-ground. 'Evidence has been given,' the judge in the Lewis divorce was to say, 'that Mullally had said his greatest ambition was to sleep with all the beautiful women in London.'

Today Mullally remembers how he met John Lewis' wife. 'She and Lewis had lots of fights, rows and walkouts. And on one occasion she went out in great distress, and didn't know what to do, and called Stephen. And he put her up for the night at his place. It was a totally friendly gesture on his part . . .'

Ironically, says Ward's friend Warwick Charlton, it was not the wife's affair with any man that really enraged Lewis. It was later, when he discovered that Ward had introduced ————,* a female associate of Lewis, to a lesbian affair with another *woman*. 'He went potty,' Charlton recalls, 'when he found Stephen had fixed her up with a Swedish beauty queen, a lesbian, with whom she had an affair. This, he thought, was an assault on his manhood . . . He had a heart attack over it. I was with him when he got the news. He said, "I will get Ward whatever happens." I remember he took out a revolver, and said, "I'll shoot myself, but not before I get Ward." From then on, the most important thing in John's life was his burning hatred for Ward, which went on year after year.'

The judge in the Lewis divorce case noted that it had 'been fought with a consistent and virulent bitterness which could rarely have been excelled . . .' He excoriated Stephen Ward, who gave dubious evidence, apparently in an effort to protect Mrs Lewis. Lewis himself stopped at nothing to have his way in the case. According to two

*Name deleted for legal reasons.

sources, Lewis asked several witnesses to perjure themselves, and bribed some to do so.

This then was the man Christine Keeler encountered in late 1962. According to Paul Mann, she met Lewis at a party, and simply poured out her story of the love triangle with Profumo and Ivanov. That is probably a censored version. Warwick Charlton offers another version of the savage fate that brought Keeler to the doorstep of Ward's worst enemy. Once again, the common denominator was lust.

'It happened because Christine was broke,' says Charlton. 'When she went to Profumo all he gave her was £15 and a bottle of scent. A mean person. So she did what she always did when she was broke. She went round the clubs picking people up. John used to go to a Baker Street club which supplied girls to customers. One night he was just sitting at home at his place, and he sent for a woman. The girl they sent was Christine Keeler. She came along with no idea who he was or what he had against Stephen Ward, and, during the evening, she began spilling the beans about Ward, Profumo, everything . . .'

John Lewis had all the time in the world to listen to Keeler pouring out her worries. The Lewis she saw was a nice middle-aged gentleman who made her see the funny side of her tale of woe. Just as she had once found security in Stephen Ward, she now felt safe with Lewis. He, of course, revealed nothing of his vendetta against Ward. Keeler told him that Lord Astor and Michael Eddowes had failed to help her – they only worried about Profumo. Now Lewis offered to find her a solicitor. 'Everything,' he told her, 'would be all right . . .'

Others were not at all sure things were going to be all right. Lord Astor called, fretting about rumours that Keeler was going to bring up Profumo's name when the Edgecombe shooting case came to court, that she was going to 'drag everyone into it'. He came round to dinner, offered to pay Keeler's legal costs, and she said she had no plans to mention big names in court. 'He never telephoned again,' says Keeler.

One wonders how the latest developments were received at the headquarters of the Secret Intelligence Service, MI6, in Queen Anne's Gate. For, as we reveal here for the first time, MI6 had long been watching the Lewis vendetta against MI5's man, Stephen Ward. Indeed, so far as MI6 were concerned, Ward had been *their* man long before MI5 came on the scene – even if he did not know it.

Outrageous though it may seem to the British public, who pay the bills, MI5 – responsible for internal security, and MI6 – supposedly limited to foreign targets – have often failed utterly to coexist and cooperate with each other. The sister services have frequently behaved like rivals. Operations by MI5 have run head-on into those run by MI6 and the two organisations have ended up at loggerheads. Government oversight has been poor, except in wartime, and this lamentable situation has sometimes persisted for years at a time. According to fresh information, the handling of Stephen Ward was one example.

As we have seen, MI6 on occasion 'played at home' rather than abroad, and part of the game included providing women for visiting foreigners. By the fifties, Ward's potential in this area was obvious, and – a full decade before MI5 began contacts with Ward – MI6 'marked' him.

This information comes primarily from former MI6 contract operative ——— ———.* He has a track record of providing reliable information. ———, today a plump, bespectacled figure in his sixties, came to MI6 after wartime service with RAF Intelligence. His first task was to establish himself in journalism, which was to be his long-term cover. Thus, from beginnings as a photographer on the *Derbyshire Evening Telegraph*, he was moved to London in 1952, to be planted in the *Daily Mirror*. His true role was known only to an MI6 'friend' at the paper, Managing Editor Cyril Morten.

Not surprisingly, since he had other fish to fry, ——— was disliked at the *Mirror* because of his odd ability to write

———
*Name deleted for personal security.

his own schedule, and his lack of interest in doing much real work. Colleagues noted, however, that he did take a great interest in 'the vice scene'. Today ——— is frank about it – his MI6 task was to spot people who could be compromised or actually recruited, or might become useful to MI6. As early as 1952, he got to know Stephen Ward.

'Ward was a social climber,' ——— recalls, 'someone who needed to "get on" . . . Sex was the entrée. We learned that Ward wasn't that interested in participating in sex. He liked to watch girls being screwed, especially adult women dressed up as underage girls. Ward would obtain girls, and a boost for us came when he met Lord Astor – and capitalised on Astor's perversion . . . For us, here was a thriving little London setup with all sorts of big names and diplomats and others swimming in and out . . . MI6 has tentacles everywhere, and someone spotted Ward and felt the setup might become useful, that some interesting people might walk into it. We could get to know them, do little deals, so that they'd be friends of ours . . .'

Nobody, says ———, mentioned this interest to Ward himself. Instead, a 'bagman' was placed close to Ward, someone who could, for instance, help out occasionally with funds. Ward, as we have seen, was hopeless at living within his budget. The money supplied would never be much, just enough to tide Ward over, and to make him feel indebted. The bagman would then have some control over Ward, and a small investment would harvest a trickle of intelligence. Then Ward came up against the vengeful John Lewis.

Logan Gourlay, the veteran *Daily Express* journalist, remembers the first Lewis plot to discredit Ward. So does Frederic Mullally, the reporter who had the affair with Lewis' wife. In 1953, says Mullally, 'Lewis got hold of an *Express* reporter, a young untrained boy, and gave him what purported to be an exclusive story that Stephen Ward and I were running a call-girl business in Mayfair . . .' That story was scuppered when the editor of the *Express*, Arthur Christiansen – who was, conveniently, a member of the Thursday Club – intervened.

'The problem,' says ———, was "How do we negate
Lewis, and stop him spoiling this promising setup?" My
case officer assigned me to get in with Lewis, and I did, by
pretending I wanted an interview for the paper or something. Soon I was going nightclubbing with him – we went to
a place called Eve's quite a lot. He was quite open about his
hatred for Ward. And I got in with him to the extent that I
was helping him to plan his anti-Ward campaign, but in
such a way as to make sure it didn't come off . . .'

Lewis' private war against Ward sputtered on until
1961, with MI6 man ——— watching from the sidelines.
The MI6 man was aware, meanwhile, of a continuing MI6
interest in Ward – and in his patron Lord Astor – but his
case officer offered no details. Ward was never actually
recruited, so far as ——— knew, just observed and kept on
ice as an available asset.

Then, in 1961, two developments occurred. Ward,
goaded by Lewis' scheming and aware of Lewis' association with 'Mirrorman' ———, threatened to sue the *Mirror*. At about the same time, to the irritation of MI6, Ward
began contacts with MI5. ——— says, 'Ward approached
security, offering help prior to any of the contacts mentioned in the Denning Report. He approached 5, not 6, and
with some disastrous consequences . . .' According to ———
—, MI6 learned of this at an inter-service meeting, but told
MI5 nothing of its own long-standing interest. The word
went out, says ———, 'Scatter. Everybody drop it. And we
did.' Soon ——— was overseas, working undercover on a
foreign paper. MI6 washed its hands of Ward, and stood
back and chuckled when MI5's contacts with him led the
service into embarrassment and difficulty over the Profumo
case.

With ——— gone, there was no one to restrain Ward's
bitter enemy, John Lewis. In late 1962, when Christine
Keeler came his way with her astonishing story about
Ward, Profumo, and Ivanov, he at last had the perfect
opening. The sordid secrets of this teenage Nefertiti came
as a gift from the gods. Keeler's information could not only
destroy Ward but also resurrect Lewis' broken political

career. Warwick Charlton understood what was happening at the time. 'John was an able politician,' he said. 'He had held pretty high office, but because of the way he was living he had lost his seat. He was desperate to get back in. He had two motives delivered to him by Christine: one, the Russian security thing, and, two, evidence that Stephen was a ponce. He'd have his revenge, and he had little presents to give Wigg to beat the Tory Party with, and he might get back and re-establish his reputation with Labour . . .'

Who made the anonymous call to Labour MP George Wigg in November 1962, telling him: 'Forget about the Vassall case. You want to look at Profumo'? According to Chapman Pincher, the writer on intelligence affairs, MI5 files contain evidence that the caller was a Soviet agent fronting as a contributor to the *Evening News*, Victor Louis. A year later, the *Cambridge Evening News* was to receive an anonymous call twenty-five minutes before the assassination of President Kennedy, warning of 'big news' and suggesting the paper call the US Embassy. A CIA telegram, London to Washington, dated 23 November 1963, noted: 'SOME SIMILAR PHONE-CALLS OF STRANGELY COINCIDENTAL NATURE PREVIOUS RECEIVED IN THIS COUNTRY OVER PAST YEAR, PARTICULARLY IN CONNECTION WITH DR WARD'S CASE.'

It is conceivable that the Soviets arranged a call to Wigg, to provoke an embarrassing investigation and to damage the Conservative Government. Surely, though, they would have given him some titbit of information to go on, not just one meaningless sentence with no follow-up message? No responsible source has ever laid the Profumo Affair at Moscow's door.

John Lewis, though, is another matter. Did he learn something about the case as early as November, when the call was made? Given what we now know of Lewis' scheming, of his political ambitions, his purple passion against Stephen Ward, and his track record of deviousness, he must be considered a candidate for the role of anonymous caller to his former Labour colleague. Certainly, in the weeks to come, it was Lewis who was to give Wigg the ammunition for his formidable attack on the Government over the Profumo case.

Wigg and Lewis were not close friends, but they shared a keen interest in horse-racing. Wigg had long been involved in the supervision of racecourse betting, and Lewis was a race-horse owner. As Wigg's secretary recalls, the two men often engaged in horse talk together, and that gave Lewis an opening to start pouring out his venom about Profumo, Ivanov and Stephen Ward. He went to Wigg for the first time on 2 January 1963, and outlined what Keeler had told him. Wigg, mindful of his anonymous telephone caller, was interested. He was cautious, though, and asked for more information. Lewis asked Keeler to come and see him at his home in St John's Wood.

According to Keeler, she had originally turned to Lewis for advice. She says that – from this man – advice did not come free. He wanted sex, and when she argued, he pulled a gun. In spite of this melodrama, Lewis managed to get more information out of Keeler. She talked about Ward's connection with a man from MI5 – and about Ward's request that she ask Profumo when nuclear warheads were to be delivered to West Germany. Lewis tape-recorded it all, without telling Keeler. Then he called Wigg again.

Wigg's secretary remembers, 'Mr Lewis constantly rang up during the day when Mr Wigg was about his parliamentary business. I frequently got the impression he wasn't completely sober. But he was insistent . . .' On 7 January, Lewis brought Wigg the troubling story about nuclear warheads. Still Wigg hesitated. It seemed so far-fetched somehow, and – although Wigg thought Profumo 'politically untrustworthy' – he could not see him as a security risk. 'It seemed to me,' Wigg said later, 'that the man to keep an eye on was Ivanov. Lewis agreed that the matter must be handled exclusively on the issue of security.' Quietly, Wigg began building a dossier.

While the battle-lines were being drawn, Stephen Ward carried on as though nothing had changed. During Christmas, he and Ivanov had gone down to the country home of Lord Ednam (later Lord Dudley). 'We had two extra women staying with us,' says Lord Dudley today, 'and we were giving a big dinner party for Boxing Night so we had the idea of asking Stephen, and Stephen had told us that Ivanov was spending Christmas with him, so it solved our problem.'

Lord Dudley thought Ivanov 'a very attractive man, very jolly, drank incredible quantities of vodka without turning a hair, a great *bon viveur*, with a lot of charm, a gold tooth that flashed, quite typically Russian . . . I knew that he was a naval attaché, and I knew that naval attachés have to do a certain amount of intelligence work. I used to make sort of jolly jokes and say, "Have you been to Portsmouth lately?", and that sort of thing. And he would roar with laughter.'

There was a more serious interest in the man with the flashing gold tooth. When Lord Dudley learned Ivanov would be present, he called a relative who would also be coming, a senior Foreign Office officer called Edward Tomkins. 'Look,' Lord Dudley told Tomkins, 'our mysterious Russian friend is coming to dinner, and I shall quite understand if you don't feel like coming, being in the FO and all that . . .'

Tomkins, who worked in a department with responsibility for Germany, asked for time to think about it. A day or two later, Lord Dudley recalls, he rang back to say, 'It's all right. I've talked to the FO, and they rather want me to go to dinner, because they are quite anxious to find out what this chap's up to . . .'

Tomkins, now Sir Edward, remembers the dinner. He had been posted to Moscow during the war, and spoke Russian. Ivanov, he noted, 'showed great interest in the details of the Polaris missile deal – it was immediately after Macmillan's visit to America in connection with Polaris.'

Ivanov also brought the conversation round to West Germany's prospects of acquiring nuclear armament, the very question he had been pursuing during Profumo's affair with Christine Keeler.

Dr Stephen Ward — a sexual enigma, 'provider of popsies for rich people' — died when the rich people abandoned him.

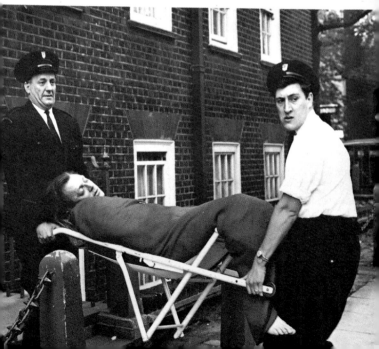

The young Stephen Ward explored sex in brothels around the world, then obsessively cultivated high society in Britain. (*Above*) with actress Celia Lipton at a London premiere, 1948. Less openly, in his white Jaguar (*below*), Ward cruised the streets picking up women.

(*Facing page*) The Manipulator. Ward the osteopath treated the famous at his Devonshire Street surgery, and — as an accomplished artist — drew their portraits in his spare time. At his cottage on Lord Astor's estate, Ward entertained a stream of female protégées, like Maggie Brown (*below*) who became a top international model. This picture, Ward confirmed, was taken by Soviet diplomat and spy Eugene Ivanov, probably in 1961.

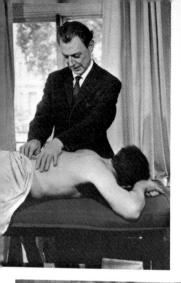

Did the Profumo Affair come close to destroying the President of the United States? In 1963, when the President was visiting England (*above*), Prime Minister Macmillan was startled when John F. Kennedy confided that he got a headache if he went long without a woman. The White House scrambled to suppress rumours that he was linked with women named in the Profumo scandal.

Mariella Novotny (*below left*) at her marriage to Ward's friend Hod Dibben, and Suzy Chang during shooting of the film *Nudes of the World*.

'I have been one of the most successful men in London with girls', bragged Ward.

Ronna Riccardo (*top right*) was one of the whores. She was bullied by the police into giving false testimony. There were the models, like Ilya Suschenek (*below right*) who claimed a 'perfectly harmless' association with Ward.

Ward turned Pat Marlowe (*below*) into a rich woman, but she committed suicide in 1962.

The Right Honourable
John Profumo, MP, Fifth
Baron of the late United
Kingdom of Italy and Her
Majesty's Secretary of
State for War, until 1963
when he resigned because
of his affair with Christine
Keeler (*facing page, top
right*) — here drawn by
Stephen Ward. Ward also
sketched Captain Eugene
Ivanov, the Soviet spy
(*facing page, below right*).
MI5 ran a 'honeytrap'
operation against Ivanov,
in the hope that he would
defect. Keeler, it seems,
was the honey. (*Below
right*) Ivanov — a
contemporary photograph.

A place to bring the girls — Lord Astor giggled when he talked about Spring Cottage (*above*) the house he provided for Ward in the grounds of Cliveden. Guests included many women — and Eugene Ivanov.

Pornography — these sex photographs (*below*) allegedly taken by Stephen Ward, are part of a batch that surfaced mysteriously in 1986. Ward collected pornography, and some of his known female associates are recognizable in the pictures. Some were taken in the open near Spring Cottage.

Lord Dudley admits that having Ivanov to dinner was 'slightly what you might call an intelligence operation.' Stephen Ward, for his part, made some odd remarks 'about having contacts with MI5'. He also 'dropped some hints about Ivanov and Profumo'. Dudley remembered this, not least because Profumo was a friend of the family. Ward, says Dudley, was 'fairly cryptic – but he hinted that there was something brewing.'

Something was brewing all right. On 16 January, Johnny Edgecombe was committed for trial on the Wimpole Mews shooting charges. The press, sensing now that this was more than a simple case of armed assault, were buzzing around Christine Keeler. In secret, Ward's nemesis, John Lewis, went on dripping his poison into the ears of George Wigg.

It was an uncomfortable New Year for Stephen Ward. The flat at Wimpole Mews was the focus of press interest because of the shooting and was also proving too expensive. He moved out, into the Bryanston Mews flat once used by Mandy Rice-Davies' sugar-daddy, Peter Rachman.

Lady Astor, who saw Ward down at Cliveden, thought he was going downhill. 'I noticed a physical deterioration,' she says now. 'Whether it was too much coffee-drinking I don't know, but when things were getting difficult, you could see his hands were trembling. He looked dreadfully ill sometimes . . .'

Long envied for his magnetic effect on women, Ward suddenly seemed pathetic. 'Don't go,' he said one weekend to Jon Pertwee, who had dropped in at the cottage, 'Wait. You must meet my new friend.'

'Oh my God,' said Pertwee. 'Who is it now?'

'It's the baker's daughter from the village,' Ward replied.

'I can't believe it,' groaned Pertwee. 'Aren't you ever going to stop?'

On 18 January, Ward saw Ivanov, and within days the Russian was planning to leave. These facts were supposedly picked up by MI5 on a tapped telephone, though they may well have come from MI5's loyal servant, Ward himself. On

29 January, just two months short of the end of his three-year posting to London, Ivanov left London. 'His departure,' said the diarist in the *Guardian*, 'was much regretted by his many friends . . .'

Ward, the soul of everybody's party, was about to find himself short of friends. 'The first intimation I had that any underground work was afoot,' he wrote, 'was from Lord Astor, who is always well informed about these things. He had heard a story that the police were interested in me, that it was being said that I had seen people as patients and then charged them high fees for introducing them to girls. I just laughed . . . I did not think for one second that anyone would take such an idea seriously . . .'

John Lewis – reviving the libel he had invented against Ward years earlier – was spreading his falsehoods with skill. The great manipulator was being swept to disaster on a current of events he could not control. Very soon now, the British Establishment would be looking for a scapegoat. Take Lewis and his lies, frighten a few witnesses into giving phoney evidence, rig a trial – and Ward was their man. John Profumo, though, was one of their own. The Establishment would stand by him to the last.

THIRTEEN

PROFUMO AT BAY

'When there is an almost universal conspiracy to lie and smother the truth,' wrote the American columnist, Walter Lippman, of another scandal, 'I suppose someone has to violate the decencies.' The US Ambassador to London, David Bruce, was to report to President Kennedy that, in the Profumo case, 'the truth trickles, instead of gushing forth.' It trickled – and has remained only partially revealed until today – because of the massive effort made to conceal the facts, and John Profumo's personal arrogance in deceiving his high-ranking colleagues.

The panic started, ironically, over the newspaper story that never was. On 22 January 1963 came the logical outcome of Christine Keeler's contacts with the *Sunday Pictorial*, the newspaper that had infiltrated Keeler's circle through her friend Nina Gadd. For a down payment of £200 – and the promise of £800 to come – Keeler told the *Pictorial* everything. With the deft help of professionals, an accurate draft story was assembled. The truth was told better in this first draft than it ever would be when Fleet Street finally broke into print. Speaking of her relations with Profumo and Ivanov, Keeler said: 'If that Russian . . . had placed a tape-recorder or cinecamera or both in some hidden place in my bedroom it would have been very embarrassing for the Minister, to say the least. In fact it would have left him open to the worst possible kind of blackmail – the blackmail of a spy . . . This Minister had such knowledge of the military affairs of the Western world that he would be one of the most valuable men in the world for the Russians to have had in their power . . .'

The article referred to the request that Keeler ask Profumo about nuclear-armed weapons for Germany. Finally, as proof that there really had been an affair, Keeler gave the journalists Profumo's letter of 9 August 1961, addressing her as 'Darling'. A copy was placed in the safe at the office of the *Pictorial*. The story was dynamite, but, as is the way with Sunday newspapers, the editors did not rush into print. What with cross-checking, and the need to have Keeler authenticate the final version, nearly three weeks slipped by – time for much skulduggery.

Four days after telling all to the *Pictorial*, on Saturday 26 January, Keeler had a tiff with Stephen Ward. It happened when Ward, not knowing that Keeler was listening in, had a telephone conversation with Keeler's current flatmate. The Edgecombe shooting incident was proving a nuisance, and he burst out: 'I'm absolutely furious with her . . . she's ruining my business. I never know what she'll do next, the silly girl . . .'

Keeler was angry. What she did next was to tell the Profumo story all over again, this time with Ward as the villain of the piece, the man who had made all the introductions. She told the story to the next person who came to the door, who by unhappy chance was an officer in the Metropolitan Police calling to say that Keeler and Rice-Davies would have to appear at John Edgecombe's trial. The detective listened to Keeler, then went back to the office and filed a report. It included all the main elements of the story, along with the allegation that 'Dr Ward was a procurer for gentlemen in high places, and was sexually perverted,' and the fact that the *Pictorial* already had the story. The detective's report went to his Inspector, and – given the content – he passed it on to Special Branch, the police unit which liaises with MI5.

That same Saturday, Stephen Ward learned from a reporter of the impending story in the *Sunday Pictorial*. He was the first of the principal male characters to learn of impending disaster. Ward at once demonstrated a loyalty to his friends that none of them would ever show towards him. 'I was anxious,' he said in his memoir, 'to save Profumo and Astor from the consequences . . .' Within twenty-four hours, although it was a Sunday, Ward hurried to the home of a barrister friend, William Rees-Davies.

Rees-Davies, then the Conservative MP for Thanet, had long mixed socially with Ward and those in his circle. Variously nicknamed 'Count Dracula' and 'The One-Armed Bandit' because of a wartime amputation, Rees-Davies had lines to the top officers in the Government. Next morning, Monday the 28th, Ward called Lord Astor. The two men met, Astor also took legal advice, then personally took the bad news to the Minister for War. The time was 5.30 p.m.

Profumo's immediate response was remarkable – he urgently contacted the Director-General of MI5, Sir Roger Hollis. It was an unusual procedure for a minister of Profumo's rank to call in the head of MI5. Yet Hollis was sitting in Profumo's office in just over an hour. Both men, of course, remembered the occasion in 1961 when MI5, through the Cabinet Secretary, asked Profumo to take part in the Honeytrap operation to make Ivanov defect. Now, so far as Hollis could tell, Profumo wanted help in getting a 'D Notice' – a Government gag – slapped on the *Sunday Pictorial*. Hollis failed to oblige.

MI5 had been having a hard time of late, in spite of strenuous attempts to paint a rosy picture. There was a second suspect in the Vassall spy case, at the Admiralty – and he had simply been moved to a less sensitive post, to avoid the embarrassment of another trial. A month earlier, an assistant controller at the Central Office of Information had been jailed for passing information to her Yugoslav lover. An Italian atom scientist working in England, Dr Guiseppe Martelli, was facing trial on espionage charges. It was suspected that a Government minister, one of the Prime Minister's friends, had left himself open to blackmail by Soviet agents. And last, but worst of all for British Intelligence, one of its own had just defected to the Soviet

Union. Less than a week before Profumo's cry for help, MI6 traitor Kim Philby had departed for Moscow.

If that were not enough, MI5 had its own selfish reasons for running for cover from the Profumo deluge. It had not only recruited Stephen Ward in its efforts to entrap Ivanov – it had done so in spite of doubts in its own ranks as to whether Ward could be trusted. Those who thought Ward untrustworthy because of his leftwing opinions had been overruled by those who thought those very sentiments made him more likely to gain Ivanov's confidence. The exposure of Ward's MI5 connection could prove highly embarrassing.

MI5 learned from the police Special Branch of Christine Keeler's statement to the Metropolitan Police officer. After conferring, the two services decided the best thing was to leave well alone. 'I think it is wise for us to stay out of this business,' the Special Branch commander noted in a written minute, 'and the Security Service agree.' The police cancelled plans to interview Keeler again.

As head of MI5, Hollis had blocked one way the matter could come to light. He did not, however, come to Profumo's rescue with a gag to silence the *Sunday Pictorial* – even though, as we have learned, an MI5 operative under journalistic cover sent warning that the *Pictorial* had the story. MI5 already knew that Ivanov, the Soviet diplomat, was about to leave the country, and on 29 January he did. It was therefore possible to argue that, with Ivanov gone, there was no worry about a security leak. It was a weak argument – the presence or absence of Ivanov did not change Profumo's vulnerability to blackmail – but it was one accepted later by Lord Denning.

On 1 February, the Head of MI5 issued this instruction, as reproduced in the Denning report:

> Until further notice no approach shall be made
> to anyone in the Ward galère, or to any other
> outside contact in respect of it. If we are
> approached, we listen only.

Sir Roger Hollis had cut Stephen Ward and John Profumo adrift. They could drown in a sea of scandal, but MI5 wanted nothing to do with them. These brutal tactics succeeded – MI5's Honeytrap operation, and its use of Ward, was to remain secret.

John Profumo, Lord Astor and Stephen Ward were out on their own. One of them, though, held real power, and both Profumo and Astor were millionaires. Power and money might yet save the day. The three men met for lunch at Astor's London residence, then Profumo and Ward talked at the Dorchester Hotel.* By 1 February, a Friday, they knew the fuses were burning down on twin disasters: the Edgecombe trial, due to start in a few days with Keeler as the key witness; and the *Sunday Pictorial* story, which would be ready to publish as soon as Keeler put her signature to its authenticity, something she was expected to do within days.

There followed another frantic weekend. Ward's barrister friend, William Rees-Davies, met with Profumo's solicitor on both Saturday and Sunday. On the Saturday afternoon, Profumo's solicitor visited Christine Keeler to suggest a solicitor through whom she could negotiate a deal – in Denning's words – 'not to publish her story'. Canny for her years – she was still only twenty – Keeler did not fancy being represented by a lawyer picked by the Profumo side. Soon though, she did accept the services of Gerald Black, a solicitor suggested by Ward's counsel, William Rees-Davies.

That deal was done through the mutual friend shared by Stephen Ward and Christine Keeler, Paul Mann. 'I think,' he told Ward's lawyer, 'that Christine should be made to deny everything and talk propositionwise and to what it is worth for her to be quiet. I think she is open to a higher bid. She is not satisfied with £1,000.† I told her she ought to have obtained a good deal more.' Mann offered to take Keeler

---

*In his memoir, Ward refers to a meeting with Profumo at the Grosvenor House Hotel.
†The sum due to her under her deal with the *Sunday Pictorial*.

away, as soon as the Edgecombe trial was over, to separate her from the press – so long as somebody else paid the bill.

On Monday 4 February, solicitor Gerald Black, speaking for Keeler, telephoned Profumo's solicitor. After some fencing, Black suggested that the sum of £5,000 might be sufficient to persuade Keeler to abandon the *Sunday Pictorial* and go abroad, to the United States.

Was this a blackmail attempt, an effort to extort money from John Profumo? Behind the scenes, according to Mandy Rice-Davies, there were private discussions. She had already, she says, called Lord Astor and his friend ——— ———*, with both of whom she claims to have slept, to say, 'Something dreadful's brewing. We're all going to be thrown into it.' 'The idea,' says Rice-Davies today, 'was that ——— should give £1,000, Bill £1,000, and Profumo £2,000. Christine put the figure up to £5,000, because she had Profumo's letters.'

'It was not a matter of blackmail,' Christine Keeler told Lord Denning. 'I would have asked for £50,000 if it was.' Profumo could easily afford the sum requested of £5,000. 'Let no one judge her too harshly,' Lord Denning wrote later, '. . . if she had been minded to blackmail Mr Profumo, she would have kept the "Darling" letter herself and not handed it over to the *Sunday Pictorial*.'

Lord Denning also discounted the possibility of any improper conduct on the part of Christine Keeler's solicitor. Quite what was going on remains unclear. It is possible that Keeler was being lured into a trap, to leave herself open to a charge of extortion, and thus be silenced. At any rate, Keeler only ever received £500.

The deal fizzled out on 5 February, when Keeler's solicitor went to collect £5,000 from William Rees-Davies. He was given an envelope which turned out to contain only £450, for 'expenses', and this Keeler rejected. She now went ahead with her plans to cooperate with the *Sunday Pictorial*.

Profumo was by now engaged in complex discussions

---

*Name deleted for legal reasons.

with the senior Government law officer, Attorney-General
Sir John Hobson. He lied, telling Hobson that he had not
slept with Keeler, that the 'Darling' in his letter signified
nothing – he had simply got into the habit of calling people
'Darling' because he was married to an actress. Fatuous
though that sounds, contemporary events gave Profumo
some grounds for hoping he would be believed. In the
Vassall case, another minister, former Civil Lord of the
Admiralty Thomas Galbraith, had resigned partly because
of a letter in which he addressed the homosexual traitor as
'My dear Vassall'. Many had assumed an intimacy, but
there had been none. On the rebound from the Galbraith
episode, Profumo might just have been able to swing it. At
a further meeting, attended by both the Attorney-General
and the Solicitor-General, Sir Peter Rawlinson, he repeated that he was 'totally innocent . . . a victim of mal-
evolent gossip . . .'

It was a classic confrontation of upper-class chaps operating under the Old School code. Both Profumo and Hobson
had been to Harrow, where Hobson – not quite three years
older than Profumo – had been Head of School. Both had
gone on to Brasenose College, Oxford. It was almost as
though Profumo were up on some tuck-box pilfering offence in the Head Boy's study. Had he done it or was he
innocent? Hobson was suspicious. Then Profumo came up
with a supreme piece of bravado. He said he would sue for
libel if Keeler's story was published, and was ready to
prosecute Keeler over the request for £5,000, which some
might construe as extortion. If Profumo was prepared to
declaim his innocence on oath, reasoned the Attorney-
General, he must surely be telling the truth.

John Profumo was now wholly dependent on the trust of
his public school colleagues, and he proceeded to abuse it –
right to the top. On Friday 1 February, just as Profumo and
Ward were gearing up to persuade Keeler not to publish
her story, a top executive of the *News of the World* asked to
see the Prime Minister. The paper's General Manager,
Mark Chapman-Walker, now brought his questions to the
Prime Minister's Private Secretary and close friend, Old

Etonian John Wyndham. The Prime Minister was away in Italy until Sunday, so Wyndham took up the matter himself.

His immediate concern was whether there had been a security risk, and he at once summoned Graham Mitchell, the Deputy Director-General of MI5 (a Wykehamist and a veteran, like Wyndham, of the Conservative Party Research Department). Mitchell told Wyndham that MI5 was aware of the matter, had discussed it with Profumo a few days earlier, and that the Minister for War seemed to want MI5's help in gagging the press.

'Why,' Wyndham asked Mitchell, 'have we not been told about this before?' 'This is a free country, not a police state,' replied the deputy head of MI5, as quoted by Wyndham in his memoirs five years later. The inference was that, given MI5's opinion that there had been no security leak, the bedroom antics of ministers were of no concern to British Intelligence. MI5 had told Macmillan nothing when the affair started – during its Honeytrap operation in 1961 – and it did not enlighten him now.

The failure of British Intelligence to alert the Prime Minister would leave Macmillan open to savage criticism. 'It would imply,' Opposition leader Harold Wilson was to say in Parliament, 'that the sixty million pounds spent on these services have been less productive than the security services of the *News of the World*.' John Wyndham, later Lord Egremont, thought the intelligence services a waste of time and money. 'Much better,' he opined a few years later, 'if the Russians saw the Cabinet minutes twice a week. Prevent all that fucking dangerous guesswork.'

On 1 February 1963, less than satisfied by his MI5 briefing, Wyndham decided to see Profumo himself. Late that night the Prime Minister's Private Secretary – Eton and Cambridge, confronted Profumo – Harrow and Oxford. 'The Private Secretary,' Profumo suggested hopefully, 'need not bother the Prime Minister with all this at this stage . . .' Wyndham urged him to see the Chief Whip, Martin Redmayne, whose business was to keep the Prime Minister advised of potentially embarrassing rumours. Profumo saw Redmayne, with Wyndham, on Monday 4 February – and lied some more. It was a contorted story of his relationship with Keeler, no more than 'a giggle in the evening' that had never led to sex.

'Look,' Redmayne told Profumo doubtfully, 'nobody would believe that you didn't sleep with her.' 'Yes,' replied the Minister disarmingly, 'I know they wouldn't believe it, but it happens to be true . . . I didn't sleep with her.' Profumo lied even to Iain Macleod, the Leader of the House of Commons and one of his best friends. Macleod did not entirely believe him. Yet what was one to do? Profumo was so adamant that there had been no affair. The Chief Whip told Profumo he need not resign, and need not inform the Prime Minister. What the Prime Minister was or was not told, and when, has become a matter of controversy.

When Did Harold Macmillan Learn the Truth?

The Prime Minister returned to London from Italy on Sunday evening, 3 February. According to the official version, he was briefed on the Profumo problem the next day, when his Private Secretary, John Wyndham, and the Chief Whip, Redmayne, informed him of the rumours and of what Profumo said about them.

Macmilllan told Lord Denning that he did not bring up the matter with Profumo at all. There were two reasons, said Denning:

1. 'If a Prime Minister sees a Minister and asks a question of this kind, there is no "follow-up". The Prime Minister could either believe it or disbelieve it, and if he disbelieved it, he could not do business again as a Prime Minister with him.

2. He thought it better to get friends of his own age, the Attorney-General, the Chief Whip, and others to talk to him: and if there was anything in it, he would say it to them.'

The Prime Minister remained 'satisfied completely', he

told Lord Denning months later, that Profumo's denials were truthful.

Some believe, though, that the Prime Minister was told about the Profumo–Keeler–Ivanov triangle – by credible sources – in early 1963, or even earlier, and still did nothing.

William Shepherd, the Conservative MP who knew Profumo and Ward and had been a customer at the club where Keeler first appeared as a showgirl, says he wrote to the Prime Minister six months before the affair blew up telling him he was 'sick and tired of immorality in the Government'. Macmillan, he says, asked him to discuss his worries with the Chief Whip, and he did – including his opinion that Profumo had slept with Keeler. Shepherd, however, has not kept copies of his exchange of letters with Macmillan, and his account of the conversation with the Chief Whip indicates that it took place no earlier than February 1963.

Much more troubling is a long series of reports in American official files, released only recently and never analysed by historians. They cover the last days of January and early February 1963.

This was the very time Profumo and his friends, including Ward, began rushing about trying to suppress the truth. It was also, to the day, the time that Eugene Ivanov left London. If accurate, the reports suggest the Prime Minister was briefed on the Profumo problem by an American source, on 28 January.

As we have seen, the Prime Minister was told about the allegations by the Chief Whip, Martin Redmayne, on 4 February, and – according to Denning – decided to accept Profumo's word that they were untrue. But if the Prime Minister was given the information at the time the FBI file specifies, he should *already* have been aware that Profumo was lying. Yet he did nothing. This leads to the worst possibility of all, that Macmillan was a silent accomplice to Profumo's later lie in the House of Commons.

The new evidence comes from a mass of FBI documents, some heavily censored. They focus on Thomas Corbally, a forty-two-year-old American then living in London. He

was a businessman, with a major holding in a company
linked to Pearl and Dean, the cinema advertisers. He was
also, according to the press, something of a playboy. His
marriage to tennis star 'Gorgeous Gussie' Moran had
caused a stir a few years earlier – it was annulled on the
grounds of non-consummation. The columnist Taki
Theodoracopulos, writing in the *Spectator* following first
publication of this book, has reported a more serious side to
Corbally. 'He also had great contacts in very high American government circles as well as security services,' wrote
Taki, claiming first-hand knowledge.

In early 1963, Corbally was living at a flat in Duke Street,
Mayfair, rented by another American. Both men were
involved in the bizarre chain of events, reported here for
the first time, that may have led to Macmillan hearing about
the Profumo–Keeler–Ivanov triangle from the American
Embassy. Both were contacted during the writing of this
book, and clearly still regard the matter as highly sensitive.
The second American cannot be named here – he gave an
interview only on the basis that he remains unidentified.
Thomas Corbally began talking openly, but then excused
himself on the advice of his lawyer, who happened to arrive
while Corbally was talking. He subsequently replied to
questions in writing, through the lawyer. From him and the
'second American', and from the files, we learned the
following story.

In late 1962, at Duke Street, Corbally was suffering from
a knee injury, one so serious, he was told, that only surgery
would help. Then says Corbally, 'I was at a party one night
and some bloke I didn't know looked at me and said,
"What's wrong with your knee?" It was about as big as my
head . . . he put his hand on my knee, and within about
thirty seconds I was in some place in the flat with my
trousers pulled up to my knee. And fifteen minutes later I
walked back into the party with nothing, no swelling.'

The miracle worker was Dr Ward, and Corbally gratefully invited him round to Duke Street. 'He knew a lot of
pretty girls,' says Corbally, 'and I like pretty girls. He liked
to gossip and talked incessantly about the things he knew

. . . I entertained a lot, and Stephen was around my flat a lot . . . I certainly liked him and I considered him a friend.'

Corbally met Mandy Rice-Davies, and liked her – she has not lost touch with him to this day. He had once, reportedly, been engaged to construction heiress Valerie McAlpine, whom Rice-Davies knew well. The second American also knew Rice-Davies, and met John Profumo through a mutual friend, another British minister. Corbally met Christine Keeler, briefly, at a party. He sums her up as 'petite, pretty face, and dumb'. Michael Eddowes, the solicitor who knew Ward and Keeler, recalls a party at Duke Street where Corbally 'had Keeler and Rice-Davies sitting on each side of the armchair'.

It seems that Ward not only knew the two Americans, but had reason to visit Duke Street on 28 or 29 January. It was the 28th, a Monday, that – according to the FBI files – the Profumo case was brought to the attention of Prime Minister Macmillan.

On that day, disaster struck for a young London model called Sylvia Parker. Her lover, Antonio Mella, was shot dead outside a Soho club called the Bus Stop. In her distress, Parker turned to a German girlfriend, Elizabeth Brunley, then staying at Corbally's flat. She herself was then given shelter and comfort at Duke Street, and Stephen Ward – in the midst of his own troubles – came round to see her.

The twenty-eighth of January was the very day that Ward, Profumo and Lord Astor began mounting their attempt to silence Keeler and stop the truth coming out in the *Sunday Pictorial*. It was the foremost thing in Ward's mind, and at Duke Street, he confided in his American friends.

'Stephen', the second American recalls, 'proceeded to tell me that Christine had been seeing Ivanov, that he had taken Ivanov to the Astors' place at Cliveden, that she met Profumo, had an affair with him, and so on . . .'

It was an extraordinary story, and the second American decided to do something about it. He placed a call direct to the most senior American in London, Ambassador Bruce.

They knew each other socially, and there was no problem getting through. Bruce listened carefully. It was the first he had heard of the story, and he was interested. He had met Ward himself, eighteen months earlier, when the osteopath sketched him for the *Illustrated London News*. Bruce was also a personal friend of the Astors, and had visited Cliveden. The Ambassador was interested all right – the information was clearly explosive.

Thomas Corbally told us about this part of the episode through his lawyer. The lawyer states: 'Mr Corbally was asked to visit the American Ambassador, and did so on or about the 28th or 29th . . . this was at the Ambassador's invitation . . . The Ambassador had been told that Mr Corbally knew Stephen Ward as his patient and friend. When the Ambassador asked Mr Corbally about Ward's knowledge of the Profumo affair, Mr Corbally told the Ambassador that Ward spoke about it incessantly . . . Mr Corbally felt that the truth would be served better by the Ambassador talking to Ward direct rather than through him . . .'

Bruce wanted Ward's information, but was about to leave London. 'I can't follow up myself,' he told the second American. 'I'm just about to go to Washington. Wells can handle it.' Alfred Wells, the Ambassador's Assistant, did follow through.

On 29 January, according to the FBI dossier, Wells wrote a memorandum. As regurgitated by the FBI, it supposedly quoted Corbally as saying that Christine Keeler had sold an article to the *Sunday Pictorial*. It then stated, as summarised for the FBI Assistant Director in charge of Counter-Intelligence, 'that the impending scandal had been brought to the attention of the Prime Minister on the evening of January 28, and a letter had been written to the [*Sunday Pictorial*], putting the paper on notice that the Government is aware of the story, and that under British law the story could not be published until after the trial of the Jamaican [*John Edgecombe*] . . .'

Another FBI memorandum, sent from London at the height of the scandal, in June, repeats that the Prime

Minister was advised on 28 January. Corbally categorically
denies that this information came from him. His lawyer
says, 'Mr Corbally did not know the Prime Minister, he had
no contact with him or others in his government . . . he
would deeply resent his name being used to besmirch the
reputation of a distinguished prime minister who is now
dead and unable to answer for himself.'

Corbally points out, however, that he was 'not aware of
what Ambassador Bruce or anyone else told the Prime
Minister'. The evidence is that the information was at some
stage passed on by the Ambassador's office. Weeks after
the January meetings at the Embassy, on 13 February,
Bruce's assistant, Wells, sat down to lunch with Stephen
Ward. The meeting, confirmed by Corbally, the second
American, and by a woman who was present, took place
at Simpson's-in-the-Strand. 'Mr Wells,' according to
Corbally, 'obtained answers to all the questions he put to
Mr Ward'. 'Stephen,' says the second American, 'went into
everything about Mr Profumo, absolutely A to Z. You
couldn't shut him up.'

Astonishingly the Ambassador's Assistant Wells, contacted in retirement in France says he 'cannot remember'
anything at all on the subject, neither about the 29 January
memorandum, nor about his later meeting with Stephen
Ward. According to the second American, though, Wells
said at the time exactly what he did after the lunch at
Simpson's. He reported that he had contacted the British
Prime Minister's office with the information. A senior
official later called back to say that he had passed the
information to Macmillan. The Prime Minister, the official
told Wells, dismissed the Profumo story as 'absolutely
ridiculous'.

In Washington, later in the year, the matter was taken
seriously. On his American lawyer's advice, Thomas Corbally went to see the head of the FBI's New York office,
John Malone, and subsequent documents, albeit heavily
censored under national security classification, indicate
that there was an unholy flap in Washington once the
scandal broke. On 20 June, the matter was discussed at a

meeting attended by the Defense Secretary, the Director of the CIA, the head of the Defense Intelligence Agency, and an Assistant Director of the FBI. The documents involved are censored almost out of existence, except for a couple of lines. At one point they appear to indicate that the London Embassy failed to react to the information they were given in January. Another, dated the day after the high-level meeting, shows that Secretary of State Dean Rusk decided to send an emissary to London to sort out what had really happened.

A few days later, on 25 June, the FBI was told that the emissary, Deputy Assistant Secretary of State William Burdett, was 'en route London to look into this matter'. He was to take the problem up with Ambassador Bruce. Again, even today, much of the cable is censored for national security reasons. And again, memories are strangely faulty. William Burdett, contacted recently, could recall no details of the London visit.

What of Bruce himself? He was the man who originally saw both Thomas Corbally and the second American. He was on excellent personal terms with the Prime Minister. Also, as Ambassador, he was the American in London who could get straight through to the Prime Minister at any moment of the day or night. Did Bruce brief Macmillan in late January?

A recently released State Department document, an 'Eyes Only' report sent in June by Ambassador Bruce to President Kennedy, reads as follows: 'Few people believe that Macmillan, whose private integrity has never been questioned, would have connived at a clumsy attempt to avoid an almost inevitable disclosure if he had known that Profumo had lied. Nor would it consort with the character of the PM to have done so.'

Is it conceivable that Bruce would have championed Macmillan's innocence in a personal briefing to the President several months later, unless he really believed the Prime Minister was blameless? Yet Bruce himself had been given information on the Profumo case, as early as January. He had ordered Wells, his own Assistant, to investigate, and Wells had reportedly informed the Prime Minister's office of what Corbally and his friend had learned from Ward – many weeks before Profumo's lying statement to Parliament. Did Ambassador Bruce cover up for Macmillan?

Bruce is dead, but in 1987 we were able to examine not only his papers as released by the State Department, but also his journals, now held by the Virginia Historical Society. Bruce kept a meticulous record of each day's activity, down to details of food served at dinner and precise comments on people he spoke to or met each day.

The Bruce journal is almost pedantically detailed, and on 28 January – the day Macmillan had supposedly been informed – there is no reference to Profumo. Nor is there on the next day, the 29th, but a whole page is missing from the day's coverage. Some of the journal is censored, blacked out by the State Department, but at this point a page is missing in its entirety. There is no way of knowing whether it contained material on a tip-off to the Prime Minister.

It may be no coincidence that, later in the year, Bruce's response to an FBI report of its interview with Corbally is also missing. So is a letter on the subject to the Secretary of State, Dean Rusk. The FBI files state, moreover, that the original information given to Ambassador Bruce was not even passed on to the State Department in Washington. The Wells memoranda stayed in the file, in the Ambassador's office. It seems possible, therefore, that – until the case blew up in public – Bruce simply decided to sit on it.

Whatever Bruce did or did not tell Macmillan personally, the British government did learn what the Americans knew about Profumo. According to the FBI report of another memorandum by Bruce's Assistant, the word was also passed to Clive Bossom, Parliamentary Private Secretary to the Secretary of State for Air, Hugh Fraser. Their meeting took place on 5 February, according to an FBI report, with Bossom, Wells and Corbally present. Today Corbally says he never met Bossom, and Wells – consistent with his responses on the whole affair – 'cannot remember'.

Clive – now Sir Clive – Bossom does better. He remembers someone at the US Embassy telling him, 'in a stupid way, at the end of a dinner, that there was a case pending against a minister of the Forces'. Bossom was told the essence of the story, told that it involved a minister and Cliveden, but he was not told which minister. There were only three ministers for the armed forces, one each for Army, Navy, and Air Force. Bossom says he reported at once to his own Minister, Secretary for Air Hugh Fraser. 'I knew my Minister had a cottage at Cliveden,' says Bossom. 'I asked him, "Are you involved?" and he said, "No, not at all."'

For Fraser, then married to Lady Antonia – the present wife of Harold Pinter – this was a timely warning. He was indeed friendly with Lord Astor, had met Ward, and, like him, had been given the use of a cottage on the Cliveden estate. Soon, realising that these circumstances might prove embarrassing, he stopped using the cottage. One of the Prime Minister's secretaries, Sir Philip Zulueta, who also used an Astor cottage, was to do the same. There is, of course, no suggestion that either of these officials used the cottages in any improper way.

Air Minister Fraser, however, was a close personal friend of his opposite number at the Ministry for War, John Profumo. The information now went full circle – Fraser's secretary passed it on to John Profumo himself. 'There are always rumours', was the Minister's lofty response, 'about men in the limelight.'

The stories, from this and other sources, continued to reach Harold Macmillan's office in the weeks following the initial flap. The Prime Minister was informed, but – we are told by Lord Denning – he maintained his belief that Profumo, his young friend and protégé, was telling the truth. 'His lie', Macmillan's secretary John Wyndham wrote later, was believed 'because his story was so incredible that it must be true. It was as simple as that . . .'

Perhaps not quite so simple. Macmillan had at some stage been tipped off by the American Embassy to the fact that Stephen Ward, a man better qualified to say so than anyone except Profumo and Keeler themselves, had described a triangular situation involving Profumo, Keeler and a Soviet diplomat. By that time he had also been warned by his own Private Secretary and his Chief Whip. Why then did he simply snort 'Ridiculous', and pass on to other things?

The Prime Minister knew Profumo well, and those who knew him knew his reputation as a ladies' man. It may be that Macmillan preferred to play the ostrich, to Hear No Evil, See No Evil, in the hope that the affair would blow over. Failing fresh evidence, that is the only rational explanation. The truth was staring him in the face – his young friend, a potential Prime Minister, was lying. If this was blind faith, it was to cost Macmillan his career.

Hard though it is to comprehend now, John Profumo's guilty secret had so far remained entirely hidden from the general public. And in early February, happily for him, two perilous events failed to occur. The trial of John Edgecombe, scheduled for the 8th, was postponed because a key witness was unavailable. The taxi driver who had driven Edgecombe to Wimpole Mews was allegedly ill following a heart attack. It has been impossible to establish whether this was a genuine illness – it certainly brought a heaven-sent delay to a trial in which embarrassing truths might have bubbled to the surface.

Meanwhile, deft manœuvring by Stephen Ward brought Profumo a temporary reprieve from the publication of Christine Keeler's story in the newspapers. First, he managed to persuade an assistant editor of the *Sunday Pictorial*, Fred Redman, that there were major inaccuracies in the story provided by Christine Keeler. Redman decided to go for a relatively harmless story about Ward and young girls, and to drop the Keeler story altogether. Second, somehow Ward also prevailed on the *News of the World* to hold off. The twin miracle was not entirely due to Ward's diplomacy – Fleet Street was scared stiff of libel actions, and of Government reprisals.

When the headline did appear it came as a sneak attack. On 8 March the tiny readership of a mimeographed handout called *Westminster Confidential* was offered the Profumo story, only slightly disguised under the headline, 'That was the Government That Was!' So thin was the veil that Profumo was called 'Jack ——— the Secretary for W–r.' *Westminster Confidential* was a political broadsheet that went to two hundred subscribers, a small but influential group made up of politicians, diplomats and reporters. The man with the guts to publish was an expatriate American called Andrew Roth, and he had based the story on information supplied by – of all people – a rightwing Conservative MP.

Roth's source was Henry Kerby, a huge man with a cannonball head filled with an independent pugnacity that spared no one, least of all his own party. He had worked for MI6 during the war, and still maintained the intelligence connection. Kerby detested the élite of the Foreign Service – 'those Foreign Office boys rogering their own rectums' was his description. He was deeply scornful of the self-serving core of the British Establishment and also intensely patriotic. All these characteristics combined to make him exceedingly dangerous to John Profumo. 'He was scandalised,' recalled *Westminster Confidential* editor Roth, 'that a millionaire War Secretary from the Establishment "kissing ring" should make himself so vulnerable through a "tart".'

There was a nice justice in the fact that the stick now used to belabour Profumo was coloured both pink and blue. Roth, the journalist, had left the United States during the McCarthy witch-hunt. His source, Kerby, was a right-winger, and the damning article was eagerly distributed by the Conservative Right. Kerby, moreover, produced a steady stream of political intelligence for Labour, in the shape of the bloodhound colonel, George Wigg – the very man now consolidating his evidence on the Profumo case.

It is now known that Kerby was regularly used by MI5, and some of George Wigg's information seems to have come from intelligence sources. In 1987, as the public finally learns of MI5 plots to oust a later Government, one wonders whether the Profumo scandal was not, in the end, deliberately triggered, for specific political purposes, by forces within British Intelligence who saw him as sexually compromised.

During the scandal, Home Secretary Henry Brooke received information that MI5 finally lanced the boil by sending anonymous letters about the Keeler affair to Mrs Profumo. The Head of MI5 denied it, of course, but the same possibility was raised by Stephen Ward, a tool of MI5. 'I think,' he wrote in his memoir, 'the matter was ended by MI5 leaking the story of Profumo's affair to Valerie Hobson through some roundabout route.'

'British sources who should know,' wrote *Washington Post* correspondent Flora Lewis, 'are convinced that it was neither accident nor their ingenuity that provided . . . the knowledge gradually used to oust Profumo. Their suggestion is that British Intelligence themselves determined that if he could not be removed one way, another way must be found . . .'

FOURTEEN

TRUTH IN A TIGHT CORNER

For John Profumo, it now mattered little who was fanning the flames of his destruction. For him, March was the cruellest month, in 1963. On 14 March, when the Edgecombe case finally came to trial, a witness was again missing – and this time the vanishing trick worked against the War Minister. It was Christine Keeler herself who failed to appear. She had run off to Spain with a girlfriend, and Stephen Ward's bridge partner, Paul Mann.

'It would be a question for a jury to decide,' Lord Denning was to say, 'whether they did intend to obstruct the course of justice.' While Denning was unable to discover hard evidence that Keeler had been deliberately spirited out of the country, that is clearly what happened. If the intention was to protect Profumo, the plan misfired. Today Keeler herself believes the trip was dreamed up by those determined to expose Profumo. That, certainly, was the effect.

In the event, Edgecombe was found not guilty on the slashing and shooting charges, but guilty – in spite of Keeler's absence – of possession of a firearm with intent to endanger life. For this he was sentenced to seven years in jail, of which he served five years and two weeks.

The police did not pursue Christine Keeler, from whom Edgecombe had obtained the gun in the first place. Nor did they look up the chain of possession of the weapon, a 'hot' gun that had been used in two hold-ups.

For Edgecombe, the prison sentence seemed racially

inspired. 'The Englishmen,' he says, 'didn't mind having a black guy for a brother, but they didn't want him as a brother-in-law. The British people wouldn't wear a situation where a Government minister was sleeping with the same chick as a black guy. I was an embarrassment to the Government, and they had to put me away and shut me up. If I had been a white guy, it would have blown over.'

For John Profumo, who must long have wished the earth would open and swallow up Christine Keeler, her disappearance now spelt disaster. It provided a way, at last, for the press to link the Keeler–Edgecombe case with the name of Profumo. The *Daily Express* did it, on 15 March, by means of a clever layout trick. One column away from a picture of Keeler, captioned 'VANISHED', the *Express* ran a picture of Profumo and his wife, under the headline 'WAR MINISTER SHOCK – Profumo, He Asks To Resign For Personal Reasons And Macmillan Asks Him To Stay On'.

The story was not accurate. Profumo had discussed resignation weeks earlier – with the Chief Whip, not the Prime Minister – and had decided against it. Profumo was able to tell reporters, now gathered outside his home, 'There is no truth in this story at all – I have not seen the Prime Minister. I have been working on the Army estimates.' It did not matter that the story was garbled – Fleet Street had been chafing at the bit for weeks, and now they were off and running. The story remained front-page news from now on. It was fuelled by some curious burglaries.

The break-ins had started in early February during Profumo's efforts to suppress the truth. Two photographs, both taken at the Cliveden swimming-pool, vanished from Ward's London flat. One picture, showing Ward with three girls, had been snapped by Profumo. He had later added a caption, 'The new Cliveden Set. "J".' The second photograph showed Profumo with two girls, one of them Christine Keeler. Ward, who thought the photos had been stolen by Paul Mann, reported the loss to the police. Then came more break-ins, one at Lord Astor's London home, another at Ward's cottage on Astor's estate.

The thefts excited interest, but the truth about one of them is far from sinister. Trevor Kempson, then a twenty-six year old freelance journalist, now admits that he was the culprit in the burglary at Ward's country retreat. With a photographer friend, he mounted a commando-style raid, approaching Spring Cottage by boat. They broke in, turned the place upside-down, and finally found pictures of Ward and Keeler inside a jar of coffee. Kempson nearly sold the photographs to the *Daily Mirror*, but the paper cried off when it realised they were stolen. Kempson hid the pictures in the loft, inside some Christmas decorations, and eventually destroyed them.

By now, few in the world of politics believed the dam could hold. It was about now that MP William Shepherd wrote to the Prime Minister, demanding action on the 'immorality in the Government'. Macmillan asked him to give his information to the Chief Whip, Martin Redmayne, and he did. 'I went through a list of men then in the Government,' says Shepherd, 'some of them at a very high level, whose conduct – mostly in the homosexual field – gave rise to anxiety. I said to the Chief Whip, "You really ought to have contact with the people across the road, at Scotland Yard" . . . One of these men was involved with children, you see.'

'And as I was about to leave I said, "What are you going to do about Jack?" and he says, "If anyone says a word about Jack in public, we will sue for damages . . . Iain Macleod [Leader of the House] is very strongly of the view that we must resist this under all circumstances." This was really the culmination of so many things. There had been the Ian Harvey case,* and two or three others at the same time. And another member of the Government had been involved in homosexual activity and had been let off by the police . . . so they were nervous – they didn't want any more.'

What the mandarins of the Conservative Party wanted

---

*Ian Harvey was a Foreign Office minister who resigned in a homosexual scandal.

would soon be academic. Labour MP George Wigg had shown his bulging dossier to his political boss, Harold Wilson, and Wilson cleared him to bring the matter into the open. Wigg now looked for a way to raise the Profumo case under protection of parliamentary privilege, and fate offered an ideal opportunity.

On the evening of 21 March, the House debated the jailing of two reporters who had refused to reveal their sources during the Vassall enquiry. As midnight approached, Wigg rose to deliver his bombshell. 'Here,' he said, referring to the Vassall case, 'was a set of rumours that gained and gained in strength, consumed men's reputations – might, in fact, have destroyed them – and which here infringed on the security of the state. But are we sure that the same thing is not happening again? There is not an Honourable Member in the House, nor a journalist in the Press Gallery who, in the past few days, has not heard rumour upon rumour involving a member of the Government Front Bench. The press has got as near as it could – it has shown itself willing to wound, but afraid to strike. That being the case, I rightly use the privilege of the House of Commons – that is what it is given me for – to ask the Home Secretary . . . to go to the Dispatch Box. He knows that the rumour to which I refer relates to Miss Christine Keeler, and Miss Davies, and a shooting by a West Indian – and, on behalf of the Government, categorically deny the truth of these rumours . . .'

The Home Secretary, Henry Brooke, closed the debate that night by criticising Labour for raising such things under privilege. 'I do not propose to comment,' he said bravely. Behind the scenes though, there was pandemonium. The Prime Minister was woken after 1 a.m. by Chief Whip Martin Redmayne. He told Macmillan that nothing less than a personal statement by Profumo could contain the damage – and it must be done within hours, before the newspaper splashed Wigg's speech across the front pages. Profumo's telephone was off the hook, so an official car was sent to his home in Regent's Park. The Minister for War had taken a sleeping pill, and was deeply asleep. In a stupor, he climbed from the marital bed he had once shared with Christine Keeler and drove to the House of Commons.

The five men Profumo faced that night were the commanding officers, the ruling élite of the British Establishment personified. There were Sir John Hobson, the Attorney-General and a former lieutenant-colonel in the Army. He and Minister without Portfolio William Deedes were both old Harrovians, like Profumo. There, too, were Chief Whip Redmayne, Radley School and honorary brigadier; Solicitor-General Sir Peter Rawlinson, Downside, Cambridge and former Army major; and Leader of the House Iain Macleod, Fettes and Cambridge, and also an ex-major. The Home Secretary, the man responsible for police and security matters, was conspicuous by his absence. Profumo was up before the school prefects of the Conservative Government, but this was no inquisition.

Profumo, a fellow Conservative was to say later that year, 'was not a man ever likely to tell the absolute truth in a tight corner . . .' The school prefects of the Government were not now questioning his word, although several of them thought it likely he was lying. For this was a secret cabal, convened in the small hours, expressly to stage-manage Profumo's next move.

By 4.30 a.m. a statement had been concocted. Everyone went home, Profumo to a house still besieged by reporters and a wife who had sat up all night in the drawing-room, with a cat on her lap. After breakfast, at Downing Street, the Prime Minister was shown the draft statement, made a couple of amendments, and gave his approval.

Shortly after eleven o'clock, flanked by Harold Macmillan, R. A. Butler, Iain Macleod, and the Attorney-General, Profumo rose to tell the lie that would never be forgiven.

My wife and I, [said the key part of the Minister's statement] first met Miss Keeler at a house party in July 1961, at Cliveden. Among a number of people there was Dr Stephen Ward, whom we already knew slightly, and a Mr Ivanov, who was an attaché at the Russian Embassy . . . Between July and December 1961 I met Miss Keeler on about half a dozen occasions at Dr Ward's flat when I called to see him and his friends. Miss Keeler and I were on friendly terms. There was no impropriety whatsoever in my acquaintance with Miss Keeler . . . I shall not hesitate to issue writs for libel and slander if scandalous allegations are made or repeated outside the House.

The lie perpetuated, John Profumo left the Chamber to the cheers of the Conservative faithful. The Prime Minister walked with him, his hand on the younger man's shoulder. That same afternoon, Profumo found time to go to the races, at Sandown Park, with the Queen Mother. He allowed himself to be photographed with her, a liberty which, in a way, was as outrageous as his lie in the Commons. The Minister's face in the pictures is that of a middle-aged schoolboy daring the world to call his bluff. That night he went to a dance at Quaglino's with his wife, Valerie Hobson.

'Look, I love my wife, and she loves me, and that's all that matters. Anyway, who's going to believe the word of this whore against the word of a man who has been in Government for ten years?' It was a few days after his parliamentary statement, and Profumo was tying up loose ends, taking lunch in the Savoy Grill with Chapman Pincher, the influential defence correspondent. 'But what about the letters?' Pincher responded, knowing that at least one was in the safe at the *Sunday Pictorial*. 'Letters? There are no letters,' Profumo shot back confidently. In fact, Christine Keeler had kept at least two other letters, but she says she handed them over to her friend Michael Lambton. Lambton, cousin of rightwing Conservative MP Lord Lambton, proved impossible to contact during research for this book.

Profumo was all bravado. His statement to the House had been a masterpiece of ambiguity – with the exception of the outright falsehood about the innocence of his relations with Keeler. Just as he now paraded around with his wife to demonstrate marital bliss, the speech had three times used the royal phrase 'My wife and I'. One could even infer from

it that Mrs Profumo had been on friendly terms with
Keeler. There were rumours to that effect. 'Certainly,'
Keeler herself was to say on her return from Spain, 'both he
and his wife were friends of mine. But it was a friendship no
one can criticise.'

Profumo's former Head of School, Attorney-General
Hobson, played a key role in drafting the statement. 'His
understanding of the complex art of the parliamentary
draughtsman,' Hobson's obituary was to say, 'was the
result of years of study . . .' His expertise paid off in the
short term, but it was flimsy armour on a battlefield now
crowded with enemies.

George Wigg left the Commons later that morning, he
remembered, 'with black rage in my heart, because I knew
what the facts were. I knew the truth and I knew that just as
over the Kuwait operation, I had been trussed up and done
again.' Wigg would not rest now until he had forced the
Government to face the truth. In the background were
other men, with more dubious motives, all dedicated to the
exposure of either Profumo, or Stephen Ward, or both.
There was Ward's deadly foe, John Lewis, solicitor
Michael Eddowes, intervening for his own complex
reasons, and the chiefs of MI5, scheming to mask their own
involvement without regard for those they had dragged into
the Honeytrap.

George Wigg was back on the offensive after the affront
of Profumo's statement. On BBC Television on *Panorama*,
he spoke of a continuing security issue. One of the viewers
was Stephen Ward. Stung by the implication that his actions had endangered national security, Ward saw Wigg the
next day. He provided a briefing that Wigg recorded on
paper. It was, Harold Wilson was to say later, 'a nauseating
document, taking the lid off a corner of the London underworld of vice . . . blackmail and counter-blackmail . . .
together with references to Mr Profumo and the Soviet
attaché . . .'

What precisely Wigg learned from Ward that day was
never revealed. Wigg's papers, now deposited at the London School of Economics, remain closed to researchers.

Harold Wilson reportedly gave his documents on the case
to the archives of *The Sunday Times*. That newspaper
searched for the papers at our request, but said they had
disappeared.

On 29 March, Eddowes, the solicitor in whom Keeler
had confided after the Edgecombe shooting, called Scotland Yard to say he had important information. Then, at his
Knightsbridge home, he gave a Special Branch officer an
aide-mémoire alleging that Ivanov – not Ward, as all other
accounts have it – had personally asked Keeler to pump
Profumo for information about the delivery of nuclear
warheads to Germany. 'This is a hot potato,' said the
Special Branch man, according to Eddowes. 'It will be on
the Prime Minister's desk in the morning.'

Five days later Eddowes called Special Branch to enquire
about progress. 'It is out of my hands now,' replied the
officer, whom Eddowes names as Dickinson. 'Why don't
you drop it?' A few days later, when Eddowes' assistant
met Dickinson by chance at King's Cross Station, the
officer repeated his feeling that Eddowes should drop the
matter. Special Branch, which takes its lead from MI5 on
security matters, was following the line taken by MI5 head
Sir Roger Hollis – deny, drop all contacts, run for cover.

On the day of Eddowes' meeting with Special Branch, 29
March, Hollis was called in by Home Secretary Henry
Brooke. MI5, of course, knew Profumo had lied to Parlia-

ment – as we have shown, its agents had known about the Keeler affair at the time. Hollis, however, did not share his knowledge with the Home Secretary. To do so would have revealed MI5's use of Ward in the Ivanov Honeytrap scheme. Instead, the head of MI5 threw Ward to the wolves. He told Brooke Ward had asked Keeler to get information from Profumo on nuclear warheads. Was there, the Home Secretary wanted to know, a case for prosecuting Ward under the Official Secrets Act? As well he might – since Ward had been the tool of MI5 – Hollis told Brooke the evidence was shaky. But he had planted a deadly seed. In the mind of authority was born the idea that the buck should be passed, not to the foolish Minister, Profumo, but to the foolish 'provider of popsies', Stephen Ward.

Brooke – Marlborough and Balliol – now turned the guns of the Establishment on Ward, the man from a minor public school and an obscure American college of osteopathy. Was there, he asked the police commissioner, Sir Joseph Simpson, a police interest in Ward? Simpson said there might well be some basis for prosecuting Ward in connection with his girls, but the evidence would be hard to get. It would indeed, for Ward was no criminal. Yet there now began an almost manic police investigation of the man. Suitably enough, it began on April Fool's Day.

The police pump had already been primed. Two days before the Brooke meeting on 25 March, the Criminal Investigation Department began receiving anonymous mail. It alleged that 'Ward was living on the immoral earnings of girls'. Significantly, the public was never allowed to see the letters. There is only one serious candidate for the poison-pen writer – John Lewis. It was he who, years earlier, had sent anonymous information to the Inland Revenue regarding Ward's tax affairs.

George Wigg later recalled that weeks earlier, when Ward's obsessive enemy came to see him, he 'advised him to talk to Commander Townsend at Scotland Yard . . .' Lewis did, and with a vengeance. A year later, when he faced drunk driving charges, Lewis called Townsend as a character witness. Townsend revealed that Lewis had been a great help to the police 'on a matter of very considerable public importance'. Roy East, the reporter for the *People* who spent months on the Profumo case, remembers Lewis introducing him to Commander Townsend. Arthur Townsend, in charge of the Serious Crimes Division, was to run an implacable police effort to get Ward's scalp – and his alone.

The very first police statements, taken from Christine Keeler, contained details of her relations with Profumo which – as Lord Denning admitted in his laborious prose – 'one would think . . . not likely to have been invented'. The police now knew, if they had not known already, that Profumo had lied in Parliament – but that was not the issue. Their job was to get Ward.

'I became aware that the police had started asking questions,' Ward wrote. 'It only came home to me most gradually that these questions were directed against me. Originally the police had told people they were trying to end the rumours. Of course, this had the opposite effect. The police, people reasoned, could not be investigating like this unless there was substance. Now the full horror of the situation came home to me, and I started to feel hunted.'

Trapped in a new nightmare, Ward flailed around for help. True to his old form in the days of Missile Crisis diplomacy, he tried to get to the top. On 7 May he telephoned the Prime Minister's office and spoke to the Principal Private Secretary, Timothy Bligh. They met that evening, with an MI5 man sitting in – there was no getting away from MI5.

'You see,' said Ward hopefully, 'the facts as presented in Parliament were not strictly speaking just like that . . . I made a considerable sacrifice for Mr Profumo . . . I feel I should tell you the truth of what really happened. You probably know as a matter of fact anyway . . . I don't know whether you have any feelings about this, whether there is anything you can do. I know myself here that there is a great deal of potentially extremely explosive material in what I've told you.'

On this evidence, Lord Denning was to call this an attempt 'to blackmail the Government' into calling off the police. Bligh – Winchester and Balliol – was of no help. The pursuit of Ward went on.

During May the Director of Public Prosecutions, Sir Theobald Mathew, Oratory and Sandhurst, received an interim report. As the Commissioner had predicted, it said there was not enough evidence to charge Ward. Someone, as yet unidentified, insisted that the investigators press on – evidence or no evidence. At six o'clock each evening, the senior American FBI man in London, Charles Bates – eventually to become an Assistant Director – went to the Red Lion pub opposite Scotland Yard to drink a pint with his counterparts in the British police force. A key contact, during the Profumo affair, was Joe Jackson, Assistant Commissioner for Crime. 'I was told,' says Bates, 'that someone was going to take a fall . . . That someone was Ward.'

On 19 May, more desperate by the day, Ward wrote to the Home Secretary, Henry Brooke:

The Marylebone police [he complained] are questioning my patients and friends in a line, however tactful, which is extreme-ly damaging to me both professionally and socially . . . The instruction to do this must have come from the Home Office. Over the past weeks I have done what I could to shield Mr Profumo from his indiscretion about which I complained to the Security Services at the time . . . Possibly my efforts . . . might make it appear that I had something to conceal myself. I have not . . . The allegations . . . are malicious and entirely false . . . That I was against this [Profumo] liaison is a matter of record in the War Office [MI5] . . . May I ask that the person who has lodged the false information against me should be prosecuted.*

On 20 May, Ward fired off two more letters, to his MP, Sir Wavell Wakefield, and to Harold Wilson. His hopes of a

*Presumably a reference to John Lewis.

positive response were to be raised, and then to fizzle out. Two MPs tabled parliamentary questions, then withdrew them.

Ward's anguished revelation that MI5 had been briefed on Profumo's affair with Keeler – from him – ran into a brick wall. 'There is no truth,' MI5 Director-General Hollis had long since reported to the Prime Minister's office, 'in the story that the Security Service was informed of . . . anything . . . in connection with Mr Profumo's alleged visits to Ward or to Miss Keeler.'

It was a lie, of course, as several former MI5 officers would shamefacedly confirm nearly two decades later.*

Labour leader Wilson did do something. He wrote to the Prime Minister, then secured an interview with him at the House of Commons. Profumo's lie, which should by now have been obvious to the office cleaners let alone the Prime Minister, was apparently not discussed. Wilson's concern, drummed into him by George Wigg, was national security. Macmillan said he would ask MI5 to 'look again'. On 29 May, Hollis told him about the effort to have Keeler get the 'bomb-heads' information out of Profumo. Though Macmillan still felt there had been no security lapse, he ordered the Lord Chancellor, Lord Dilhorne, to review the dossier.

Had Macmillan at last decided that a way must be found to clear the air, that the Government could no longer get away with turning a blind eye to Profumo's lie? The *People* newspaper, under its editor Sam Campbell, was now ready to step into the gap left by the *Pictorial*'s decision to drop the story. Campbell intended to expose Profumo as a liar in his paper on the Sunday following the Whit weekend. He said as much to the Police Commissioner, and the Commissioner warned the Government.

On Friday 31 May, Lord Dilhorne told Profumo he would interview him in a week's time. The Minister responded by going to Venice with his wife – on holiday. Before the weekend was over, a telegram from Dilhorne

*See Chapter 9.

destroyed any illusion that his lie would hold up: would he please return to London earlier than planned? Profumo talked through the night with his wife, then decided to go home at once. He came back quietly by train and boat, then owned up at last.

In the absence of the Prime Minister, who was relaxing in Scotland, Profumo told his Secretary, Timothy Bligh, that he had indeed slept with Christine Keeler. His resignation letter, written at once, read in part:

> Dear Prime Minister,
> . . . I said that there had been no impropriety in this association. To my very deep regret I have to admit that this was not true . . . I have come to realise that, by this deception, I have been guilty of a grave misdemeanour . . . I cannot remain a member of your administration, nor of the House of Commons. I cannot tell you of my deep remorse . . .
> Yours sincerely
> Jack Profumo

Harold Macmillan wrote back from Scotland:

> Dear Profumo,
> . . . This is a great tragedy for you, your family and your friends. Nevertheless, I am sure you will understand that in the circumstances, I have no alternative but to advise the Queen to accept your resignation.
> Yours very sincerely
> Harold Macmillan

The Leader of the House, Iain Macleod, was in the United States when the news came through. 'I was, and am,' he told the Washington press, 'a friend of Valerie and Jack Profumo. I think it is a personal tragedy that this should have happened.' Five years earlier, Macleod had used virtually the same words about the resignation of his friend, Foreign Office minister Ian Harvey, compromised by his homosexuality. In October 1969, as Conservative Shadow Chancellor, Macleod would be appointed a director of the Provident Life Association, controlled by the Profumo family.

In London, Christine Keeler was sitting at home with the
man who had become her 'manager', Robin Drury, when
Profumo's resignation was announced on television.
'Christine was furious,' Drury recalled. 'She had planned to
make an announcement herself, about the relationship.'

To the public, the resignation was a gentlemanly affair,
handled more in sorrow than in anger, almost as though he
had been bowled out by a googly at cricket. It was all very
public school. John and Valerie Profumo successfully went
into hiding for several days. The 'folk of the village', Lord
Denning noted with obvious approval, knew where they
were, but kept it a secret. Astonishingly quickly, as one
observer noted, 'Profumo was far from the stage, heading
back fast towards obscurity'. It would not be long before he
was forgiven altogether, praised for his good works, and
spoken of as 'Poor Jack Profumo'. The Establishment had
no such mercy for Stephen Ward.

Ward was at Bryanston Mews when the resignation news
came through, with the press at his door. He was now at his
wits' end, harried by reporters and abandoned by his rich
friends. When a former patient, film producer Bill Lang,
offered Ward sanctuary at his home in Watford, Ward
gratefully accepted.

He emerged blinking into the light and squeezed into his
Jaguar, only to find the street blocked by press cars.
Frantic, Ward drove straight into one of the other vehicles,
bulldozing himself an escape route. The man with the
unflappable charm was finally snapping. For a couple of
days, ensconced with the Langs in Hertfordshire, he had
time to think.

Ward had made friends with a few of the newspapermen,
those who dealt straight with him. By the end, they would
be virtually the only people still talking to him. One
journalist, *News of the World* Features Editor Pelham
Pound, was hoping to buy Ward's story for his paper. He
had also promised to help Ward get away somewhere for a
rest – perhaps in the United States.

On 7 June, on Ward's behalf, Pound went to Scotland

Yard to see Commander Townsend, the man running the Ward investigation. 'I asked him,' Pound remembers, 'if it would be all right for Ward to go on a holiday abroad. Ward wanted to know if it would be in order. He said that, apart from a few formalities, there would be no problem.'

It was a lie. The next day, when Pound arrived in Watford to tell Ward all was well, two policemen appeared – to arrest Ward. 'It was,' says Pound, 'another example of police deviousness and lying.' Ward went courteously. To avoid embarrassing his hosts, he walked a little distance away from the house, dressed in open-necked shirt, dark glasses, and carpet slippers. There they arrested him.

Five hours later, at Marylebone Police Station, Dr Stephen Ward was charged: 'That he, being a man, did on divers dates between January 1961, and 8 June 1963, knowingly live wholly or in part on the earnings of prostitution at 17 Wimpole Mews, London W., contrary to Section 30 of the Sexual Offences Act, 1956.' Other charges were to follow, a total of nine in all.

While Profumo, the man who had put the nation's security at risk, faded from the limelight, Ward was detained like a felon in Brixton Prison. He would not be granted bail for weeks to come.

'Ward,' the respected commentator Ludovic Kennedy was to observe, 'was a whipping boy for the humiliations the Government had suffered as a result of the Profumo affair.' While the public scourging proceeding, the private security panic continued. The exposure of Profumo's sexual peccadilloes, now placed the American presidency in jeopardy.

FIFTEEN

THE WHITE HOUSE TREMBLES

On the day Ward was arrested, 8 June, an FBI official in Washington opened a new file. Its first title, CHRISTINE KEELER. JOHN PROFUMO. INTERNAL SECURITY – RUSSIA, GREAT BRITAIN, was soon to be replaced with a codename, BOWTIE. Some code clerk, perhaps, imagined that bow ties, like bowler hats, are the hallmark of the English gentleman.

More than a thousand pages of the BOWTIE dossier, along with many others from the Air Force, Immigration Service, and CIA files have been obtained during the writing of this book under the Freedom of Information Act. Many of them are largely blacked out by the censor's pen, in the name of national security or personal privacy, but what survives gives us a glimpse of the true gravity of the Profumo Affair. One man's folly in the bed of a teenage girl opened up a can of American worms, a scare about Air Force security, and the discovery that the President himself was implicated.

The day before BOWTIE was opened, the *New York Post* ran a story on 'the notorious British prostitute, Christine Keeler'. 'Information had been forwarded,' said the report, 'on the possibility that American diplomats or politicians may have been compromised.' That worry was kept out of the written record as much as possible, but the Profumo Case received prolonged attention at the highest level. There was a series of meetings, attended by Defense Secretary Robert McNamara, CIA Director John McCone, Defense Intelligence Agency boss General

Joseph Carroll, and usually one of the senior aides to FBI Director J. Edgar Hoover. Two Assistant Directors handled the case at the FBI: William Sullivan of Counter-Intelligence, and John Malone of the New York Field Office. Progress reports, which remain almost entirely censored, went to Hoover, Attorney-General Robert Kennedy, and the office of the President.

'There is a possibility,' Hoover informed Robert Kennedy on 14 June, 'that some Air Force enlisted personnel may have had relations with Christine Keeler.' Hoover had learned from Air Force investigators that one airman admitted spending several nights with Keeler, for money. In England, frantic enquiries, particularly at USAF Ruislip, soon established that several airmen had 'closely associated' with Keeler. All were black, and had met Keeler at London nightspots.

According to Albert Hammond, who in 1963 served as an airman at Mildenhall airbase, the investigation was 'heavy . . . thirty or forty guys were flown back to the States under tight security'. The Air Force never did admit the true size of the security flap – public statements only mentioned the investigation of three airmen. They were, we now know from the files, Technical Sergeant George 'Hoppy' Hopkins, aged twenty-nine, Airman Charles Wright, twenty, and a colleague identified only as Hamilton. There are also references to a fourth man, but his name is always blanked out by the censor, for reasons that will become apparent.

Airman Hopkins told investigators he had frequented the All-Nighters Club, where Edgecombe and Lucky Gordon had their fight over Christine Keeler, and the Roaring Twenties Club. 'Many girls go there,' he said, 'and are picked up by the GIs. These girls are usually well-dressed and attractive and have wealthy boyfriends – sugar-daddies – who provide their flats and clothes. Usually these girls come in late at night after going out with their sugar-daddies . . .'

Johnny Edgecombe well remembers visits to the All-Nighters Club. 'Ward used to accompany me and Keeler there,' he says. 'The attraction was drugs. Many of Ward's upper-class friends wanted to try drugs, and the only way to get them was to go down to the shady side of life.'

'Sometime in 1961,' Sergeant Hopkins told his inquisitors, 'I was introduced at the All-Nighters to a girl by the name of Ronna . . . Ronna knew this year that my birthday was coming and arranged a party for me on 6 February 1963, to be held at her flat . . . At the party Ronna introduced me to a girl called Christine, whom I later saw in the newspaper as Christine Keeler . . . Christine came to the party with a girl known to me as Paula.'

'Ronna' was Ronna Riccardo, a prostitute who had known Ward since about 1960. She was later to figure prominently at his trial. 'Paula' was Paula Hamilton-Marshall, the convicted prostitute then spending much time with Keeler.

Riccardo, interviewed today, well remembers the nights of the All-Nighters. 'We'd start in the Club, on Fridays,' she says, 'take some pills, crash out during the day, go to another club on Saturday night, take some more pills, then go to a Sunday afternoon dancing session . . . Stephen didn't like to dance, but he liked to mix.'

According to the records, both Riccardo and one of her friends had babies by American servicemen – though Riccardo today denies bearing an airman's baby. Keeler had had her American baby as long ago as 1959.[*]

The other airmen questioned told similar stories, including references to some of the key characters, like Lucky Gordon and Paul Mann. Investigators were satisfied that no classified information had been discussed with Keeler or her friends. Within twenty-four hours of the interrogations, a senior Defense Department spokesman told a news conference there had been no security leak. What was never revealed is that investigations continued for months, tracing people who might have known Keeler, the other girls, or Stephen Ward himself. Enquiries connected with Ward reached right back to World War II, and included a

*See Chapter 4.

reference to a 'Miss Kolb', of the OSS, the wartime fore-runner of the CIA.

The Defense Department spokesman did not mention a fourth man questioned. One of the men of interest to the FBI, it appears from the records, was an Air Force man, rank unknown, called Hawkins. At Ward's trial, in a reference that meant nothing at the time, Riccardo said: 'I never met a man in Stephen Ward's flat except my friend "Silky" Hawkins . . . the only man I have ever had inter-course with in Ward's flat.' Clearly, one airman at least visited Stephen Ward's home during the year Keeler first met War Minister Profumo. Why he was there, and why this whole area was so sensitive to the US Air Force, remains unknown. On the day the other three airmen were returned to duty after questioning, Hawkins received an honourable discharge from the service.

The US security enquiry caused a rash of newspaper stories in June 1963, notably in the New York *Journal-American*, a Hearst paper, which gave the Profumo case blanket coverage. Some of its stories, indeed, appear to have been inspired by deliberate leaks from someone in authority, and its editor, Guy Richards, was a rightwinger with excellent intelligence contacts. In mid-June 1963, in the wake of the Air Force enquiry, he invited one of the stranger figures in the Profumo case to come to America – Michael Eddowes.

Eddowes had been angry and suspicious when Special Branch failed to follow up the dramatic information he had passed on, that – according to Keeler – she had been asked to get secret nuclear information out of Profumo. On 13 June, Eddowes wrote a letter to the Prime Minister. 'The apparent disregard of my report and suggestions,' he said, 'has been a matter of deep concern to me from the security angle, and in case the whole contents of my report did not reach you, as Head of the security forces, I feel it is now my duty to draw your attention to it.'

No sooner had he raised the security bogey than Eddowes inexplicably clammed up. He pulled out of a planned television appearance, on *World in Action*, and flew to the United States courtesy of the *Journal-American*. With a 'no comment' to the horde of other reporters at the airport, Eddowes was hustled off to a New York hotel. An article in the *Journal-American*, the first in a planned series of six, claimed that 'Anglo-American security and the Anglo-American alliance had been jeopardised by the affair.'

Within two days, FBI Assistant Director John Malone, head of the Bureau in New York, came personally to see Eddowes. He was then driven to the FBI office, and questioned at length. What Eddowes told the Americans went to the office of the President, to the Attorney-General, the Secretary of State, and the Director of the CIA. The content of the interview is entirely censored in the document, and Malone cannot be interviewed – he died recently.

Eddowes himself will not say exactly what he told the FBI, nor what he learned from American officials. He does say, however, that the FBI was keenly interested in 'the Ward–Keeler relationship with Thomas Corbally'.

Corbally, the man who had given information on the case to the American Embassy in London, was by now back in the United States. Like Eddowes, he spoke briefly to the press, then went silent. Scotland Yard, it was reported, were keen to interview him. To clear the air, Corbally hired the prominent New York attorney, Roy Cohn, a friend of J. Edgar Hoover since the red-hunting days of the McCarthy era. The information Cohn gave the FBI is entirely censored in the BOWTIE dossier, as is a seventeen-page interview apparently conducted with Corbally himself.

The FBI's man in London, Legal Attaché Charles Bates, was an Anglophile. Affectionately known to his friends as the 'Legal Beagle under the Eagle', he liked his posting so much that Hoover had difficulty persuading him to leave. He eventually stayed in Britain for eight years. Now a security consultant in California, after leaving the FBI as an Assistant Director, Bates remembers the Profumo Affair well. In June 1963, he found himself bombarded with requests from Washington for more information. Bates had a direct line to Scotland Yard, and a scrambler telephone to MI5. He had been cultivating his British contacts for five years, and his close friend, Assistant Police Commissioner Joe Jackson, was usually an invaluable source of sensitive information. Now, though, Bates found his contacts strangely reticent.

'I knew Washington was worried,' says Bates. 'There had been some references to high-level or prominent Americans involved and of course my HQ sent cables saying "Is this true? What can you find out?" I didn't know the extent of it – they weren't transmitting to me all they were picking up in the States, they often didn't. But I began to feel that I was kind of all alone on a desert island someplace. I couldn't raise a thing out of MI5. Some of the time I couldn't get much out of Scotland Yard. But my friends at MI5, they'd just pulled the blankets over their heads.'

The CIA Station Chief in London was Archibald Roosevelt, a relative of the late President. He obviously had a direct line to British Intelligence, but for once it was virtually useless. 'I took it up with Roger Hollis at MI5,' Roosevelt remembers, 'and made myself a nuisance. But they never came up with anything.' Something about the messages from Washington puzzled Roosevelt. 'As far as I was concerned,' he says, 'it was a strictly British scandal. But Washington persisted. They asked me all the time – "Are you sure there isn't any American involvement?" But they never spelled it out to me, so that I could understand what they were on about.'

One of those pushing in Washington was Walter Elder, Executive Assistant to CIA Director John McCone, who was attending key meetings on the subject. Elder remembers the case as 'painfully hilarious'. 'There was great excitement,' he says, 'and we kept pushing to find out what the American involvement was . . .' Elder knew the scare about the American airmen had come to nothing.

Elder also knew that the Ambassador to London, David Bruce, had sat for a portrait by Stephen Ward, but that seemed harmless enough. He also heard that 'some Americans may have met the ladies in question', but that was all he was told. Elder had no information on a security leak, so he kept his peace.

The man at the FBI's listening post, Charles Bates, was shown the police interviews in which Christine Keeler and Mandy Rice-Davies claimed they had slept with Fairbanks, and he noted the wife's brave response. 'What do you think about this story?' someone asked Mary Lee Fairbanks at a reception. 'My husband,' she replied, 'doesn't have to pay for anything. He can get any woman he wants for free . . .' During June, Fairbanks also discussed the case with the US Naval Attaché. An FBI document, released to us in 1988, quotes Fairbanks as saying he 'met Christine Keeler on two occasions, and as he "touched wood", said he was not one of her customers. In passing, Fairbanks stated that half of the House of Lords could be named between the Ward –Keeler combination.'

The FBI man in London, Charles Bates, heard much more on the American angle, as the days went by, from his Scotland Yard contacts. It was mostly hard information, he remembers, some of it referring to 'high-level Americans involved'. None of it, though, turned up in the Denning Report. For that matter, nor did parts of the British side of the story.

On 20 June, back in the United States, a crack appeared in the wall of silence. The New York *Journal-American*, which had been interviewing British solicitor Michael Eddowes, disinterred the story of Harry Towers and Mariella Novotny. It was now two years since Novotny had spent her hectic few months in New York City, months in which – she claimed at the time – she had been bedded by the man who was now President, John F. Kennedy.*

At first, the public furore in the United States gave no hint of the underlying scandal. The *Journal-American* simply raked over the facts about Novotny's arrest for prostitution, and the flight abroad of her and her alleged pimp, British television producer Towers. The paper drew

*See Chapter 5.

attention to Novotny's Czech connection – her father, as we have seen was Czech – and the fact that Towers had vanished behind the Iron Curtain. Towers was by now sunning himself in South Africa, producing the film *Sanders of the River*.

The press coverage, based on leaks from law enforcement sources, went further. In the same breath as its references to Keeler and Ivanov, it referred to the 'espionage' activities of an unnamed Hungarian woman, reporting to a Soviet contact. The Hungarian, identified in FBI files as ———— ————,* had been identified by Mariella Novotny as one of the prostitutes she had 'done dates with'.

The Novotny case, it was now reported, was linked to a vice-ring that had been active two years earlier, with United Nations diplomats as customers. On 24 June, Congressman Harold Gross called for an enquiry into the UN angle. Gross was a rightwing member of Congress, often used as a mouthpiece by FBI Director, Hoover. Then U Thant, the Secretary-General of the UN, called for further investigation. A woman called Evelyn Davis was arrested on vice charges, and then three girls linked to the UN case – one English, one American, and one Hungarian – were reported to have arrived in Prague. The bottom line, in a complex story, was the theory that Soviet puppets, notably the Czechs, had been using the sexual compromise ploy in New York – the Honeytrap technique.

As we have seen, American officials suffer remarkable memory lapses on this subject, even allowing for age. Ambassador Bruce's Assistant, Alfred Wells, who dined with Ward more than once, says his mind is a blank. Dean Rusk's trouble-shooter, William Burdett, has a similar problem. In California, we talked to John McCone, the man President Kennedy chose as CIA Director when Alan Dulles failed him. McCone, now in his eighties, listened silently to what we had to say. Then, watching through hooded eyes, he said he was sorry. He had 'no recollection'.

*Name deleted for legal reasons.

The CIA Director's Assistant, Walter Elder, was mystified. 'Washington,' he says, 'was terribly interested, but I didn't quite know why. Because I didn't have the background.'

The only people who really had 'the background' were the President of the United States himself, perhaps his brother Robert and some trusted male friends – and at least one of the young women close to Stephen Ward. Humans hide to have sex, a fact that has saved many a potentate. It is clear, though, that the explosion of the British scandal shook the White House.

In December 1962, as the Profumo case was about to break, Kennedy had met the British Prime Minister in the Bahamas. The President was no longer intimidated by the older man, whom he addressed jovially as 'Mr Prime'. In the heat of a Nassau evening, as he chatted over the whisky with Macmillan and his Deputy, R. A. Butler, reporters were eavesdropping. 'You know, it's funny,' Kennedy confided, eyeing a young woman nearby, 'but if I go too long without a woman, I get a headache . . .'

Years later Macmillan criticised Kennedy for 'spending half his time thinking about adultery, the other half about second-class ideas passed on by his advisers'. Adultery was a sore point with Macmillan, whose own wife betrayed him for years with one of his own friends.

Kennedy was an Anglophile, with what one female friend called the 'aristocratic English attitude' towards women. A favourite book was Lord David Cecil's *Young Melbourne*, a heady celebration of sexual adventure and politics. In spring 1963, as the Profumo case began to break, the President showed an almost obsessive interest. The first anecdote comes from a surprising source, Mandy Rice-Davies.

In the wake of the scandal, Rice-Davies met the future Israeli Prime Minister, Shimon Peres, who in 1963 had been Deputy Defence Minister. Peres told her how, in March 1963, he had visited President Kennedy at the White House, on the same day as British Opposition leader

Harold Wilson. 'Everyone was allotted a certain time with the President,' goes the story as told by Rice-Davies. 'Shimon was waiting in the antechamber, and Wilson was supposed to be in there for just a little while. But he stayed in there about two hours, and Shimon couldn't believe it. "What the hell have you and Kennedy been talking about?" he asked Wilson when he came out at last. And Wilson said, "I couldn't believe it. The man just talked and talked about the Profumo business. He really grilled me on what I knew . . ."'

During those crisis weeks, in London, Lord Astor came hurrying to see Stephen Ward – at that point still a free man. 'Astor was just back from Washington,' Warwick Charlton recalls. 'He had been to see President Kennedy for lunch at the White House. Partly JFK was joking, asking Astor about the girls, and saying he was disappointed Astor denied having had them himself. He also wanted to know everything that was coming out . . .'

Kennedy discussed the Profumo case with David Bruce, his London ambassador, and ordered all London Embassy cable traffic on the subject sent to him personally. The messages from Ambassador Bruce, recently released at our request, are long and colourful descriptions of developments and political implications for the Macmillan Government.

'He felt terribly sorry for Profumo,' remembered Kennedy's friend Charles Spalding, 'and he sympathised with the way Profumo was caught. Jack also thought the girls involved were kind of cute.' The President's wife, Jacqueline, was heavily pregnant at this time, but his advisers had more reason than that to distance him from stories of girls in England. They were struggling to protect the first Catholic president, projected to the public as a family man incarnate, from his own indiscretions. A year earlier, at an embarrassing luncheon in the White House, FBI Director Hoover had confronted Kennedy with evidence of his affair with starlet Judith Campbell, a woman then also seeing a top Mafia leader. A few months later, when Marilyn Monroe died, he and his brother Robert had only barely prevented the exposure of their affairs with the actress. The Kennedys' womanising had their advisers worried.

In June 1963, as the Profumo Affair unravelled, the President prepared for an important European tour. 'With the case of the British War Minister and the call girls building up', said the *Washington News*, 'we can think of no better time for an American President to stay as far as possible away from England.' 'Strong pressure was exerted', it was later reported, 'to postpone a visit to London, for fear President Kennedy might become in some way involved.'

The State Department, however, was keen that Kennedy should visit London, to show that the 'special relationship' with Britain was as strong as ever, in spite of the crisis. When the President left Washington on 21 June, London was on his itinerary. He went first to Germany, there to make the famous speech on visiting the Berlin Wall. 'Two thousand years ago,' said Kennedy, 'the proudest boast was *Civis Romanus sum*. Today in the world of freedom, the proudest boast is, *Ich bin ein Berliner*. There are some who say that communism is the wave of the future. Let them come to Berlin.'

As Kennedy captured the hearts of Berliners, a twenty-two-year-old called Mariella Novotny began making dangerous noises. 'Now,' she said, answering a London reporter's questions about the Americans and the Profumo case, 'they are just trying to put up a smokescreen . . . in case they blundered over two years ago . . . I suppose the Americans will want to interview me.' In New York, someone noticed. The New York *Journal-American* fired off a telegram, pressing Novotny for an interview. Before she could respond, another troubling story came out of London.

On 28 June, as Kennedy visited Ireland, home of his forebears, the *Washington Post* ran a story from Dorothy Kilgallen, the powerful columnist. 'The Novotny story,' Kilgallen wrote from London, 'may challenge Christine Keeler's saga before the international call girl scandals become history.' Kilgallen suspected, according to her biographer, 'that the British counterpart of the CIA knew a whole lot more than it was telling about the international ramifications of the case . . .'

Next day, as the American President arrived in England, the *Washington Post* dropped a heavy hint of skeletons yet to be uncovered. 'Britishers who read American criticisms of Profumo,' wrote Drew Pearson, 'throw back the questions "What high American official was involved with Marilyn Monroe?" '

Kennedy arrived at Macmillan's country residence, Birch Grove, by helicopter. 'I can see him now,' the old Prime Minister remembered, 'stepping out from the machine, a splendid, young, gay figure . . . the excitement was intense . . . The roads were packed outside the front gates. The crowd included a hundred CND marchers, with banners demanding that we should abolish nuclear tests. Since it was the main purpose of our meeting to achieve this, the demonstration seemed hardly necessary.'

The President found the British Prime Minister worn out by the Profumo Affair, 'tired and lacking in ideas. Macmillan could not convey any sense of excitement and optimism for the future, because he did not feel any . . .' Kennedy was hiding his own exhaustion – the chronic back problem was giving him hell. That Saturday evening, as he dined with Macmillan, he learned that the Profumo case was about to touch his presidency.

At home in the United States that day, the noon edition of the New York *Journal-American* carried this teaser: 'One of the biggest names in American politics – a man who holds "a very high" elective office – has been injected into Britain's vice-security scandal . . .' The headline read: 'HIGH US AIDE IMPLICATED IN V-GIRL SCANDAL.' In 1963, anyone in the political know understood that the story referred to the President.

The story stayed in the paper for only one edition. In Washington, the President's brother Robert, the Attorney-General, took urgent action. Without explanation, the

Journal-American dropped the item from its next editions. FBI Assistant Director, Courtney Evans, who acted as liaison between Hoover and Robert Kennedy, told the FBI's weekend supervisor that the Kennedys wanted to know what was going on. A phone-call disturbed the President at Macmillan's home in England. Through his brother, he expressed his 'concern'.

In London, FBI man Charles Bates was told to give the President a personal briefing. Next day, Sunday, he drove down to Sussex, to find the President in characteristic pose, feet on the desk and tie askew. 'Charles,' said Kennedy, 'if anything develops on this case, anything at all, we'd like to be advised. Get it to us in Rome.'

The President was on his way to Italy, and the FBI man watched as the helicopter bore him away to London Airport. So did Macmillan. 'Hatless, with his brisk step, combining that indescribable look of a boy on holiday with the dignity of a President and Commander-in-Chief, he walked across the garden to the machine. We stood and waved . . .'

At home in Washington, Robert Kennedy took swift action over the *Journal-American* story. On Monday 31 July, within forty-eight hours, its authors faced the Attorney-General. As we learned from a former *Journal-American* staffer, the two reporters were hauled from their homes in New York and flown to Washington in the Kennedys' private plane, the *Caroline*. The two journalists were James Horan, the paper's Managing Editor, winner of the Pulitzer Prize and numerous other awards, and a younger reporter called Dom Frasca. In the words of a senior colleague, 'Horan was the best investigative reporter they ever had. If he wrote it, it was true.'

Both Horan and Frasca are dead, but their ordeal at the hands of Robert Kennedy survives thanks to Courtney Evans, the FBI liaison man with the Attorney-General.

According to Evans' memorandum, the President's brother asked the newsmen to name the 'high US aide' who, according to the article, was being linked to the Profumo scandal. Horan replied that the reference was to the President, and that – according to the newspaper's information – he had 'been involved with' a woman – not Novotny – shortly before he was elected President.

The meeting between Kennedy and the reporters was less than cordial. 'It is noted,' Evans wrote afterwards, 'that the Attorney-General treated the newspaper representatives at arm's length . . . in fact, there was almost an air of hostility . . .'

Nothing was resolved. The reporters refused to reveal sources other than those already mentioned in print. Kennedy offered no information to the reporters, and the meeting ended in frosty deadlock.

Afterwards, the Attorney-General did something rather odd. He 'admonished' Hoover's liaison man, Courtney Evans, 'not to write a memorandum' on what had occurred. Evans promptly reported the matter to J. Edgar Hoover orally. When Kennedy learned that, the following day, he said he hoped Evans 'had not misunderstood' his earlier instruction not to write a report.

According to Mark Monsky, now a vice-president of NBC News, the Kennedy response was vicious. Monsky was a godson of Randolph Hearst, owner of the *Journal-American*, and says he observed the way the Attorney-General resolved the matter. At a meeting in Manhattan, Kennedy threatened the paper with a Government antitrust suit if it did not cease to pursue the story. The story was dropped.

On 2 July, Robert Kennedy asked J. Edgar Hoover to find out what Christine Keeler and Mandy Rice-Davies had been up to during their visit to the States a year earlier. Nothing untoward was discovered. The next day, as John Kennedy met the Pope in the Vatican, his brother learned of yet more trouble. Now there were allegations linking 'highly placed Government officials' with a woman of East German origin called Ellen Rometsch.

'Robert Kennedy definitely knew,' Vice-President Johnson's assistant Bobby Baker wrote in his memoirs, 'that Ellen Rometsch had been one of the women Jack Kennedy had asked me to introduce him to. I accommodated his request.' Following an FBI enquiry, Rometsch was packed off back to Germany.

President Kennedy's endless womanising was catching up with him all in a rush. In England, weeks earlier, Christine Keeler had spent four evenings putting her experiences on tape for Robin Drury, the man now acting as her business manager. The tape was eventually handed to the police, under a court order, but the contents were never made public. 'You know,' Drury later said, 'there were a lot of big American political names involved in this thing. It never came out because it was hushed up by the British Government for political reasons.' What Drury learned was passed on to Washington by the FBI – as an 'allegation against President Kennedy'. A related document remains entirely blanked out by the censor.

The 'big flap' – as FBI man Charles Bates remembers it – was not about Christine Keeler herself. The only John Kennedy she knew was the manager of the pop singer, Tommy Steele. Nor was it just about Mariella Novotny, and her claim to have slept with Kennedy. 'One of Novotny's closest girl chums,' columnist Kilgallen had written during Kennedy's European visit, 'was involved with a very big man on the other side of the Atlantic.'

On the evening of 29 June, as Kennedy dined with Macmillan, Bates had sent coded telegraph 861 to FBI headquarters. It was rated VERY URGENT, and concerned the President. Of twenty lines, seventeen have been cut out by the censor. What remains reads: '. . . [NAME CENSORED] TALKED ABOUT PRESIDENT KENNEDY AND REPEATED A RUMOUR THAT WAS GOING AROUND NEW YORK . . .' Again, no names but a second document provides more background. A report addressed to the FBI's Assistant Director in charge of Counter-Intelligence, William Sullivan, offers – between the censored chunks – information that 'ONE OF [NAME BLANKED OUT] CLIENTS WAS JOHN KENNEDY, THEN PRESIDENTIAL CANDIDATE. [NAME] STATED THAT MARIE NOVOTNY, BRITISH PROSTITUTE, WENT TO NEW YORK TO TAKE [NAME]'S PLACE,

SINCE SHE WAS GOING ON PRE-ELECTION ROUNDS WITH KEN-
NEDY.'

Today Charles Bates throws some light on the censored cable traffic. His information, he says, came from Assistant Commissioner for Crime Joe Jackson, at Scotland Yard. 'They had questioned a woman,' says Bates, 'apparently Mariella Novotny. She had taken the place of another woman, who had looked after Kennedy during the campaign.' Bates cannot remember the name of the other woman. Who was she?

Dorothy Kilgallen had written of a 'girl who could "tell all" . . . reported to have committed suicide not long ago.' Stephen Ward's girls had a tendency to suicide. Yvonne Brooks, who knew Lord Astor and was kept by an American businessman in London, attempted to kill herself just as the Profumo Affair was breaking. Another Ward protégée, Pat Marlowe, a regular visitor to the United States and friend of another presidential mistress, Marilyn Monroe, had succeeded in killing herself in August 1962 – within days of Monroe.

Research suggests, however, that the mystery woman was neither Brooks nor Marlowe, and that she survived the events of 1963. Before it was silenced, the New York *Journal-American* said she was 'a beautiful Chinese-American girl now in London'. The highest authorities, said the paper, 'identified her as Suzy Chang . . . who later went to London and operated as a call girl from the fashionable layout of Dr Stephen Ward . . .'

Who was Suzy Chang?

SIXTEEN

THE WORLD OF SUZY CHANG

For a long time during the work on this book, Suzy Chang remained a mere name on an old newspaper clipping, a frustrating enigma. Then, gradually, we began to put a face on the woman alleged to have been mistress to John Kennedy. We obtained immigration records covering Chang's comings and goings in the United States. Using them, we started to reconstruct a life.

Chang, who has used a string of different names, was born at Tientsin, China, in 1935. Her parents, both doctors, came to Hong Kong in the wake of the Communist take-over. They settled in Delaware, in the United States, during the fifties. Suzy, for reasons unknown, did not follow immediately. At the age of nineteen she was in England, starting adult life as a nurse in Birmingham. Then she headed for the bright lights of London.

By 1960, when she reportedly spent time with President Kennedy, Chang was a strikingly lovely model and aspiring actress. She got a part in the film *Nudes of the World*, and publicity shots show her in the pose one would expect: slinky Oriental-style dress cut to the thigh, fitting tightly on a figure to make any man take a deep breath. The film's producer, Arnold Miller, says Chang knew who was who in the world of London nightclubs. She was, he remembers, 'always elegantly and expensively dressed. And she obviously wasn't doing the film for the money.'

For three months in 1961, Chang was acting in the film *Road to Hongkong*, made at Shepperton Studios. The lead parts were played by Bob Hope, Bing Crosby, and Joan Collins – and the glittering list of guest stars included Frank Sinatra and Dean Martin. For us, here was a first hint of a link between Chang and the people in the Profumo case. Bob Hope and his manager, Louie 'Doc' Shurr, were shortly to become friendly with Mandy Rice-Davies.

In California we traced Glen Costin, who knew Chang in London in the early sixties and was later married to her for a while. He remembers a woman who 'moved in very wealthy circles'. Indeed she did, but in 1963, at the height of the Profumo Affair, Chang was involved in some strange adventures. In May that year she was in court giving evidence against Alfred Davis, an Olympic Airways official accused of stealing her handbag, contained cash and a ring worth £900. This unrelated case produced a tenuous connection to Stephen Ward. Alfred Davis was described to us by his friends, Tony and Barbara Pistalo (both of whom were patients of Ward's), as 'a big gambler who always had money, and hung about in Chelsea. He was more or less living in Nell Gwynne House at the time . . .'

Suzy Chang, moreover, was staying at Nell Gwynne House herself. More than one call girl lived at that address, but there is no evidence that Chang was ever a prostitute. Those who knew her say she was in a much higher league.

Ronna Riccardo, the London prostitute who was close to Stephen Ward, knew Suzy Chang. 'I remember Suzy,' she says, 'from when I was living in Nell Gwynne House. She had long hair down her back. We all stayed there at one time or another, me and Paula and Suzy. Stephen knew Suzy. We were a tight little clique.'

Chang's tangle with Alfred Davis – he was said to have taken the handbag during a car ride from Nell Gwynne House – led to another odd coincidence. Davis' defence counsel was James Burge, the barrister shortly to defend Stephen Ward. Burge persuaded Chang, in court, to reveal whose flat she had been in that day at Nell Gwynne House. She said it belonged to a 'Mr Slazenger'. 'I had been staying there a few days,' said Chang.

'Slazenger' was in fact John Schlesinger,* a multi-millionaire American-born film producer and business-man. In South Africa, where Schlesinger lived later, we found a film distributor who remembered him as 'the best-known womaniser in the history of South Africa'. In 1958, when he was thirty-five, Schlesinger was involved in a particularly messy divorce.

Another curious aspect of the handbag theft case was Suzy Chang's use of another name. 'Film actress Jackie Chang,' a newspaper reported after the case, 'is deter-mined not to change her name. "Why should I? It's my name, and the one I've always had . . ."' It wasn't, of course – Chang told the court she had been calling herself 'Jackie' only for the past few years. Another lady of Oriental extraction, however, took great exception to Chang using the name – and with reason.

Jacqui Chan, star of the film *World of Suzie Wong*, began a libel action against a newspaper that had mistakenly printed 'Chang' as 'Chan' in connection with the Davis handbag theft case. Why did she bother? The silly little episode throws a little more light on Suzy Chang.

Jacqui Chan, as is well known, had been the girlfriend of Antony Armstrong-Jones, now Lord Snowdon, in the late fifties, before he married Princess Margaret. Snowdon, then a young photographer, appears to have been fascin-ated by Chinese girls – he produced two portfolios of photographs on the theme. He also knew Suzy Chang. And Chang seems to have begun using the name 'Jackie' at about the time Snowdon broke up with Jacqui.

We wrote to both Snowdon and Jacqui Chan asking about Chang, but they did not reply.

Lord Snowdon knew Stephen Ward from the early fifties. After he left Cambridge, he began his photographic career as assistant to Ward's good friend, court photo-grapher Baron.

*This is not the celebrated John Schlesinger who made *Far From The Madding Crowd*, *Yanks* etc.

Ward did not much like Armstrong-Jones. Not long before the Profumo case broke, when he did portraits of numerous members of the Royal Family, he sketched Princess Margaret – 'probably the most difficult face to draw' he had ever attempted, Ward said later. Armstrong-Jones told him he had 'got the nose too long'. The Princess's husband was Ward's next sitter, but somehow he never finished the sketch.

Suzy Chang – friend of Armstrong-Jones and alleged mistress of John Kennedy – herself knew Stephen Ward. Thomas Corbally's friend, who knew Ward and his circle, remembers Chang as 'one of Stephen's girls', and heard rumours about her and Kennedy at the time. Chang's former husband, Glen Costin, remembers her telling him, at the height of the Profumo Affair, that she was acquainted with the people in the case. 'I know them, I know them,' she told Costin. She also said, specifically, that she knew Ward. She did not, however, tell him anything about the Kennedys. Was Chang really involved with John Kennedy?

Those heavily censored FBI and Immigration Service documents reveal that Chang did travel to New York in 1960 – the year she is alleged to have gone with John Kennedy. She was also there in 1961, and over the Christmas period at the end of 1962. Earlier in 1962, she applied to get on to the Chinese visa quota for the United States. Chang's mother – already living in America – filed a petition to the Immigration Service on her daughter's behalf. The record shows that she did so through the prestigious New York law firm of Donovan, Leisure, Newton and Irvine. William Donovan, the founder of the firm, was the founder of the OSS, the precursor of the CIA, and the firm always had strong connections with the government in power.

This was a law firm at the very top of the tree, a surprisingly powerful helping hand for a minor actress called Suzy Chang. 'Someone,' says a former FBI official, 'was protecting her ass. They wanted someone with real clout to carry the ball, to run interference for her . . .' Suzy

Chang got on to the visa quota, within a fortnight.

A report in the Immigration Service file, dated 19 July 1963 – immediately after the Washington flap over the *Journal-American* – reflects an extensive investigation of Chang. The report lists nine people, most of them British models, who had been linked to Chang. All the names are blanked out. Another document shows that the authorities had gone through the file on the Mariella Novotny prostitution case, looking for a connection to Chang. They did not find one.

The most revealing document is dated well after the Profumo case, in 1965. It notes that Chang 'arrived in US at New York, via Flight 701, on 22/12/63. She was the [blanked out section in report] . . . she was questioned regarding the "Profumo Affair", and alleged to be a close friend of Stephen Ward.'

As this book went to press, we finally traced Suzy Chang, who has now taken a new name and lives on the eastern seaboard of the United States. She confirmed that she indeed knew Stephen Ward, Antony Armstrong-Jones, and John F. Kennedy.

'Stephen was a good, good, good friend . . . I knew him a long time,' said Chang. 'He used to come to my house to eat . . . I loved Stephen . . . I knew all the people Stephen knew . . . I really cared about him.'

We asked Chang about the reports linking her to John F. Kennedy. She paused, then said, 'Well, John – John was the President of the United States . . . Well, I used to come and visit my mother. And well, anyway, we'd meet in the 21 Club. You know, everybody saw me eating with him. It wasn't behind anybody's back. I know Stash Radziwill, but I don't know Lee very well, you know what I mean? . . .'

'Stash' was Prince Stanislas Radziwill, married to Lee, sister of the President's wife, Jacqueline. The President did visit the 21 Club, between his election and his inauguration. Asked whether she had an affair with him, Suzy Chang denied it. She said, 'I think the President was a nice guy, very charming.' Then she laughed. 'What else am I going to say?' she said.

Two British journalists, Alastair and Sheila Revie, covered the Profumo case in depth in 1963. Unlike others, who concentrated on Keeler and Rice-Davies, they went to great pains to interview as many women as they could trace who had been close to Ward.

'The Ward girls,' say the Revies, 'were all talking about Kennedy. And Chang was one of the girls discussed. A coloured girl, a Eurasian, who lived at Nell Gwynne House, was believed to have gone with the President.'

Charles Bates, the FBI man in London during the Affair, remembers being shown Scotland Yard reports on the way Kennedy's name came up in the Profumo case. 'I saw something about a couple of girls who went over to the US in 1960, during the JFK campaign. They went to New York, they were in a hotel there. One or both later rode the campaign train to furnish her wares to those who wanted it. Also, one of them was given an assignment to meet a man in a certain hotel room. Then the other girl was sent over to take her place. That's vivid in my mind – the business about the hotel in New York, and the report referring to the man by the initials JFK . . .'

On 22 July, nearly a month after the flap had started, the President's brother had a meeting with FBI Assistant Director Courtney Evans, who had sat in on the encounter with the *Journal-American* reporters who had written the Chang story. Now Evans reported to Hoover:

The Attorney-General was contacted last evening and orally advised of the information developed by [name blanked out] that [name blanked out] had lived with [name blanked out], a New York City callgirl, and that one of her clients was alleged to be the then presidential candidate John F. Kennedy. He was further informed that Mariella Novotny had allegedly gone to New York to take [name blanked out]'s place, as she was travelling on pre-election rounds with the presidential candidate. As a matter of fact, Novotny did not enter the United States until 14 December 1960, nearly six weeks after the

election. The Attorney-General was appreciative of our bringing this matter to his attention personally. He said it did seem
preposterous that such a story would be circulated when a
presidential candidate during the campaign travels with scores
of newspapermen. He added that with the next presidential
election now less than eighteen months away, he anticipated
there would be more similar stories and he would like us to
continue to advise him of any such matters coming to our
attention on a personal basis, as he could better defend the
family if he knew what was being said.

Donald Stewart, an Espionage Supervisor in Washington at the time, remembers Robert Kennedy's intervention
during the Profumo Affair. 'Everything we got,' says
Stewart, 'had to go through him. One night I got a call
from Courtney Evans [FBI Assistant Director] and he
said "Bobby wants everything," and everything went to
Bobby from then on . . .'
Who inspired the press leaks about Novotny and Suzy
Chang? It may well have been Robert Kennedy's arch-
enemy, J. Edgar Hoover himself.

The FBI Director has been called the 'keeper of the keys to
the closet where our skeletons are stored'. For nearly four
decades now, Hoover has been building an astonishing
dossier on smear material on some of the most influential
men in the United States. These were the 'O and C' –
Official and Confidential – files, kept by Hoover in his own
office, and not fully available to researchers to this day.
They contained damning ammunition that gave the Director a lasting hold over many men of power – including the
Kennedy brothers.
    The FBI file on John Kennedy had been opened at the
start of World War II, based on British MI5 reports on the
young Kennedy's activity while visiting his father Joe, then
Ambassador to London. Almost certainly, those first reports included material on the Kennedy family's association with the Cliveden Set. During the war, Hoover had
personally ordered tape-recorded surveillance of Kennedy
as a Naval Intelligence Officer. The recordings included

coverage of the hotel bedroom in which Kennedy had sex with Inga Arvad, the Danish woman suspected of being a German agent. From then on the apparently insatiable Kennedy had provided Hoover with a stream of compromising material – culminating most recently in his prolonged affair with starlet Judith Campbell. Now there was Mariella Novotny, Suzy Chang, and the mounting information linking the Kennedys and their friends to the Stephen Ward circle in London.

This last information was manna from heaven for Hoover, for it apparently touched not only John, but also Robert. Hoover's greatest disdain was for Robert, whom he regarded as an upstart Attorney-General, the first ever to treat Hoover as his subordinate, to dare to dictate FBI policy. Sexually, Robert had been more restrained than his brother the President. In 1962, though, it was Hoover who had come to his rescue to suppress evidence of both brothers' affairs with Marilyn Monroe. Now came the links to women in the British scandal – Hoover's hold over the Kennedys was strengthened yet again.

It was probably Hoover who saw to it that the *Journal-American* got its stories on Novotny and Chang. It was a Hearst Corporation newspaper, and throughout the fifties Hoover had seen to it that Hearst papers fanned the flames of the Red Menace. Some of the Hearst star writers – like Walter Winchell – were personal friends of Hoover. There were even former FBI men on the paper's staff. In 1963, this cosy relationship was still flourishing. Red-baiting continued, as did fierce editorial opposition to the policies of the Kennedy administration.

The *Journal-American* folded four years after the Profumo Affair, so there is now no way to discover how it got its inside information. With the deaths of both reporters involved, we are left only with coded references in a novel written by one of them, managing editor James Horan. Entitled *The Right Image* and written on a theme of political fixing in the White House, it includes barely veiled allusions – to the Novotny affair, and to an Oriental girl called 'Suzy Chu'.

Hoover's knowledge of Kennedy secrets dovetailed neatly with his obsession about communist subversion and his conviction – ever since the defection of Burgess and Maclean – that British security was hopelessly unreliable. In 1957, when Britain was trying to come to an agreement with the United States on sharing nuclear secrets, Hoover's British specialist, Charles Bates, had told him just the sort of thing he wanted to hear. Bates wrote of a 'British counter-espionage service full of inexperienced "old school-tie" men who feared probing suspects because of possible political rows . . .'

On Saturday 29 June 1963, in the same edition that carried the Novotny–Chang story, the *Journal-American* gave first news of yet another security fiasco for Britain. On the Monday, the same day the Government at last admitted that Kim Philby had defected, the *Guardian* spoke of 'a new spy sensation . . . a startling new espionage case which is likely to break momentarily and may bring down the Conservatives'. George Wigg, in the midst of harrying Macmillan over the Profumo case, told reporters there were 'bigger scandals to come'. He referred to 'American sources' for his information.

Newsweek, one of the two most powerful American weeklies, went for the story hard, basing its information 'on an unchallengeable security source in Washington' – probably Hoover himself. According to *Newsweek*, the new case involved 'leaks of a US Skybolt missile critique and other military documents. A Skybolt document was left by Secretary of Defense Robert McNamara with the British Defence Ministry last December.'

The Skybolt missile programme was highly controversial during the Kennedy presidency. Its cancellation, communicated to the British Prime Minister at his Nassau meeting with Kennedy in 1962, threatened political disaster for Macmillan. Without Skybolt, and with no British-built alternative, Britain's days as a nuclear power seemed numbered. As a sop, Kennedy gave him the Polaris missile, and War Minister John Profumo went to Washington for talks on the technical details.

So great was Macmillan's chagrin, supposedly, when he learned of the alleged British leak about Skybolt, that he called President Kennedy, close to tears. He said he would understand entirely if Kennedy cancelled his forthcoming visit to Britain. *Newsweek*'s London correspondent, pursuing the Skybolt story, was Eldon Griffiths, soon to become a Conservative MP. According to Macmillan's press secretary, Harold Evans, Griffiths went to George Wigg to get information from him on his 'further dossier'. With Wigg's papers still locked up, we can only guess at the nature of the dossier – he had recently been in close touch with Stephen Ward.

On 7 July, just after President Kennedy's visit to Britain, there was yet another embarrassment. A newspaper revealed that a key Soviet defector, one of the CIA's most prized assets, was in Britain. The defector, Anatoli Golitsin, was hastily flown back to the United States. The newspaper that had revealed his presence was the *Daily Telegraph*, edited by Colin Coote – by now Sir Colin – the man who had almost certainly been used by MI5 to bring Stephen Ward and Soviet Assistant Naval Attaché Ivanov together.

The FBI firmly believed that the Skybolt leaks were coming from London, and Hoover's men said so to the press. A few days later the Defense Department joined the chorus, telling correspondents that 'it would be dangerous to allow the sale of Polaris missiles to Britain'.

The Profumo Affair left Charles Bates, Hoover's man in London, deeply disillusioned about British security. When he went to see the Director-General of MI5, Sir Roger Hollis, Bates could not get him to consider the security implications. 'I will never forget going to see Hollis one time,' says Bates. 'I said, "Roger, you guys haven't come up with anything since World War II." He said, "Oh, sure we have." I said, "No you haven't. We gave you almost everything, either us or the CIA." When I asked what he could give us on the Profumo thing, he just said, "Oh, we looked at that, and there's no security angle." '

In 1986, shown the BOWTIE file and the research produced

for this book, Bates said, 'In the Profumo case, MI5 kept telling me there was no intelligence angle. Now I can see they were deliberately misleading me. Yet MI5 kept telling me, "We don't have any interest . . ."'

Courtney Evans, the FBI Assistant Director charged with the delicate task of liaison between Hoover and Robert Kennedy, is legendarily tight-lipped. He rarely talks to the press. On the Profumo Affair, though, he is blunt. 'This was a time,' Evans says, 'when there was a feeling that we had been deceiving ourselves, that we had felt more secure than we should have done, not least because we depended a great deal on the security capability of the British. And then to find that the President was perhaps involved with somebody in the British security scandal. Nobody was grinning . . .'

SEVENTEEN

DAMAGE CONTROL: THE DENNING ENQUIRY

'The capital and whole nation was mad with hatred and fear,' Macaulay wrote of a scandal in another century.

In the summer of 1963 there was certainly a feeling that the world had gone mad, and real fear that the Profumo Affair would topple the Government. 'The "popular" Press had been one mass,' Harold Macmillan wrote in his diary, 'of the life of spies and prostitutes, written no doubt in the office. Day after day the attacks developed, chiefly on me – old, incompetent, worn out.'

Macmillan was sixty-nine and suddenly weary of it all. His younger Labour opponent, Harold Wilson, however, did not want to be seen to be kicking the Prime Minister when he was down. Further Opposition attack on Macmillan, Wilson confided to the First Secretary at the American Embassy, 'could easily have the effect of alienating the public and consolidating Conservative ranks in a demonstration of sympathy'. 'Wilson believes,' the First Secretary reported to Washington, 'that Labour can safely allow the post-Profumo plot to boil in a "natural" way. He mentioned several – he said six – ministers who may be mixed up in the Keeler business. Wilson was not certain when (or if) all these floating rumours about high-placed persons could be stilled. But it could take a long time, smudging the Prime Minister's hopes of carrying on . . .'

Ambassador Bruce himself was briefed by Robert Allan, the Conservative Party Treasurer, on the rumours linking more ministers to the scandal. 'Names mentioned,' Bruce informed President Kennedy in note form, 'are Selwyn Lloyd, Sandys, Hare and Marples. Has been told Marples naked masked man who served at banquet. Allan thinks allegation against Selwyn Lloyd ridiculous.'

The allegation involving Selwyn Lloyd, former Chancellor of the Exchequer, was in fact not against him personally – Stephen Ward was alleged to have had an affair with a member of his family. As we have seen, Ernest Marples, the Transport Minister, was not the Man In The Mask at Mariella Novotny's notorious party. Rumours were flying, though, that he was, and some Conservatives said the stories were being spread by Stephen Ward. There is no evidence he did any such thing. It would have been difficult, since Ward was languishing in Brixton jail when the rumours were circulating.

One man who did tell tales about the Man In The Mask was ——— ———,* a Chelsea solicitor who knew Ward, Novotny and her husband Hod Dibben. Dibben remembers how, before the scandal, ——— was forever hanging around outside the house in Hyde Park Square, and once threatened Novotny with rape. He claimed to have been at the Mask Party, though he was not. According to Roy East, the *People* journalist, ——— was 'one of the people mainly responsible for putting around false tales . . .' East thought the rumours were 'deliberately encouraged by Special Branch, to divert attention from other aspects of the scandal they wanted to hide'.

On Wednesday 12 June the Chief Crime Reporter for the *News of the World*, Peter Earle, was at Christine Keeler's flat – his newspaper had now bought her story. 'She had been out with her black lovers,' Earle remembers, 'and was lying in bed, naked and asleep.' Then Earle's boss, General Manager Mark Chapman-Walker, rang to ask if Keeler had slept with any ministers other than Profumo. Dragged from her bed at the Editor's insistence, Keeler 'burst into tears, declaring that she wasn't involved with anyone else'.

*Name deleted for legal reasons.

The call to Keeler had been inspired by Randolph Churchill, then a political columnist for the *News of the World*, who had been tipped off about a turbulent Cabinet meeting. After discussion of the Dilhorne report, which said there had been no security leak, some ministers expressed concern that more embarrassments would come to light. One of them – supposedly Enoch Powell, though he denies it – reportedly threatened to resign rather than remain a member of a tainted Cabinet. Then another minister, the Secretary of State for the Colonies, the late Duncan Sandys, offered to resign, because he had indeed been embroiled in a lurid, though somewhat ancient divorce case.

German newspapers had reported that Duncan Sandys had been the 'headless man' having sex with the Duchess of Argyll, as shown in a photograph produced at the Duchess's sensational divorce hearings beginning in March 1963. In fact, according to Drew Pearson, the Washington columnist, 'a former Hollywood movie-star, with a very famous name, who has now adopted the life of England . . . an amateur photographer of parties', had 'paid quite a bit to get his photos kept out of the Duchess of Argyll's divorce case. Notwithstanding, the naming of the Minister caused panic in Conservative ranks.'

On 20 June, Macmillan's secretary, Harold Evans, arrived at work 'to be greeted with a warning at the 11.30 lobby I should almost certainly have to announce a Ministerial resignation. The Minister . . . was not the headless man, but he had been involved with the lady and apparently felt he must expiate the indulgence by resignation . . .' He decided to ponder his final decision for a few hours.

Next day, in the House, Harold Macmillan announced that he was appointing Lord Denning to hold a one-man enquiry into the security aspects of the case. There was no word now of a new resignation – the Minister had changed his mind overnight. But Macmillan asked Denning to look into the 'headless man' rumours. Denning obliged – and reported that the man was not Duncan Sandys. Denning had established this after Duncan Sandys submitted to a

medical examination. His physical characteristics did not
match those of the man in the lewd photograph. Denning's
Report discreetly avoided mentioning what Sandys had
already admitted to the Prime Minister, that he had indeed
been involved with the Duchess of Argyll.

Denning's handling of this fringe matter was one example of the way Stephen Ward's name came to be smeared –
even more than it was already – by the Report. Denning
gave publicity to the notion that Ward had been in possession of one of the Argyll pictures, and that Ward had acted
as go-between in a deal to keep the Minister's name out of
the divorce case. While the Report left the Minister looking
whiter than white, the allegation against Ward was simply
left hanging.

Denning, incidentally, always called Profumo 'Mr',
while Dr Ward was not given any title at all – he was just
plain Ward. Profumo's adultery, with a girl he had
observed cavorting with a Soviet diplomat was called an
'indiscretion', and balanced against a record entitling him
to 'the confidence of his colleagues'. Ward was dismissed as
'utterly immoral', a man of 'vicious sexual activities'. His
efforts as a diplomatic go-between were 'misconceived and
misdirected'. Ward, of course, had no way of answering
back. He was long dead by the time the Denning Report
dragged him through the mire.

The purpose of the Denning Report led, Macmillan
wrote later, to 'at least some check in the flood of accusation and rumour'. Britain's senior Appeal Court judge
accepted his task as a patriot. 'It was my duty,' he wrote
later, 'to do what I was asked.' There were, he noted in his
Report, 'unavoidable limitations'. First, since it was in
secret, his work 'had not the appearance of justice'.
Second, it was a one-man band. He had to be 'detective,
inquisitor, advocate and judge'. 'My enquiry,' Lord
Denning wrote, 'is not a suitable body to determine guilt
or innocence . . . No witness has given evidence on oath.
None has been cross-examined . . .'

Then Denning noted the advantages. He thought that,
because he heard witnesses in private, they were honest

with him. He could check their testimony one against the other, and allegations made received no publicity. 'It is, I believe,' Denning wrote at the end of his Report, 'better for the country . . . that this unfortunate episode should be closed.' The Report did just that.

Profumo, the Government, and British Intelligence were let off lightly. Stephen Ward, in death, was left to carry the metaphorical can. 'The Report was a disgrace,' says Ludovic Kennedy, who wrote a highly regarded book on the case in 1963. 'Lord Denning produced all sorts of dirt, with no evidence. It was a shambles.'

Denning operated from a room at the Treasury in Whitehall. 'There,' he wrote later, 'I saw Ministers of the Crown, the Security Service, rumour-mongers and prostitutes. They all came in by back doors and along corridors secretly so that the newspapers should not spot them. Some of the evidence I heard was so disgusting – even to my sophisticated mind – that I sent the lady shorthand writers out, and no note of it was taken.' The reader must decide for himself which is more important – the sensitivities of female ears or a complete record of the most serious security investigations in British history.

The disgusting evidence included Stephen Ward's pornographic photographs. There were pictures of numerous men at sex parties, some of them clearly identifiable. Ward had given his collection to his friend Warwick Charlton after the Affair broke, and Charlton entrusted them to his employers, Odhams Press, when Ward was arrested. 'I gave them for safekeeping to the accountants,' says Charlton. 'They thought they were valuables. They were shocked when the safe was opened.' The pictures were given to the police, 'after lots of pressure on Odhams'. Ward himself, it appears, had told the police where the photographs were being kept.

In late June Richard Crossman, a member of the Labour Party's Executive Committee, went to the Café Royal to meet Hugh Cudlipp, then Editorial Director of the *Daily Mirror*. 'I said to Hugh,' Crossman wrote in his diaries, 'well, how are those photographs that the Secret Service took? . . . When Scotland Yard had received the evidence from George [Wigg], these had been taken back as evidence . . . Every one of Hugh's staff around the room was uneasily aware that I was on to something . . .' Hugh Cudlipp did not respond to an interview request for this book.

Charlton remembers the photographs well. 'They were hardly dirty pictures,' he says, 'but people naked, yes. They would have been considered rather daring. They showed Vasco Lazzolo, ——— [a member of the Royal Family],* and other people, —— ——— [a Conservative MP],* and the photographer Baron, with his withered arm. There were all these girls around, stark naked. It was horrible, actually.'

The photographs, we understand, were taken in the early fifties, at a 'safe house' in St John's Wood.

On 18 June, in New York, an FBI Supervisor declared that there were 'some thorny problems involved inasmuch as there are indications that Prince Philip and Douglas Fairbanks may be involved in the Keeler affair'.

On the day Denning started work, 24 June, the *Daily Mirror* devoted its entire front page to a new story. 'The foulest rumour,' it said, 'being circulated about the Profumo Scandal, has involved the Royal Family. The name mentioned in this rumour has been Prince Philip's.' The *Mirror* failed to say what the rumour was, but said it was 'utterly unfounded'.

The *Mirror* story led to a complaint to the Press Council, which finally decided the piece had been in bad taste. The Council could not, however, 'judge whether the stage had been reached when the *Daily Mirror* was justified in the public interest in repudiating [the rumour], and thereby giving it great publicity'.

'Stephen,' says Charlton, 'was quite friendly with Prince Philip in the early days. When Denning was doing his stuff

*Names deleted for legal reasons.

he was very worried about it. I think he had a brief to stop any fall-out from that. Stephen protected people he had known. He was proud of that relationship.'

Denning was indeed concerned about the injection of Prince Philip's name. He made a point of interviewing Michael Parker, the Prince's former equerry and close friend.

Denning was told about the American connection in the Profumo Affair, but there is not a word about it in the Report. Michael Eddowes, the solicitor who gave his information on the case to the FBI, was interviewed by Denning. He says he submitted detailed memoranda on the security aspects of the scandal. There are no references to such documents in the Denning Report.

Hod Dibben testified to Lord Denning – not only about the Man In The Mask Party, but also about Novotny's visit to New York and her liaison with John Kennedy. There is nothing about the American episode in the Report – which does not mention the Dibbens' names. 'I do remember,' Denning told us in a letter, 'that a woman called Mariella came and gave evidence . . . and also Mr Horace Dibben, but I'm afraid I cannot add anything of use . . .'

The police were fully informed on another matter which made no appearance in the Report – and yet is suggestive of a criminal aspect to the Affair. This has never been covered at all, anywhere. We learned about it from Dr Eric Dingwall, anthropologist and former Keeper of the Private Case at the British Museum, who was called in as a consultant when Scotland Yard handled bizarre sex cases.

'One of the key figures behind the sexual side of the Profumo scandal,' said Dr Dingwall before his death in 1985, 'was a woman who calls herself "Carmen". She originally ran an expensive sex service in Washington. Elaborate sexual displays were put on, covering every conceivable anomaly and perversion, and elaborate charades were enacted. At some time Carmen moved her operation to England. She owned a large country house in Berkshire, catering to people with the money to participate. This was in the late fifties and early sixties. The front for their activities was that they posed as antique dealers.'

We were unable to trace 'Carmen', but one of our contacts, a prostitute, expert in 'S and M' – flagellation and the like – was familiar with her operation. One of Carmen's customers was ———,* a Conservative Secretary of State in 1963. Dr Dingwall confirmed this. '——— used to go down there quite a lot,' said the former British Museum official, 'but I wouldn't imagine he would wish to talk about it. I heard that he favoured a "babies and nursemaid" scene in which he played the nursemaid . . .'

During or soon after the Profumo Affair, 'Carmen' moved back to the United States. This may explain why George Wigg, on 17 June 1963, spoke of three people, 'actively connected with blackmail on an international scale, who got out of London last weekend as quickly as they could when they knew that Dr Ward had been arrested . . .' American police investigators believed that one of those involved in blackmail during the scandal was a thirty-one-year-old woman from Glasgow. She had set up an apartment in Soho specially equipped for unusual sexual practices. It was the haunt of numerous influential men during the early sixties.

'The Americans are worried,' one newspaper said in 1963, 'that some of the people involved in recent events are also connected with some of the highest figures in the Washington administration.' There was no reference to this, nor to international blackmailers, in the Denning Report.

The knowledge that Denning was at work, coupled with Stephen Ward's arrest, contained the damage. The newspapers ceased to be dominated entirely by the Profumo story. In the second week of June, the American Embassy reported that the British press now planned to take the heat off the Government. According to the late Lord Rothermere, owner of the *Daily Mail*, 'the *Telegraph*, *Express*, *Mail* and *Mirror* were joining forces to reduce the Profumo coverage . . . if the Government was going to be brought

*Name deleted for legal reasons.

down, the socialists didn't want it to be a landslide. The motive here was not to attract all types of leftwing support to the socialist cause.' If this report was true, it was an exceptionally rare example of cooperation between newspapers.

While the Denning enquiry created the illusion that something was being done, the Establishment staged a successful diversion. The prosecution of Stephen Ward shifted attention away from the Government, on to one lone individual.

Following his arrest, Ward was kept in prison for four weeks. The charges – of living on prostitution – were relatively minor. Yet the authorities kept Ward in Brixton for an inordinately long time. The police opposed bail, on the grounds that Ward might flee abroad or interfere with witnesses. When bail was granted, it was in the sum of £3,000, a huge amount at contemporary values. It is worth recording who put up the bail money, once Ward was abandoned by his high and mighty friends. The donors were Pelham Pound, the journalist acting as Ward's agent; Dominic Elwes, son of artist Simon Elwes and himself a controversial society figure; and, reportedly, Claus von Bülow, then executive assistant to oil millionaire Paul Getty, now known for the trials in which he was accused, and eventually cleared, of trying to murder his American wife.

Ward's trial began at the Old Bailey on 22 July 1963. It was a staged trial, an outrageous abuse of the judicial system.

EIGHTEEN

SMOKESCREEN: THE TRIAL OF STEPHEN WARD

'All I now have left between me and destruction,' Ward wrote before the trial, 'is a handful of firm friends, my legal advisers, the integrity of a judge, and twelve men on a jury.'

Ward went on trying to shield his former friends from exposure, to draw the fire on himself, to the bitter end. Even in court, he covered for his friends, minimising the damaging testimony.

Ward hoped from the start that Lord Astor would come to his aid. 'I had always believed,' he told Warwick Charlton, 'that Bill wouldn't let me down. I thought he could do something to restore my good name. I thought he might hold a party at Cliveden, collect some notables, and have me down as a sort of gesture of solidarity. Imagine my shock when he at once asked me to let him have a letter vacating the cottage . . . I was absolutely flabbergasted. I then began to realise that the waves were coming aboard and soon I would be clinging to the mast. And all the time there was no one at all to turn to . . .'

'Expect nothing from the Establishment,' Charlton had warned. Ward had spent nearly twenty years cultivating these 'friends'. Now they dumped him, and Ward belatedly realised their true calibre. 'They are all the same,' he told Charlton. 'They all thought you could buy it with a cheque book.'

Lord Astor, says his widow, stayed silent not only on the advice of his solicitors, but on the 'spiritual direction' of a bishop. 'He could not defend either of them, Ward or Jack Profumo,' says Lady Astor, 'without incriminating both of them, and involving more people as witnesses to his statements.'

Astor paid Ward's legal expenses, according to his wife, but he kept his mouth shut. 'Silence,' the bishop told him, 'is the only possible course.' Astor had recently become a fervent Christian, and his 'model' for keeping quiet, says Lady Astor, was Jesus Christ. Like Christ, says the widow, he did not want to 'start having to involve other people as witnesses . . .'

'By the time the balloon had gone up,' Ward noted, 'no one looked like the same people any more . . . I have lost hope of the basic simplicity of the matter ever emerging . . . The car is out of control. Anything may happen now.'

The trial began on 22 July 1963, at the Old Bailey. The setting was Court No. 1, where so many celebrated defendants have entrusted their fate to a jury. Outside the building, the crowds were ten deep.

The authoritative account of the trial is that of Ludovic Kennedy, the campaigner for the righting of judicial wrongs. To his irritation, Kennedy found that the authorities refused him access to full official transcripts. The decision was taken by Lord Parker of Waddington, the Chief Justice, though transcripts of other trials had been made available. In 1987, after repeated application, we did obtain a partial transcript, and will draw on it in this chapter.

'The tiny, tubby judge,' wrote Kennedy, 'came billowing in like a small Dutch *shuyt* under a full spread of canvas, grey and black and scarlet . . . a keen, determined mole, all set for a good day's burrowing . . .' The judge was Sir Archibald Marshall, aged sixty-four, a former President of the Oxford Union, nicknamed 'The Hen'. 'As a judge,' his *Times* obituary was to note, 'he was an unusual mixture; his upbringing and beliefs perhaps led him to pass or at any rate form, moral judgements which would no doubt be regarded as old-fashioned in this day and age, and yet he never seemed to be out of sympathy with a modern jury. He had the knack of talking to the men and women of a jury as if he were on neighbourly and equal terms with them.'

'Marshall could hardly be expected to make allowances for the renegade son of a canon,' wrote a chronicler of the Old Bailey. 'He conducted the trial without overt bias, but his demeanour and the very inflection of his voice implied moral disapproval, emphasised by the scratching of his pen as he laboriously entered questions and answers on a huge pad like the Recording Angel.'

Judges for trials at the Old Bailey are sometimes selected by the Lord Chancellor's office. The Lord Chancellor, at the time, was Lord Dilhorne, the man who initially investigated the security side of the Profumo Affair. It may be, though, that a word from the Lord Chief Justice can ensure the selection of a judge to his liking. It turns out that the then Chief Justice Parker had his own reason to dislike Ward and his circle.

Parker – Rugby and Cambridge – was sixty-three in 1963. In summer that year, travel writer Robert Harbinson was having his portrait painted by Gwen le Gallienne, the well-known lesbian artist and close friend of Ward. 'At the time she was doing my portrait,' Harbinson remembers, 'she was also doing the Lord Chief Justice. And she came back from the Strand one day, and told me that Parker had discovered her in bed with ———.'*

The prosecuting barrister was Mervyn Griffith-Jones – Eton, Cambridge and the Brigade of Guards. 'Square,' wrote Ludovic Kennedy, 'is the word that suits him. He is so ultra-orthodox that some aspects of modern life have escaped him altogether . . . during the *Lady Chatterley's Lover* trial, as prosecuting counsel, he solemnly asked the jury whether it was a book they would wish their servants to read . . .' At Ward's trial, Griffith-Jones was to tell the jury that the accused was a 'thoroughly filthy fellow . . . a wicked, wicked creature'.

*Name deleted for legal reasons.

Defence counsel was James Burge – Cheltenham and Cambridge. He was not a Queen's Counsel, but was respected as a criminal barrister. Kennedy thought him 'a jovial, sunshiney, Pickwickian sort of man, who always seemed to be smiling . . .' Some of his practice was devoted to licensing cases. 'Beer and Burgundy,' said Kennedy, 'seemed to blend with his beaming face . . . I had been told by one of his colleagues that he was one of the few men at the Bar who could laugh a case out of court.' Burge had a bad back, and Dr Ward treated him on the sofa in his chambers.

Burge, it has been said, was a model for the character of John Mortimer's Rumpole, and Mortimer does not deny it. He and his staff soon began to feel that there would be no laughing this one out of court. 'No one liked the trial or the procedure,' says a former colleague of Burge. 'It was too political, and it was felt that Ward was a scapegoat . . .' 'Ward said to me, "The dice is loaded," ' says the defence counsel, now retired in Spain, 'and it was. On the other hand, with an English jury, he had a good chance.'

Ludovic Kennedy watched the man with a chance come into the vast dock of Court No. 1. 'There was no mistaking the now familiar figure,' wrote Kennedy, 'the roué of fifty who looked thirty-five, perceptive eyes set in a face rather too full to carry them, boyish hair swept back like the wings of a partridge . . . He was dressed in a sober heather-mixture suit, and one's first and most striking impression was that he was a man of intelligence and dignity.'

'Right at the end,' Ward wrote in his memoir, 'I realised they were out to get me, at all costs.' Now, like some heterosexual Oscar Wilde, he listened to the charges against him. He was accused of living on the earnings of prostitution of Christine Keeler between June 1961 and August 1962, on those of Mandy Rice-Davies in late 1962, and on those of two other women between January and June 1963. There were two other charges: of procuring a girl under twenty-one to have intercourse, and attempting to procure another underage girl.

There had at one stage been no fewer than nine charges –
including one of keeping a brothel. Two had been that
Ward introduced girls to an abortionist – probably his
friend Dr Sugden. Abortion was still illegal in those days.
Those charges were dropped for the time being, with the
possibility that they might be revived later. It was all out
of proportion. The 1956 Wolfenden Report – ironically
Ward had met Sir John Wolfenden at Cliveden – shows
how such cases were normally treated. Of 131 people
found guilty of living on immoral earnings in one year, 117
were dealt with in magistrates' courts, and thirteen were
conditionally discharged, fined, or put on probation. It was
unheard of to pursue such an offender in the way Ward
had been pursued. Even then they failed to find real
evidence.

This is not the place to rehearse the blow-by-blow progress of the trial, which lasted eight days. Young women,
named only as 'Miss X' and 'Miss R', were brought to court
merely to speak of their sex relations with Ward, but their
evidence was just icing on the prosecution cake. The two
charges about underage girls were brought only to add to
the miasma of lechery around the defendant. But there was
worse. 'There is just one possibility that struck me,' Ward
had written to a friend, 'that is the danger of false evidence.' It was more than a possibility.

Once off the leash, the Metropolitan Police had pursued
Ward with a zeal for which these authors can find no
parallel – except perhaps the murder of a fellow Inspector. The police team for the Profumo investigation was
headed by Chief Inspector Samuel Herbert, and included
Detective-Superintendent James Axon. He was responsible for the field work, and for the painstaking trawl of
London's underworld, the prolonged search for any evidence that might tilt the scales against Stephen Ward.

Inspector Herbert revealed the fantastic industry that
had gone into the prosecution of Stephen Ward. He revealed to the court that he personally had interviewed
Christine Keeler twenty-four times, and that a senior detec-

tive had interrogated her on fourteen other occasions about the related cases of Gordon and Edgecombe.

The police installed a spy in Ward's home during the investigation. They discovered Wendy Davies, a twenty-year old barmaid at the Duke of Marlborough pub, near Ward's flat. She knew Ward, who had sketched her, and she had a policeman for a boyfriend. Davies was asked to renew her acquaintance with Ward. 'I went to Stephen's flat practically every night up to his arrest,' she later revealed. 'Each time I tried to listen in to telephone conversations, and to what Stephen was saying to friends who called. When I got back to my flat I wrote everything down in an exercise book, and rang the police the next day. I gave them lots of information . . .'

Ward knew full well he was being watched. One day, as he and his journalist friend Pelham Pound walked back to the flat, he pointed to an upstairs window opposite. 'Do you see it?' he said. 'The telephoto lens?'

'The policeman in charge,' says playwright Michael Pertwee, like his brother Jon a friend of Ward's, 'had spent most of his recent past operating in Soho against pimps and blackmailers, and his methods were pretty dubious . . .'

'Oh, my God, how dreadful!' Ward had exclaimed when he was arrested. 'I shall deny it. Nobody will come forward to say it is true.' He had no idea, then, of the savage tricks that were to be used against him.

Ronna Riccardo, produced by the prosecution on the third day of the trial, appeared with her hair dyed red and wearing a pink sweater. She readily admitted she was a prostitute. She was known as 'Ronna the Lash', and specialised in flagellation. 'She used to carry her equipment round in a leather bag,' says reporter Trevor Kempson. 'She was well known for the use of the whip, and I heard that several of Ward's friends used to like it rough.' Keeler's lover Johnny Edgecombe well remembers Riccardo and her equipment. Presumably in a more conventional liaison, she had – as we have seen – had sex in Ward's flat with American airman 'Silky' Hawkins.

The American connection did not emerge at Ward's trial. Riccardo's testimony, oddly enough, has not been officially released, even in 1987. Earlier, in a statement to the police and at the Ward committal proceedings, she had implicated the osteopath in a series of sex episodes involving money. She talked of being invited to a house party on Lord Astor's estate, and quoted Ward as saying it 'would be worth my while'. She said she visited Ward three times at home in London. On one occasion, she had supposedly gone to the bedroom with a man who gave her a 'pony' – twenty-five pounds – 'I went to bed with men at the flat . . . when this did happen . . . I had been invited to go there by Stephen.'

Two days before the Ward trial, Riccardo made a new statement to the police. 'The evidence I gave at the Stephen Ward hearing earlier this month,' she said, 'was largely untrue. I visited Ward at his flat at Bryanston Mews on one occasion. No one received any money. At no time have I received any money on Stephen Ward's premises, or given money to him. The reason the earlier statement was divergent from the truth was my apprehension that my baby daughter and younger sister might be taken out of my care following certain statements made to me by Chief Inspector Samuel Herbert.'

'Are you suggesting,' asked Judge Marshall at the Old Bailey, 'that the police had just put words into your mouth? . . .' 'Yes,' Riccardo replied '. . . I wanted the police to leave me alone . . .'

'Riccardo,' Ludovic Kennedy wrote, 'was clearly in a state of terror at what the police might do to her for having gone back on her original evidence. After the trial she seldom stayed at one address for more than a few nights for fear the police were looking for her . . .'

Lord Denning did not mention Riccardo in his Report. Ludovic Kennedy did contact her, and she revealed that, before she testified, the police interviewed her no fewer than nine times. An observation car sat outside her home for days at a time. She ended up testifying against Stephen Ward.

Today, traced during research for this book, Riccardo was even more forthright. She said flatly, 'Stephen didn't have to ponce – he was dead rich, a real gentleman; a shoulder to cry on for me, for a long time. Some of my clients were friends of Stephen's. But it wasn't business, like, more like friends. I was really into costumes then. These blokes would turn up with a costume inside their little briefcases, and I'd dress up as a nanny or a nurse, and smack their bottoms for them.'

Riccardo confirms the police pressure, and explains the quandary she was in. 'The police knew I hung around with Stephen,' she says. 'They said they would do me on immoral earnings, but Chief Inspector Herbert, who was running the investigation, was a punter of mine himself. I didn't know he was a policeman for ages. I used to wear a wig, and he always wanted me to take it off and shake my hair around. I was going with another copper, too, who was involved in the enquiry. I couldn't take this pressure by the coppers, and Stephen was a good friend of mine. But Inspector Herbert was a good friend as well, so it was complicated . . .' At the time of the enquiry, Riccardo was caring for her two sisters as well as her own baby daughter – her parents had recently separated. She said she feared her daughter and sisters would be placed in a home, unless she did as she was told.

Initially, Riccardo did give false evidence against Ward at the committal hearing. She withdrew the testimony, at the trial, after talking to *Daily Express* reporter Tom Mangold. He told her she should tell the truth, and she did. The police denied her claims. Riccardo has the letters

ACAB tattooed on her wrist. They stand for: 'All coppers are bastards.'

The court also heard a prostitute called Vickie Barrett, said to have visited Ward's flat over many weeks and to have provided sex for money for several men. Barrett appeared, a pale blonde in a green raincoat. She was, Rebecca West thought, like 'a photograph from a famine relief fund appeal'. 'I looked at her,' wrote Kennedy, '. . . and then I looked at Ward, intelligent and sophisticated, in the dock and I found it difficult to reconcile the two.'

Perhaps by coincidence, Barrett had been arrested for soliciting on 3 July, the day Ward was committed for trial. In her diary, allegedly, was the name of Stephen Ward, coupled with his telephone number and five other names. Thus the police made the connection.

Vickie Barrett said Ward had picked her up in Oxford Street that year, when he was cruising in his Jaguar. 'He said,' she testified, 'he had a man in the flat who wanted to go with a girl, and he said the man would give him the money . . . he said if I visited him two or three times a week he would save the money, and I could live in a flat.' On arrival at the flat, Ward supposedly gave her a contraceptive and sent her into a room where a man was waiting. Afterwards, she said, Ward told her the man had paid him, and he would save the money for her – for the flat.

Barrett alleged that she met other middle-aged men at the flat, that she had beaten several of them with a horse-whip – at a pound a stroke – and that Ward kept the money they paid. One of the men, Barrett said, was Ward's artist friend, Vasco Lazzolo. Lazzolo admitted meeting Barrett, but never at Ward's flat. He knew Ward was being investigated at the time he met Barrett, so – he said – it was hardly likely he would have behaved as the witness claimed in his old friend's home.

A friend of Vickie Barrett's, Brenda O'Neil, said she had been to bed with Ward for money. Oddly, although she was one of Barrett's closest friends, Barrett had never mentioned the sex scenes at Ward's flat involving other men.

Another woman, Frances Brown, said she had visited both Lazzolo and Stephen Ward along with Vickie Barrett. There had been a sex act, in which she 'helped', but she knew nothing of Ward taking money.

Ward said Vickie Barrett's evidence was 'a tissue of lies from beginning to end'. He admitted meeting her and O'Neil, and paying them for sex – two pounds each. But he vehemently denied entirely Barrett's claim that she had gone with men at his flat for money, and that he had kept the cash.

A few days later, when Ward committed suicide, he left a note for Vickie Barrett. 'I don't know,' he wrote, 'what it was or who it was that made you do what you did. But if you have any decency left, you should tell the truth like Ronna Riccardo. You owe this not to me, but to everyone who may be treated like you or like me in the future.'

Immediately after Ward's death, *Daily Telegraph* reporter Barry O'Brien called on Vickie Barrett to show her the dead man's letter. 'She read the note,' he says, and began to cry. 'It was all lies,' she said of her sworn testimony. 'But I never thought he would die . . .' She said she had been coerced into giving her evidence by the police. She agreed to go to see Ward's solicitor, then went to another room to get her coat. A few moments later, an older woman came out, and said 'Miss Barrett was not going anywhere . . .' Barrett later retracted her retraction.

The best evidence mustered against Ward came from Christine Keeler and Mandy Rice-Davies. They, too, had been under inexcusable pressure from the police. Keeler had been endlessly interrogated. To prevent Mandy Rice-Davies making trips abroad, the police had twice arrested her at London Airport. On the first occasion she was remanded in Holloway Prison for a week on a driving-licence offence. The second time she was charged with stealing a television set, which she had not. It was a device to ensure she was available for the first hearing in the Ward case.

'I've been around the Old Bailey for years and years,'

says Keeler's former solicitor, Harry Stevens, 'but I've never seen anything like the day we brought Christine to court. We had to smuggle her out of the judges' car park to get her away from the crowds. And still we got the eggs – people were throwing eggs at the girl. She was not popular. The policemen were getting their helmets knocked off right left and centre . . .'

Keeler was in a blue funk. 'The old matron was plying Christine with phenobarbitone, the Valium of the day,' says Stevens. 'She was vomiting in the room there. She was terribly upset about testifying against Stephen Ward . . . She was desperately unhappy about it. She did not want to harm him in any way at all.'

Ludovic Kennedy watched the girls enter the courtroom. 'Despite the tarty high-heeled shoes,' he noted, Keeler 'was tiny, a real little doll of a girl . . . She walked superbly on long slender legs . . . one could see at once her appeal to the animal instincts of men . . . It was a terrifying little face, vacant yet knowing, and it belonged not to a girl of twenty-one but to an already ageing woman . . .'

Mandy Rice-Davies looked more wholesome. 'Astride her golden head,' wrote Kennedy, 'sat a little rose-petalled hat, such as debutantes wear at garden parties . . . Her simple grey sleeveless dress accentuated the impression of modesty – until one looked at it closely. Then one saw that the slit down the front was only held together by a loose knot – when she walked one could see quite a long way up her leg . . .'

The testimony prised out of Keeler established that she had been given a little money by John Profumo. 'On one occasion,' said Keeler, 'he gave me money to give to my mother.' She admitted having had sex about six times, at Ward's flat, with a Major James Eynon. He paid her – fifteen or twenty pounds on each occasion.

Keeler had also had sex – for fifty pounds – with a man referred to in court only as 'Charles'. She has since confirmed that this was Charles Clore, the millionaire financier, later knighted. Clore knew Profumo and Douglas Fairbanks Jr. He had lived only a few minutes' drive from the Astor mansion at Cliveden, and had met Rice-Davies. With those connections, and his prodigious sexual appetite, the encounter with Keeler was natural enough.

Rice-Davies told the court she had sex 'about five times' with a man referred to merely as 'the Indian doctor', until someone let slip his name in the trial. This was Emil Savundra, the Ceylonese-born crooked head of Fire, Auto, and Marine Insurance. Savundra, Rice-Davies admitted, gave her money after sex, between fifteen and twenty-five pounds in cash. Rice-Davies also spoke of the one occasion she slept with Lord Astor. The prosecution tried to link that with the cheque Astor had once given Ward, which Ward had used to pay the rent, for Rice-Davies and Keeler. Rice-Davies explained that there was no connection – she had sex with Astor two years after the rent episode, simply because they both felt like it.

There were two key questions. Had the girls been prostitutes, and – the crucial issue – had Ward lived on their immoral earnings? There was no statutory definition of a prostitute. Clearly the girls had not been professionals, but equally clearly they had taken money for sex.

Osbert Lancaster produced a cartoon in the *Daily Express* at this time. The man in the picture was asking, 'If I give my wife's lover the winner of the 4.30, would I be living off her immoral earnings?' It was a daft issue, in a trial that should never have taken place, but Ward's fate now hung on such legal hair-splitting.

The girls were taken laboriously through the circumstances in which they met the named men, and the basis on which the money was paid. The prosecution did not try to make anything of the money given Keeler by Profumo – his name was kept out of the case as much as possible. As for Eynon, Keeler said she passed some of his money on to Ward – 'because I hadn't paid any rent, and things like that'.

Keeler said she had sex with Clore 'because I was in a lot of debt at the time . . . and Dr Ward suggested he knew this person who would give me this amount of money to have intercourse. He suggested if I did, that he would give me money.' With Clore's fifty pounds, Keeler said, she paid off debts to Rice-Davies and Dr Ward.

Savundra, who could afford it, had thrown his money around. 'He came round once or twice, and we did not have sex, and he still gave me money,' Rice-Davies told the court. How much did he give her?' 'It depended,' said Rice-Davies, 'because he asked me if I wanted anything. I was taking drama lessons at the time, and he gave me some money to buy a tape-recorder once, which was twenty-five pounds.'

Rice-Davies also mentioned a Mr Ropner, a wealthy man she had seen a couple of times. Ward, she said, suggested she 'borrow' £250 from him. She did not borrow the money, nor did she sleep with Ropner, because she did not fancy him. Like Keeler, Rice-Davies admitted having given Ward money occasionally – 'just a couple of pounds, or something like that, but it was not in return for him introducing me to men. You have to pay where you live.' Like Keeler, Rice-Davies had contributed to the rent at Wimpole Mews, and the food bills – 'in all about twenty-five pounds'. Rice-Davies had also slept with John Shepridge, the landlord of the flat, and once Ward asked her to get him to delay a rent demand. She did pass on the request.

The way the girls met their men became a key issue. Profumo and Astor had come on the scene as a result of Ward's socialising. Keeler met James Eynon off her own bat, but Ward, she said, introduced her to Charles Clore. He also allegedly suggested that an encounter with Clore would not go unrewarded. It was he who arranged for Rice-Davies to meet Savundra, at a coffee-bar in Marylebone. Then, telling Rice-Davies, 'He's a very rich man,' Ward supposedly arranged for Savundra to use Rice-Davies' room at the flat during the daytime, for assignations with yet another woman. Savundra allegedly paid Ward twenty-five pounds for the use of the room. Keeler had her own damaging testimony about Savundra. According to her, Ward suggested she should entertain him once a week – for money. It never came off, however.

The true facts might have come out had the men themselves been called as witnesses, yet Profumo and Astor, spoken of almost reverentially in court, were never called. Nor was Savundra, and Clore's surname was never revealed. Only James Eynon had the guts to appear. He looked, Ludovic Kennedy thought, 'typically English, a cross between Enoch Powell and the man from the Pru, a sort of poor man's David Niven,' in a grey suit and old school tie. Eynon's brief appearance established one thing for sure. In her relations with him, Keeler had been a whore. Ward, though, was in no way involved.

The trial of Stephen Ward was a national entertainment. In the pubs at lunchtime, the reporters exchanged the latest jokes. Question: 'What newspapers does Christine Keeler take?' Answer: 'One *Mail*, two *Mirrors*, three *Observers*, a *New Statesman* every week, and any number of *Times*.' Flagellation gags flourished. Question: 'What happens when you dial the speaking clock on the telephone?' Answer: 'The voice says, "At the third stroke, it will be three pounds precisely."'

The man with nothing to laugh about moved from the dock to the witness box on the fourth day of the trial. Stephen Ward repeated the oath firmly. Kennedy thought it 'a voice of quite extraordinary power, richness and resonance . . . his voice transformed him, gave him magnetism.' Ward said he had 'a pretty shrewd idea' Keeler was having intercourse at Wimpole Mews, but 'not the remotest idea' she was doing so for money.

Ward confirmed that he had only met James Eynon once. He said he could not think who the mysterious 'Charles' was. 'She is lying,' he said, of Keeler's claim that he told her to go and get money from the man we know to have been Charles Clore. Her statements about Savundra were 'all fabrication' – he said Savundra never did rent a room at the flat, and never paid him any money. Ward scoffed at the notion that he asked Rice-Davies to get money out of Ropner. 'I knew Mr Ropner extremely well,' said Ward. 'If I had wanted money from Mr Ropner I would have asked him myself.'

What of the money the girls allegedly gave Ward? The only payments, he said, had been occasional contributions to the rent, the telephone, and the electricity bill. Rice-Davies' total contribution, over two months at Wimpole Mews, had been 'twenty-four pounds, plus five or six pounds for the telephone.' This was exactly what Keeler and Rice-Davies had said. In the press seats, Ludovic Kennedy and others were impressed. 'This evidence was not subsequently challenged by the prosecution,' Kennedy wrote later. 'How *could* they go on asserting that Ward was *living* on Mandy Rice-Davies' *earnings*? It seemed so utterly absurd.'

It was absurd. Not least when Christine Keeler had said, 'I usually owed him more than I ever made . . .' The show, however, went on. 'There were times,' thought Kennedy, 'when Mr Griffith-Jones . . . became, as it were, the commentator in some mad Victorian melodrama, tracing Good and Evil in letters high enough for any child to see.' Griffith-Jones repeatedly pointed up Ward's promiscuity, which was hardly what the man was on trial for. Still, it probably influenced the jury.

'She is lying, sir,' said Ward of Vickie Barrett's claim that he got her to have sex with men, then kept the money himself. He admitted knowing Barrett, and Ronna Riccardo, and having sex with them. That was all – he had merely been their client. A defence witness, Sylvia Parker, had been staying at Ward's flat at the time Barrett claimed she was brought there to have sex with other men. She called Barrett's statements 'untrue, a complete load of rubbish'. As the confessions of both Riccardo and Barrett suggest, Ward's version was almost certainly the truth. None of this deterred the prosecution.

'This is the bottom of the bucket,' Ward cried at one point. 'A hundred and fifty people have been questioned and these are the people they found. There are other people, a hundred and fifty, who would not say anything detrimental about me. It's easy in most people's lives to find at least half-a-dozen people willing to come forward with some active malice, and they will make these statements against a person, especially a person who has some sort of irregularity in his life as I have. They lay themselves open to this type of misrepresentation.'

If any of the prosecution evidence was to be taken seriously – and this jury was required to take it seriously – Christine Keeler's truthfulness, or otherwise, was a vital issue. Almost two months earlier, in yet another related court case, Lucky Gordon had been tried for assaulting Keeler in the spring. He was found guilty, and jailed for three years. On the morning of 30 July, as Ward's trial was ending at the Old Bailey, Gordon's came up for appeal.

He was freed, and for two reasons. First the police had claimed at his trial that they were unable to locate two key witnesses – even though one of them was in police custody at the time. Second, the court was now in possession of the tape-recording Keeler had made with her business mana-ger, Robin Drury, on which she told a story different to the one she told at the Gordon trial and repeated at Ward's. In court, Keeler had denied that anyone else was present when Lucky Gordon assaulted her, and said only Gordon was involved. On the tape-recording, she admitted that two other men had been there, and that another man caused her main injuries. This was perjury. Keeler was later tried, found guilty, and served nine months in prison.

Chief Justice Parker, who presided over the Gordon appeal, telephoned the judge running the Ward trial, Sir Archibald Marshall. According to a clerk who listened in to the call, Parker warned Marshall to take care, because Keeler had lied in another court. So it was that, at the end of the Ward trial, prosecuting counsel Griffith-Jones raised the matter in a devious way. 'The basis or the grounds of that appeal,' he told the jury of Keeler's evidence in the Gordon case, 'were that her evidence was not true, and that there were two witnesses Gordon desired to call but were not at the trial and were not available . . . Gordon's appeal has been allowed.'

Then Griffith-Jones said something that was legally true, but hardly honest. 'That does of course not mean to say,' he told the jury, 'that the Court of Appeal have found that

Miss Keeler is lying. As I understand from the note I have, the Lord Chief Justice said that *it might be that Miss Keeler's evidence was completely truthful*,* but, in view of the fact that there were witnesses now available who were not available at the trial, it was felt that the court could not necessarily say that the jury in that case would not have returned the same verdict as they did if those two witnesses had been called. That is all it amounts to. The Court of Criminal Appeal have *not* found whether Miss Keeler was telling the truth . . .'

'We were all a bit gulled by these words,' Ludovic Kennedy wrote afterwards. 'Later we found out that the evidence was there' [on Keeler lying], 'but that the public were denied hearing it . . . If it had been heard publicly by the Court of Criminal Appeal (and many lawyers think it monstrous that it was not heard), if the Ward jury *had* known that Christine had lied on oath in the witness-box, not only in Gordon's trial but at this trial too, where she had repeated the lies, it is inconceivable that they would have brought in the verdict they did.'

'It was by any standards,' Kennedy went on, 'a feeble case. It consisted mainly of uncorroborated statements by proven liars: it was a hotchpotch of innuendoes and smears covered by a thin pastry of substance. It was a tale of immoralities, rather than crimes.'

Judge Marshall's summing up in the Ward trial was lengthy, and disconcerting to those who reported it. In print, in the newspapers, it seemed dispassionate and fair. Yet, said Ludovic Kennedy, 'when I first saw the summary I could hardly believe I had an accurate report of it, so great was the gulf between the words and my memory of them.' A French reporter, for *France-Soir*, put his finger on it. 'Monsieur Marshall,' he said, 'is a puritan, and Ward, the roué, the libertine, the cynic, appalled him . . . every time M. Justice Marshall explained to the jury the questions they would have to answer, his voice gave it away: M. Marshall

---

* Authors' italics.

did not like Ward, for he had brought a scandal upon England.'

Marshall told the jury they must decide three questions:
(1) Were Keeler and Rice-Davies prostitutes?
(2) Did Ward know they were?
(3) Did he knowingly receive from them or others money for the introduction and facilities for sexual intercourse which he provided?

Marshall told the jury that, to decide a man was guilty of living on prostitution, it must be shown that he knowingly assisted her, and received money for it.

Then the judge pointed out that Ward had been abandoned by his friends. 'There may be many reasons,' he said, 'why Ward has been abandoned in his extremity . . . You must not guess at them, but this is clear: if Stephen Ward was telling the truth in the witness-box, there are in this city many witnesses of high estate and low who could have come and testified support of his evidence.' Thus, somehow, the judge turned against Ward the fact that none of his high-falutin friends had had the courage to come and speak up on his behalf.

To Ludovic Kennedy, it seemed grossly unfair: 'I had no doubts at all,' he wrote, 'of the effect of such a remark on the jury.' Sir David Napley, Britain's leading solicitor, the man who defended Liberal leader Jeremy Thorpe, was on the Council of the Law Society in 1963. 'The real source of injustice,' he wrote after the trial, 'is the rumour and calumny which abounds when the name is published as the subject of a charge. Stephen Ward faced a wealth of publicity unconnected with any charge or proceedings. Once he was charged, public gossip and rumour was disposed to convict him out of hand. It was confidently disclosed that the evidence would reveal that he had been selling information to the Russians; running a brothel for important persons, procuring abortions. What effect would this currency of falsehood have on potential jurors? . . .'

The court rose at half-past four, on Tuesday 30 July with the summing-up unfinished. Ward was shattered by the judge's attitude. He asked his solicitor Jack Wheatley, for a considered opinion of his chances. 'Guilty – and a two-year sentence,' Wheatley replied. Ward was given this news by Pelham Pound. 'For once,' Pound remembers, 'Stephen had nothing to say, except a long "Oh . . ."'

The first day of the trial had been celebrated, at the Museum Gallery in Holborn, with an exhibition of Stephen Ward's sketches. In the evening the champagne had flowed, and Ward himself showed up, smiling and charming in spite of the ordeal in court. So, too, did Mandy Rice-Davies – she posed for the press in front of a Ward portrait of herself.

The collection included Ward's pictures of Prince Philip, Princess Margaret, the Duke and Duchess of Gloucester, and the Duke of Kent. Ward's friend, Robert Harbinson, was there. 'I knew certain friends would be deeply horrified,' he says today, 'so I telephoned Anthony Blunt.' Sir Anthony Blunt, of course, was the Surveyor of the Queen's Pictures, then yet to be unmasked as a traitor. 'I believe,' says Harbinson, 'that Blunt, ever anxious to keep in with Buck House, telephoned Michael Adeane [the Queen's Private Secretary] at the Palace.'

Five days later, an unidentified man, tall, distinguished, and in his fifties, arrived at the Museum Gallery. He took from his briefcase a bank draft for five thousand pounds, bought up all Ward's royal portraits, and departed. The man, we now know, was an art dealer acting as agent for Sir Gordon Brunton, then managing director of the Thompson publishing interests. Sir Gordon revealed in 1987 that the pictures had been stored for years in the safe at the offices of the *Illustrated London News*.

The BBC covered Ward's 1963 exhibition, and the osteopath watched the report on television. 'More than most of us,' says his friend Frederic Mullally, 'Stephen admired and respected the pundits of the box. The commentator on this occasion was one such pundit – a young man who would probably have botched a child's colouring book, but who reached millions daily with his special brand of urbane irony. He and his BBC masters chose this day for the most savage public mauling of an artist's work I have ever witnessed. It started with a sneer and built up to defamation. It ended with the Olympian judgement that there was nothing in the exhibition beyond the capabilities of a second-year student at one of London's schools of art. This was the day they axed through Stephen's last lifeline. He hung on, of course, for the miracle of a judge who would sum up against prejudice and hypocrisy.'

Ward went home on the evening of 30 July with his current girlfriend, a young singer called Julie Gulliver. They went to a coffee-bar, then to the Chelsea flat of the man giving Ward shelter during the trial, advertising executive Noel Howard-Jones. There, at Vale Court, in Mallord Street, Ward began writing letters – to be delivered 'only if I am convicted and sent to prison'. There were twelve of them, and Gulliver watched as Ward sealed them and handed them over to Howard-Jones. Ward's girlfriend thought him 'noticeably upset'. He was uncharacteristically restless.

That night, probably between seven and eight, *Daily Express* reporter Tom Mangold took a telephone call from Stephen Ward. Mangold had been covering the Profumo Affair for months. He was one of the few reporters Ward still trusted. Ward wrote in his memoir. The two men had spent night after night talking into the early hours. That night, Mangold was desperately tired. He also had personal problems, reaching crisis point, and this call was a damned nuisance. 'He asked me to come round to where he was staying,' says Mangold, now a *Panorama* reporter, and one of the most accomplished British journalists of our time. 'He said it was urgent. I said I would come, but I didn't want to spend another long night talking.'

Mangold drove to Mallord Street. He had been handling the prostitute Ronna Riccardo, as well as Ward. She had cried on his shoulder and told him, 'I've fitted up Stephen.' 'There were two strands running through the thing, it seemed to me,' Mangold says today. 'There was some sort of intelligence connection, which I could not understand at the time. The other thing, the thing that was clear, was that Ward was being made a scapegoat for everyone else's sins. So that the public would excuse them. If the myth about Ward could be built up properly, the myth that he was a revolting fellow, a true pimp, then police would feel that other men, like Profumo and Astor, had been corrupted by him. But he wasn't a ponce. He was no more a pimp than hundreds of other men in London. But when the state wants to act against an individual, it can do it.'

Tom Mangold knew Ward was at the end of his tether: 'He felt absolutely betrayed. Until the very last minute he was certain that Lord Astor would turn up and pull him out of the shit. But he was abandoned. That night he asked me to post the letters he had written. I said I knew what they were, suicide notes, and I refused to post them for him.' One of the letters was addressed to Mangold himself. 'Well,' Ward told the reporter, 'take your letter, but don't open it till I'm dead.'

Then Mangold left Ward, and went home. Today he is sad about what happened, but philosophical. A reporter must be compassionate, but cannot be held responsible for his interviewees. When the phone rang next morning with the news of Ward's suicide Mangold was not surprised.

Julie Gulliver stayed with Ward until about 11.30 p.m. that last night. Then he drove her home, and said 'Goodbye.' It was not like him. 'Usually,' she said, 'he would say something like "Cheerio" or "See you tomorrow".'

In the morning, at 8.30 a.m., the telephone rang at the Mallord Street flat. Ward's host, Noel Howard-Jones, heard it through the bedroom door. He knew the phone was a few feet from his guest, who was sleeping in the lounge. Yet the phone kept ringing. Howard-Jones stumbled out to take the call – it was Vasco Lazzolo's wife, calling to wish Ward the best of luck.

'It was only when I hung up,' Howard-Jones told the inquest, 'that I turned around and saw him. I thought he was dead. His face was a purple colour. His mouth was open and there was a sort of mark on his face, like dry saliva

. . . I slapped his face, and he breathed just once. I tried for a minute or so an amateur type of artificial respiration. He started breathing at long intervals, so I ran for the phone and dialled for the ambulance.'

Ward was carried from the building on a stretcher, covered in a scarlet blanket. The photographs – for the press were there – show a head lolling sideways, eyes closed. He was admitted to St Stephen's Hospital, not far away, twenty minutes after he was found, unconscious and not responding to stimuli. After an hour, though, according to one of the medical team, his condition was 'good enough for him to be transferred to a ward'. The doctors thought he might pull through.

At the Old Bailey, the court reconvened. Judge Marshall delayed for a while, then said, 'I want it to be understood that Ward shall be immediately put under surveillance. Bail is withdrawn from now, and the normal steps shall be taken to secure greater security.' Like most of his statements at the trial, the judge's words were unrelated to reality. He continued his summing-up – which included the suggestion that Ward, a prominent osteopath with additional income from art, had needed to supplement his income by living on immoral earnings. Hours later the judge told the jury, 'The ball is in your court.'

The jury deliberated all afternoon, then returned to hand the judge a long note. Marshall lectured them about prostitution and the problem of proving it. The jury wanted refreshment. Marshall said they would have to pay for it themselves, 'to avoid any suspicion of favours'.

Shortly after 7 p.m. the jury came back with a decision. They declared Stephen Ward guilty on the first two counts, not guilty on any of the others. The first two counts had concerned living on the immoral earnings of Christine Keeler and Mandy Rice-Davies. It was an extraordinary verdict. According to abstruse legal technicalities, it may have been possible to argue Ward's guilt. But he was no ponce – this was a travesty of natural justice.

The judge postponed sentence until Ward could appear.

Had he survived, he faced a possible seven years in prison.
He did not survive.

At the hospital, a sample of Ward's blood told doctors what
they already assumed – that he had taken an overdose of
barbiturates. A pill bottle had been found at his side.
Ward's friend Julie Gulliver knew he had been taking all
sorts of pills, including sleeping tablets, during the trial,
mostly Nembutal, the fashionable killer of the day. Now
Ward clung to life in Ward 3D, at St Stephen's Hospital,
with a prison officer sitting nearby. Julie Gulliver, Pelham
Pound, and Ward's temporary host, Noel Howard-Jones,
went to see him. One of his brothers, Raymond, sat at the
bedside for a long time. Bunches of flowers were delivered.
There was still hope.

Then the patient's condition began to deteriorate. A
tracheotomy was performed, and later heart massage – in
vain. At 3.45 on the afternoon of 3 August, after seventy-
nine hours in a coma, Ward died. Outside Ward 3D, a
nurse tapped the waiting prison officer on the shoulder.

'The horror, day after day at the court and in the streets,'
Ward had written in one of his suicide notes. 'It's a wish
not to let them get me. I'd rather get myself – I do hope
I haven't let people down too much. I tried to do my
stuff.'

The funeral took place a week later, at Mortlake Crematorium. The time and place were kept secret until afterwards.
Only his brother Raymond, his sister Patricia, two cousins,
his solicitor and Julie Gulliver were present. A single
wreath, with no card, lay on the paved courtyard of the
crematorium.

Ward of all people would have been touched and amused
to know that his death caused a fuss at Cheltenham Ladies'
College. The headmistress held an investigation to find out
which of her charges left a large wreath on the town's war
memorial. The note read: 'We three girls of Cheltenham
Ladies' College have laid this wreath as a tribute to dear Dr
Stephen Ward, who dared to live his life as a human being

and not just as a dummy. An outraged society revenged itself upon him.'

Another huge wreath, made of hundreds of white roses, was delivered to the Mortlake undertakers. It was sent by twenty-one writers and artists, including John Osborne, Kenneth Tynan, the singer Annie Ross, and Penelope Gilliatt. Their note read: 'To Stephen Ward, a victim of British hypocrisy.'

The trials of Stephen Ward were over.

In 1987, Lord Denning declined to be interviewed for a BBC documentary raising the possibility that there had been a miscarriage of justice. 'I refused,' he said in the House of Lords, 'because over twenty-three years ago I heard all the evidence in that case in great detail.' This was not reflected in Lord Denning's Report, which devoted only two paragraphs to the prostitution trial.

Lord Goodman, former legal adviser to Prime Minister Harold Wilson, is also – ironically – John Profumo's lawyer. Unlike Denning, he does think there was a miscarriage of justice. Ward's girls, he says, 'plainly weren't prostitutes . . . The conduct both of the judge and of the prosecution left much to be desired. It was an historic injustice.'

The truth is finally out. May its publication make those still alive who persecuted Stephen Ward, and callously abandoned him, rest less easily in their beds. More likely, they will simply shrug it off. For this is England, and nothing ever really shifts the British Establishment. Honest men must keep trying.

EPILOGUE: THE RICH WOT GETS THE PLEASURE . . .

John Profumo is now seventy-two. He is still married to Valerie Hobson. Much sympathy has been expressed for him over the years, largely because of his work for Toynbee Hall, an East London centre for the flotsam of society, alcoholics, drug addicts and drop-outs. He began this work, a 'totally voluntary three-day working week', soon after the scandal that bears his name. Profumo has a London home and a place in the country, and his family is still immensely rich. He remained Deputy Chairman of the Provident Life Association of London until its sale to a Swiss insurance company in 1982. 'The Profumos,' the *Daily Mail* City Editor reported at the time of the takeover, 'should come out with something better than £6 million.'

Once a keen racegoer, Profumo is no longer seen at the tracks. He lists his hobbies as fishing and gardening, and his London club as Boodle's. His wife has been active on behalf of Lepra, the organisation which aids victims of leprosy. She dreamed up the Ring Appeal, which prompted wealthy people, including members of the Royal Family, to hand over rings to raise money for Lepra. She wears round her neck a gold medallion, showing Profumo and herself in profile, very close, looking at each other. 'Jack made it for me,' she says.

Astonishingly, or perhaps not, the former War Minister was until 1975 a member of the Board of Visitors of Grendon Prison. That same year, he was made a Commander of the British Empire – for his work at Toynbee Hall. The CBE is awarded for Public Service. The Queen made a point of talking to Profumo when she opened a new home for social workers, established by the Attlee Foundation, of which Profumo is a trustee.

Profumo does not talk about the events of 1963. 'Jack was so greatly hurt,' says his wife. 'My husband certainly got to know about spiritual things when he retired from public life.'

Profumo has said one thing about the Affair that bears his name: 'I have my own personal papers relating to those events,' he told a reporter in 1977. 'For many years now they have been locked in a bank vault, and that is where they will stay.'

Eugene Ivanov has not been reliably sighted since he left England in January 1963. 'I was told,' said Ward's Czech friend Ilya Suschenek at the height of the Affair, 'that Ivanov is dead. It is very sad.' Press reports later said variously that he was under house arrest in the Soviet Union, working in the Navy Ministry, or in a mental hospital. Later again, he reported to be suspended from the Communist Party, pending an enquiry into his role in the Profumo case. He was also reported in Egypt, on special assignment. The journalist Brian Freemantle, who writes on intelligence matters, says: 'In no way did Ivanov return to the Soviet Union under any odium. He may have failed to obtain any military secrets from his shared liaison with Christine Keeler, but his other success was enormous – causing a huge embarrassment to a British Conservative Government and the downfall of a War Minister. His rewards would have been considerable. It has been suggested to me that he was re-posted under another name, to Tokyo.'

In the seventies, in Tel Aviv, Mandy Rice-Davies was given the oddest Ivanov theory of all. She met Herbert Atkin, a well-known FBI informant and former agent for Robert Kennedy's Justice Department, who also claims to have worked for the CIA. 'Don't you know?' he asked, 'Ivanov was an involuntary defector. Ivanov is in the United States.'

Lord Astor died in 1966. At the height of the scandal, he had the face to show up at Ascot looking – as the William Hickey column reported – 'urbane and relaxed'. His Lordship toasted the winning jockey of the Gold Cup, Lester Piggott, in champagne, then drove to Cliveden for the party he gave every year during Ascot Week.

Astor's widow paints a very different picture. At her manor house in Surrey, surrounded by books on religion, she maintains that the pressure of the Profumo case drove her husband to an early death. Ward, she says, was always an anathema to her.

Colin Coote, the Editor of the *Daily Telegraph* who introduced Ward to Ivanov, was given a knighthood a year later. He died in June 1979.

Keith Wagstaffe, the MI5 officer who handled Ward in 1961, is retired in the south of England. He was prepared to be interviewed for this book, but was denied permission to be so by MI5. 'I'm sorry about this,' he wrote. 'But I am sure you will understand that in the circumstances I cannot agree to see you . . .' 'Yes, Ward might still be alive today,' said a former senior MI5 officer, when asked if his organisation could have helped the osteopath by owning up to how they used him. 'We didn't expect the final outcome, and we were very cut up when we learned he was dead.'

Lord Denning is still active at eighty-five. He lives in a splendid house in Hampshire, with a trout stream where Isaak Newton himself once fished. He left the Court of Appeal in 1982. Denning urged in the sixties that his dossier on the Profumo case should be destroyed. In 1977 he claimed that the papers had been done away with. The then Prime Minister, James Callaghan, stated that the papers had in fact been placed in the Cabinet Office, where they will remain closed till the year 2014. One of the Secretaries to the Denning enquiry, Assistant Home Office Secretary Thomas Critchley, kept a journal during the investigation. He declined an interview for this book, citing the Official

Secrets Act. In 1964, he told Ludovic Kennedy, 'I daresay we were a bit unfair to Ward.'

A Royal Commission on Tribunals of Enquiry, chaired by Lord Justice Salmon, said in 1966: 'Lord Denning's Report was generally accepted by the public. But this was only because of Lord Denning's rare qualities and high reputation.'

Mervyn Griffith-Jones, the prosecuting counsel in the Ward trial, is dead. He wept, it is said, when told of Ward's death.

James Burge, the defence counsel, lives in retirement in Spain. 'When Ward committed suicide,' Sir David Napley has written, 'Jimmy Burge was very affected. He never seemed to be the same man again . . . It was not long after this that he left the Bar and took up residence abroad.' Ironically, Burge is a holder of the Profumo Prize, the name given to a Bar scholarship set up in 1919 by John Profumo's father.

John Lewis, the former Labour MP who did so much to bring about Ward's ruin, was delighted at the news of Ward's death. 'He was celebrating,' says Warwick Charlton. 'He made no bones about it.' He died of a heart attack in 1969, following the collapse of his business. Lewis left £63,000.

George Wigg, the nemesis of the Government in the Commons during the scandal, was appointed Postmaster-General in the Wilson government of 1964. In 1967 he was made a Life Peer, and became Chairman of the Horserace Betting Levy Board. In 1976, when he had long been out of the limelight, Wigg was charged with kerb-crawling near his home in Warwick Square. He said he had merely been trying to buy a newspaper, and was found not guilty.

Some speculate that Wigg's 1976 arrest was part of the undercover scheming against his old friend Harold Wilson. 'The possibility remained,' wrote Patrick Marnham of the

Independent, 'that he had been in some way set up.' Wigg died in 1983.

Christine Keeler is now forty-five. Her recent life has been a trail of dole queues and broken marriages. She lives now at World's End, in London, in one of the dreadful council blocks that are deemed suitable for the British working classes. Her flat has good views but little furniture. She has two sons, and they are the best thing that has happened to her since 1963. 'On the wall were her sons' school reports,' said John Mortimer, who interviewed Keeler in 1985, 'and a picture of a knight in shining armour.' She does jigsaws and crosswords, and has a meticulous filing system of everything concerning Christine Keeler. Her tragedy, perhaps, is that she can never be anyone but Christine Keeler.

'I regret it terribly,' Keeler says of her past. 'It's been a tough life, but it's something that could have happened to anybody, any good-looking girl.'

When Stephen Ward died, Keeler had 'the worst attack of asthma I've ever had in my life. And I hated people, I went to buy a paper and I heard some people say, "He's dead, the old ponce." I was so furious that I wanted to kill them. I drove my car at them, but at the last minute I hooted, and they jumped out of the way.' Ward, says Keeler, 'really was a gentleman.' Keeler's months in Holloway after the Affair, doing time for the perjury offence, were 'a bit of peace. I was psychologically exhausted . . .'

Since 1963 Keeler has had two husbands, a labourer and a company director. Asked whom she loved, of all the men she has known, she replied, 'Oh, I loved Stephen. Always, I'm very loyal.' Keeler thinks Ward was working for the Russians, not MI5. She remembers Ivanov as 'a bit of a bore really, very serious and Red . . .'

Keeler thought Profumo 'a bit overpowering, not really exciting.' She does not think he has the right to live in peace after all this time. 'He knew exactly what he was doing, even if I didn't,' she has said. 'I've never felt any remorse about what happened to him. I've had just as much trouble rebuilding my life.' In 1984, the National Portrait Gallery bought a Stephen Ward portrait of Keeler, for a thousand pounds. In March 1987 she was arrested and fined for drunkenness and causing damage near her home.

Mandy Rice-Davies is forty-three, and lives in a decent flat in North London. Unlike Keeler, she is the quintessential survivor. After the Profumo Affair, she worked on the nightclub circuit, then went to Israel, where she married her first husband – there have been two – and opened a successful nightclub and restaurant business. She helped found Israel's first glossy magazine, then returned to England to appear in plays on television and in the West End. In 1986 she had a part in the film *Absolute Beginners*. Like Keeler, she has seen her autobiography published, and is now a successful novelist.

Rice-Davies still looks good, but thinks herself at best 'passingly pretty'. She has successfully reared a daughter, now in her teens. She is extremely intelligent, and in control of her life. She sees herself, rightly, as just 'a bright, bubbly sidekick' to the events of 1963. She giggles at the memory of Eugene Ivanov telling her, 'What you've got is more powerful than the atom bomb.'

Rice-Davies has little sympathy for rich politicians who fall because of their involvement with a woman. She does not understand why people sympathise, for example, with former Conservative Party Chairman, Cecil Parkinson, who was brought down because of his affair, as a married man, with his secretary. 'Why,' Rice-Davies asks, 'is the secretary not important? Why is his career so important? I mean, is he Winston Churchill? . . . Why is the woman always told to go away in a corner and shut up? . . . She's a victim. Like Christine and myself. Victims of hypocrisy and egotism.'

Rice-Davies thinks the people who suppressed the truth about the Profumo Affair still have a hold on power in Britain. 'That group still exists in the shadows,' she says. 'The people who pressed the buttons remain a shadowy

group who inhabit the labyrinths of Whitehall. The sheer
ego of it drives me crazy to this day.'

Mariella Novotny, the woman who claimed she was bedded
by John Kennedy, and who wanted to be London's most
celebrated hostess, died in 1983. She was forty-two and still
living with her husband, Hod Dibben, her co-host at the
Feast of the Peacocks in 1961. Novotny took too many
sleeping pills, got up in the night to fetch a bowl of jelly
from the fridge, then toppled face down into the jelly.
Death was due to inhalation of vomit and the drug overdose. Novotny's psychiatrist, Dr Joan Gomez, told the
inquest that she had been suffering from a 'hysterical
personality disorder'. Dr Gomez thought it unlikely that
she was – as she claimed – involved in an operation designed to trap corrupt policemen. The psychiatrist was
wrong. Novotny was a police informant, involved in the
celebrated investigation of corrupt policemen, Operation
Countryman. Research shows that, while Novotny embroi-
dered the facts in later years, there was an element of truth
to most of what she said.

Hod Dibben survives at the age of eighty-two.

Suzy Chang, the other woman linked in the press to both
the Profumo Affair and John Kennedy, is alive and lives in
New York State under a new name.

Julie Gulliver, the young woman who stood by Stephen
Ward at the end, told the press while he was dying, 'I'll
make sure it is not in vain. He is not going to die to let a
whole lot of people get off scot-free. There is a whole crowd
of them, right now, praying for Stephen to die so their
names won't be mentioned. Stephen used to call them his
friends. But in this crisis he found out who his friends really
are.' Gulliver made a tape-recording of her knowledge of
the Affair, and was questioned by Lord Denning. Her
name does not appear in the Denning Report.
    According to Gulliver, she was pregnant by Ward when

he died. They had slept together just once. In October 1963, three months after Ward's death, she took an overdose of sleeping pills and lost her baby. She drifted through the so-called Swinging Sixties in a haze of drugs, then got married in 1972. The next year, following another drug overdose, she was found naked and dead on the floor of her home. She was given a pauper's funeral in the London borough of Southwark.

Yvonne Brooks, yet another girlfriend of Ward's, attempted suicide when she heard that Ward was dead. 'A very sweet girl,' Ward had called her. 'She knows more important men than I do. We've had a lot of fun together down at my cottage at Cliveden.' At the height of the Affair, Brooks went to Spain to stay with Lord Willoughby de Eresby, a cousin of Lord Astor and a godson of Sir Alec Douglas-Home, the Foreign Secretary in 1963. Brooks survived the 1963 suicide attempt, her second. After Lord Willoughby disappeared on a boat trip in the Mediterranean, she moved to Rome, there to live on the borderline between prostitution and the high life. In 1964, at London's Hilton Hotel, she called the switchboard operator asking not to be disturbed. Brooks then swallowed numerous sleeping pills and most of a bottle of gin, and died.

Ronna Riccardo, the prostitute whom the police pressured into giving false testimony against Stephen Ward, is now in her late forties. She has three children, all half-castes, and by different fathers. She is dramatically overweight, and – by her own admission – is still 'on the game', on a part-time basis. She says, and FBI documents confirm, that she went to the United States in the wake of the Profumo Affair, and married her American airman lover, 'Silky' Hawkins. 'I was desperate to leave England,' she says, 'because I was still under a lot of pressure from the police.' Riccardo did not stay in the States for long. She left in early 1964, says the BOWTIE dossier, on advice that 'her departure would be best for all concerned.'

'In Washington,' says Riccardo, 'I was dragged into the

offices of the CIA, and they said they knew all about me, from the cops in England.'

Riccardo says that, in the early days of the Honeytrap, she too was taken down to Cliveden by Stephen Ward. 'Astor gave us the free run of the place,' she says. The purpose, she thinks, was to involve her in the plans to compromise Soviet attaché Ivanov. She claims, 'Christine never went to bed with him. She used to lie about posing, and looking lovely, but she never went to bed with him. But he was really innocent – he'd never seen anything like it. That was the way they wanted to get someone like him involved. They wanted to blackmail Ivanov. My role in the setup was to look after Ivanov – a minder, I suppose. Stephen got involved before he knew what was happening. When he realised what was happening, he was too far in to get out . . .'

Vickie Barrett, who testified against Ward, retracted her evidence, and then retracted her retraction, has proved impossible to trace.

Frances Brown, the prostitute, did not live long after testifying that she had been involved in a sex act with Ward and the artist Vasco Lazzolo. In November 1964, Brown's decomposing corpse was found on wasteland in Kensington, apparently strangled. On her forearm was the tattoo 'Helen', over a design of red flowers and green leaves, and the legend 'Mum and Dad'. A dustbin lid had been placed over her face.

She was reportedly the seventh victim in the series of killings known as the 'Jack the Stripper' murders, in which eight prostitutes died between 1959 and 1964.

Hannah Tailford, classified as the third victim in the Stripper murders, had been – according to Brian McConnell, author of the authoritative book on the killings – one of the women supplied for the orgies held by Prince Philip's cousin, the Marquess of Milford Haven. Amongst her prostitution memories was the experience of being bought by a young man in a Rolls-Royce, near the Embankment, for twenty-five pounds, a pricely sum around 1960. She was driven to a luxurious apartment, and told to wait nude in a darkened bedroom for her client. When he arrived, she felt a strange furry outline, then the light went on and the room filled with laughing people. The man was dressed as a gorilla, and Hannah Tailford was left to find her way, in tears, out of the house.

In early 1964, police running the Stripper investigation questioned Christine Keeler. Commander John du Rose, who headed the enquiry, says: 'Every person connected with the Stephen Ward scandal was traced and questioned by the police, but all enquiries proved fruitless.'

The Profumo Affair, according to the former Labour minister, Lord Kennet, was about 'debauchery, about class, about official covering up.' With this sorry catalogue of corruption and death, a shabby history comes to an end.

POSTSCRIPT: A FINAL MYSTERY –
THE LAST HOURS OF STEPHEN
WARD

Today's Establishment roared disapproval when this book was published in 1987. Seven public figures, all former holders of high office in politics, business and the law, three of them Old Etonians and all but two products of Oxford and Cambridge, joined in a letter to *The Times*. Lords Hailsham, Carrington, Goodman, Weinstock, Prior, Jenkins and the Earl of Drogheda pontificated as follows:

> Sir, The undersigned have noted the current publicity in relation to an episode now a quarter of a century old and feel it is a good time to place on record their sense of admiration for the dignity and courage displayed by Mr and Mrs Profumo and their family in that period.
>
> This letter also records our feelings that it is now appropriate to consign the episode to history.

In the face of all the troubling evidence, here was the Establishment merely calling for three cheers for 'poor Jack', the minister whose folly caused the scandal in the first place. The strangest voice in the chorus was that of Profumo's own legal adviser, Lord Goodman. It was only weeks since he had described the judge in the Ward case as behaving in a way that 'rivalled Judge Jeffreys', and had called the trial 'an historic injustice'.

Public unease over the Profumo case persists because of the nagging sense that justice was indeed perverted, and that a citizen, Stephen Ward, was deprived of his basic rights, and died in the process. Ward should be rescued from history, not consigned to it.

In the past few months, fresh information has made the end of the Profumo case look even murkier. It suggests the possibility of yet more skulduggery by British Intelligence, and even that Ward's death may not have been a simple case of suicide.

It certainly looked straightforward at the time. The inquest jury were shown a glass vial that had contained Nembutal sleeping pills, and that had been found near Dr Ward's body, empty but for 'three or four' tablets. The autopsy pathologist, Dr Donald Teare, told the inquest that death followed softening of the brain after barbiturate poisoning. He said the softening was 'due to the deprivation of oxygen for three or four minutes'.

The autopsy indicated that Ward's system contained the barbiturate equivalent of fourteen to twenty 1½ grain sleeping tablets. Dr Teare said 'twenty grains would be dangerous and thirty very dangerous'. The medical evidence aside, there were the notes Ward left behind, twelve in all, the last – though unsigned – clearly a suicide note.*

The inquest verdict in 1963 was that Ward's death was caused by barbiturate poisoning, self-administered, and that he committed suicide. The Coroner's jury though, convened because Ward was technically in custody at the time of his death, would have been thrown into confusion had it heard the information that follows.

First there is the account of a late-night meeting between Ward and Bryan Wharton, a well-known Fleet Street photographer who recently went freelance after long service on the *Sunday Times*. In 1963, as a staff photographer for the *Daily Express*, Wharton covered the Profumo scandal.

Late on the night of Ward's apparent suicide, Wharton says, the *Express* Picture Desk told him to go to meet Ward, who had telephoned the paper – apparently following his earlier meeting with *Express* reporter Tom Mangold. The rendezvous was at Ward's own flat in Bryanston Mews, not at the Mallord Street address where Ward was currently staying, and where Mangold saw him that evening.

Wharton says he hurried to the Mews, and arrived about 11.30 p.m. Ward was there, in the company of another man dressed in a top coat with a velvet collar'. Wharton thinks the other man was Noel Howard-Jones, Ward's host at Mallord Street. Howard-Jones has refused to give us any comment for quotation on Ward's last hours.

See second picture section.

'It was clear,' says Wharton, 'that Ward was under a tremendous amount of pressure. He felt that he had been let down. I photographed him at the table. He was writing a letter to Henry Brooke, the Home Secretary. It contained a lot of names, though I don't recall whose they were. I didn't read it all – it was about three pages long. I took various shots, various angles, so that it could be seen that it was Ward who was writing. I took great care to get it right.'

'Ward was extremely upset,' Wharton says, 'and was insistent that I should meet him the next morning. He wanted me to go with him to the Home Office to deliver the letter. He kept on about me being there at 7.30 a.m., so as to be at the Home Office before going to Court.'

Wharton left Ward some time after midnight, believing he had a scoop on his hands, and headed for the *Express*. 'I processed the films,' he says, 'and hung them up. I was going to wrap up the story the next day.' Wharton did not get home till the early hours of the morning and arrived late, to accompany Ward to the Home Office – only to learn that Ward had been taken to hospital in a coma.

At the *Express*, says Wharton, he found that the scoop pictures had vanished. They never were found, and Wharton suspects British Intelligence had a hand in their disappearance. 'The *Express* in those days,' he says, 'was close to MI5, and "Five" had people in the office. The paper also had close contact with a number of policemen.'

Tom Mangold, the reporter who saw Ward at Mallord Street earlier in the evening, cannot understand why he heard nothing of Wharton's experience at the *Express* office the next day. On the other hand, the known time-frame does have a gap during which Ward's movements are unknown, a period that fits Wharton's recollection.

When he dropped his girlfriend, Julie Gulliver, at her Bayswater home at about 11.30 p.m. Ward drove straight off again – destination unclear. 'He had told me,' Noel Howard-Jones said at the inquest, 'he would go for a drive after he had run Miss Gulliver home.' Where Ward's 'drive' took him remains unknown, but Howard-Jones testified that it was not until 'about one o'clock' that he heard someone – he assumed it was Ward – enter the flat.

The testimony shows that Ward did intend to go somewhere after dropping off his girlfriend, and that he did have time to meet the *Express* photographer and return to Mallord Street by 1 a.m.

There is other evidence to suggest that, apart from the alleged letter to the Home Secretary, Ward was frantically trying to reach people in authority. Sometime that last evening he got through to Tom Critchley, a Home Office official working with Lord Denning on the official investigation. Today Critchley declines to comment on that conversation.

There is no reference to the Critchley call in the Denning Report, and it was not mentioned at the Coroner's inquest. Nor were journalists Mangold and Wharton heard at the inquest, although their evidence and Critchley's would have been very pertinent to any assessment of Ward's state of mind during his final hours.

Did something occur that night to push Ward over the edge, to contribute towards his death? And was the *Express* photographer the only other person that Ward saw during his last frantic hours?

The entertainer Michael Bentine, who knew Ward for many years, does not believe he died by his own hand. Bentine, a former Air Force intelligence officer who says he kept up his contacts after the war, quotes a police source. 'A Special Branch friend of mine,' he says, 'told me Ward was "assisted" in his dying. I think he was murdered.' Bentine declines to be drawn further.

Before first publication of this book, we had some information suggesting that Ward was murdered, or was helped on his way. We did not publish the material initially, because it appeared to fly in the face of the facts. We publish it now, for the reader to evaluate in the context of all the other information.

Earlier in this book* we reported our interviews with —————, a former MI6 contract operative who told how – under journalistic cover – he handled Ward as a potential MI6 asset. At his own request, not least in the light of the Thatcher government's actions against other intelligence personnel who have spoken out, we are still unable to name him. The operative's information on other matters has proved reliable to colleagues in national journalism and at the BBC.

'It was decided that Ward had to die,' ——— said in 1987. 'The man who was with Ward, when he took those tablets, worked for MI5. This agent told me what happened . . . He admitted that Ward was killed on the instructions of his department. He con-. vinced Ward that he ought to have a good night's sleep and take some sleeping pills. The agent said he let Ward doze off and then woke him again and told him to take his tablets. Another half an hour later or so, he woke Ward again, and told him he'd forgotten

*See pp. 203–5.

to take his sleeping pills. So it went on – till Ward had overdosed.'

'It might sound far-fetched,' says the former MI6 man, 'but it's the easiest thing in the world to do. Once the victim is drowsy he will agree to almost anything . . .'

Doctors specialising in suicide prevention say many apparent suicides are really victims of confusion, people who return again and again to the pill bottle, not realising that they have already taken more than the safe dosage. Ward, at the end of his trial, although a qualified doctor, was a prime candidate for such confusion. Behind the dark glasses there were red-rimmed eyes, the result of too little sleep and too many pills.

'He was strung out,' says his friend, Pelham Pound. 'During the trial he was taking all sorts of pills, bombers or uppers mainly.' Did Dr Ward simply miscalculate? Or could it really be that he was persuaded into the overdose by some dark emissary of British Intelligence?

The MI6 operative goes so far as to name the man who, he claims, deliberately caused Ward's death. 'Stanley Rytter is the one who killed Ward,' he says, 'I know because he told me. I don't know quite how he managed it. I wasn't there. But Rytter was with Ward the night he died, and Rytter told me he was paid to kill Ward. He was paid by our mob.'

Rytter? Our mob? Stanley Rytter, born in Poland in 1927, joined the small flood of his contemporaries who settled in England after the war. Like our MI6 informant, ———, he made his overt living as a press photographer and journalist. He specialised in 'glamour shots', the kind of slightly risqué pictures that were then the stock in trade of some Sunday newspapers.

Rytter was an associate of another Polish émigré, property racketeer Peter Rachman. He managed Rachman's '150 Club', in the Earls Court Road, lost money gambling there, and was bailed out by Rachman.

Ward, as we have shown, also knew Rachman. According to another of Rachman's Polish associates, Serge Paplinski, Ward and the racketeer were partners in the Paintbox, a London coffee bar of the mid-fifties. Like its successor, the Brush and Palette, it featured a small dais on which a nude girl would pose – as a service for artistic customers who might wish to draw her. It was there that Ward first met Noel Howard-Jones, then an impoverished law student moonlighting as a wine waiter, one day to be Ward's host on his last night alive.

British Intelligence was interested in the shadowy world of Rachman, Rytter, and their emigré friends. Peter Wright's controversial 1987 book *Spycatcher*, provides details on how MI5's D Branch, charged with counter-espionage, ran Russian, Czech, and Polish exiles as agents. They were easy to recruit, and – in the case of those already run by the KGB – had potential as double agents. Rachman himself, as a penniless post-war exile, was given the cash for his first mortgage by a British family long associated with the SAS and British Intelligence, not named here for legal reasons, but familiar to the reading public.

Our MI6 source says it was Rachman who first pointed Ward in the direction of Lord Astor. A Polish businessman, Angus Labunski, who knew Rytter well, says he received funds from mysterious sources. During recent research among Polish exiles, and in Poland itself, it emerged that Rytter was remembered for his involvement with British Intelligence. 'His link', said one Pole, 'was with MI5.'

Ward's MI6 contact, ———, says: 'Rytter had been trying to sell his services to us. But he was more likely to succeed in selling his services to MI5, he was a useful person to infiltrate the Russian and Polish émigrés here . . .'

The name 'Rytter' cropped up at Ward's trial, in an ominous context that remains unexplained. It came up in questioning, very briefly, and was forgotten till 1987, when we obtained transcripts for the first time. The prosecuting counsel, Griffith-Jones, asked Ward about an affidavit by the prostitute Ronna Riccardo, in which she admitted having given false evidence against the osteopath. Rytter's name appeared in her affidavit.

Ward referred in Court to a letter he had written, mentioning Rytter, in which he claimed 'false things were being piled up against me . . . intentional false evidence.' The letter, Ward said, also named a man called Marshall, who had allegedly been asked by Rytter to 'find a girl willing to swear an affidavit that I had employed her.' A few sentences later, Ward said Rytter had later explained the 'story' to his satisfaction. This odd exchange hangs, incomplete and mysterious, in the testimony.

The MI6 man says he first learned of Rytter's involvement in Ward's death from the man himself, years afterwards. Rytter turned up at his home, 'extremely nervous, apprehensive and sweating', and gave him a sealed package. 'He had written the whole story in Polish, and sealed it with sealing wax, and gave it to me to hold for him.'

In 1980, according to the MI6 man, Rytter came to reclaim the package. He died, following a stroke, in 1984 – in the same hospital as had Stephen Ward. His daughter Yvonne threw away all his papers, without reading them. She does recall that her father took her to wait outside St Stephen's Hospital as Ward was dying. 'Someone came to us and said, "That's it. He's dead"' she recalls, 'then we drove away . . .'

Yvonne Rytter suggested we consult a close friend of her father. This turned out to be Bill Lang, the film producer who gave Ward refuge at his Hertfordshire home, just before his arrest. When asked about Rytter, Lang requested time to think it over. Then he responded: 'I don't want to get involved. I have absolutely no statement to make. I'm going to leave things as they are. Stanley [Rytter] would have wanted that. I don't want to be rude, but I'm saying nothing at all.'

One of Rytter's fellow Poles, Serge Paplinski, is more forthcoming. He says, 'Stanley was there with Ward on the last night . . . he always said that Ward was poisoned.' Paplinski also thinks Rytter was linked to British Intelligence.

There the Rytter trail ends, as does the allegation that Ward was 'assisted' in his dying. Except for an even more dramatic allegation, by a key player in the Profumo case, Ward's friend Paul Mann. Mann, the dead man's bridge partner, a visitor to Cliveden, and a negotiator with Ward's lawyer during legal efforts to prevent the scandal from breaking, is now a businessman in the Midlands. He says he was told, shortly after the death, that 'Ward was injected with an air bubble, by hypodermic, with the intention of causing a fatal embolism. The needle broke, and the assassins left in a hurry. It was enough, though, to send the drugged Ward on his way. It was a botched affair.'

Mann claims he learned this from the individual who committed the crime, who said he did it in the company of one other person. Mann will not divulge the killer's name to us, but says he would do so to a properly constituted official enquiry.

What would the motive have been? According to the MI6 informant, Ward was a threat to the Macmillan government, the British Royal Family, and to British Intelligence. Specifically, there were sex photographs which could damage the government and the Royal Family.

As we have revealed,* Ward had entrusted some sex pictures to his friend Warwick Charlton, of Odhams Press. They were eventually seized by the police – never to be heard of again.

*See page 277.

Once these pictures were in official hands, did Ward cease to be a threat? Or did he have more evidence to reveal, more secrets to tell? The flat at Bryanston Mews, where Ward allegedly met the *Express* photographer before the fatal overdose, was where he had first stashed the photographs given to Charlton, and some jewels linked to Peter Rachman, which were found hidden in the ceiling. Did Ward have something else secreted there, something that – even more dangerously – he could have produced in Court following a guilty verdict?

There is no doubt that MI5 was intensely interested in all Ward's actions and statements. His phone calls were certainly bugged, and there were probably microphones in his various flats. Did someone in British Intelligence, eavesdropping on Ward's conversations, decide that he should be silenced?

Ward's MI6 contact, says, 'He started to make veiled threats, asking for money – he was always hard pressed for cash – and generally making himself a nuisance to the security services. The Establishment's view has always been to take a tough line against such people – squash them! Ward thought that because of what he knew, and the pictures in his possession, he was indispensable. He was wrong.'

In the light of events in 1987, surrounding the book *Spycatcher*, it would be naïve to expect any open British government enquiry into this case. Yet whether Ward was murdered or not, the information in this chapter – had it been known at the time – would have demanded an airing in any Coroner's court. There is no statute of limitations on murder.

'We were very cut up when we learned he was dead,' said a former senior MI5 officer. Many may doubt that. And there is every reason to scorn those in the British Establishment who, even today, praise John Profumo, and want to 'consign the episode to history'.

Stephen Ward not only lost his life. Thanks to an unjust trial he also lost what Shakespeare's Othello called the 'immortal part' of himself, his reputation. As in Othello, 'what remains is bestial', and that suits the Establishment just fine.

SOURCES

The following source notes are intended for the general reader, not the scholar. While every fact has been meticulously sourced, the notes are not a catalogue of each small point, more a guide to inform readers on our major sources, on who has been interviewed in person, and on the sources for specific subject areas.

A general source work, used throughout the book – though not relied upon – is *Lord Denning's Report*, presented to Parliament by the Prime Minister, by Command of HM the Queen, Cmnd 2152, HMSO, September 1963. We have also drawn on the 111-page document, entitled 'Notes for an Autobiography', by Dr Stephen Ward. This was compiled by Ward, apparently from mid-May 1963, a fortnight before his arrest. Some of it was apparently dictated into a tape-recorder, some of it typewritten in prison and carried out by journalist Pelham Pound, who was acting as Ward's agent during the last weeks of his life.

By the nature of the subject, standard reference works of national biography were used more than usual. We used especially *Who's Who* and *Who Was Who*, published by Adam and Charles Black, London; *Burke's Peerage*; *Debrett's*; Who's Who in America and *Marquis Who's Who*. We also drew extensively on *Times Obituaries 1945–1975*, in three volumes. For deaths in the last ten years, we went direct to the library collections of *The Times* newspaper.

Books referred to by authors are listed in full in the bibliography.

CHAPTER 1: Learning the Game

Interviews: Jocelyn Proby 1984; Paul Boggis-Rolfe 1986; John Doxat 1986; Dr Ellis Stungo 1987.

Ward's early life: *Torquay Herald, Daily Sketch, Daily Telegraph, Daily Mail, Daily Express* 1/8/63; *Daily Express* 5/8/63: Charlton *op. cit.*

Details of Ward's army career: extracts from his

Officer's Record of Service, supplied by Ministry of Defence.

CHAPTER 2: Pygmalion and the Popsies

Interviews: Jocelyn Proby 1984; Dr Ellis Stungo 1981, 1987; Dr W. M. McClurg 1987; Jon and Michael Pertwee 1986; Michael Eddowes 1979, 1987; Vasco Lazzolo 1982, 1983; Bill Sykes 1979; Felix Topolski 1980; Michael Bentine 1986; Dr Eric Dingwall 1986; John Lyle 1981; Brian McConnell 1981, 1986; Philip Pound 1980; Pelham Pound 1979, 1987; Hod Dibben 1986, 1987; Warwick Charlton 1987.

Prince Philip, *see*: Lane, Judd, Graham and Fisher, Baron, Bentine, Charlton *op. cits*, Lazzolo, outline for proposed autobiography; interviews: Eddowes, Stungo, Charlton and Bentine.

Milford Haven, Beecher Moore: Kearney, Fryer, Legman *op. cits*; letter British Library 27/12/80, Kinsey Institute 1981, Gernschem 1980; interviews: Dingwall, Dibben.

CHAPTER 3: Osteopath by Appointment – Wooing the Astors

Interviews: David Astor 1986; Bridget Astor 1986; Bronwen Astor 1987; Robert Harbinson 1987; John Grigg 1987; David Lewis 1987; Mandy Rice-Davies 1985; Hod Dibben 1985.

The Astors, *see*: Collis, Grigg, Sinclair, Astor, Sykes, Kavaler, Cowles *op. cits*.

Lord Astor's Intelligence career: West, Lewis, Mure *op. cits*, 'The Astor Roosevelt Espionage Ring' (article) by Jeffrey M. Dorwat, (*Journal of New York History* 1981); *Conflict of Duty*, Naval Institute Press (Lionel Lewenthal 1983).

Novotny manuscript: 'The Government Chief Whip (Retired)' and accompanying notes, undated, probably early seventies.

Letter Douglas Fairbanks Jnr 14/12/84.

CHAPTER 4: A Recipe for Scandal

Interviews: William Shepherd 1986; Jon Pertwee 1986; Philip Pound 1986; Hod Dibben 1981; Michael Mordaunt-Smith 1986; Peter Earle 1985, 1987; Connie Capes 1985.

Morgan-Dibben: *Revue*

4/8/63; *Daily Mail* Dec. 1957;
Sunday Pictorial 17/3/57;
interviews: Dibben,
Mordaunt-Smith.

Keeler: *Nothing But*; *News
of the World* series June
1963, October 1969.

Rice-Davies: *Mandy*; *The
Mandy Report*; interview
1985. Novotny: unpublished
handwritten manuscript, 'The
Girl who Paved the Way for
the Permissive Society'; *News
of the World* series June
1961; *Titbits* series June 1972;
interviews: Dibben, Earle,
Capes.

CHAPTER 5: Mariella in New York – The Kennedy Connection

Interviews: Dibben 1985,
1986, 1987; Matt White 1986;
Harry Alan Towers 1986;
Alfred Donati 1986; Peter
Earle 1985; Jeanne Martin
1984; Nina Gadd 1986; Jon
Pertwee 1986.

Novotny manuscript: 'The
Girl who Paved the Way for
the Permissive Society'.

FBI file series 31–88538.
Novotny references
declassified 1986.

CHAPTER 6: MI5 Sets the Trap

Interviews: David Floyd
1986; Intelligence sources
1986, 1987.

Berlin: Schlesinger,
Mander, Cate *op. cits*. Fay:
Jean Smith *op. cit*.

Intelligence: newspapers:
Le Monde and *Daily Mirror*
22/12/68; *Izvestiya* (p. 13
*Current Digest of the Soviet
Press* Vol. XX no. 51 1968);
Washington Post 22/12/75;
IRD: Ministry of Truth, The
Leveller, no. 64 (1981);
Kassis, Block, Coote,
Knightley *op. cits*.

MI5 & Ward: West,
Pincher, Rebecca West,
D. Lewis *op. cits*; *Denning
Report*, *Sunday Times*
28/11/82. Penkovsky: Powers,
Wynne, Penkovsky,
D. Martin, Verrier, Knightley
op. cits.

Soviet Intelligence: Corson,
Suvorov, Freemantle,
Barron, August *op. cits*.

CHAPTER 7: Recruiting Dr Ward

Intelligence: Interviews,
Intelligence sources.

MI5 & Ward: West,
Pincher, Rebecca West,
D. Lewis *op. cits*; *Denning
Report*; *Sunday Times*
28/11/82.

Penkovsky: Powers,
Wynne, Penkovsky,
D. Martin, Verrier, Knightley
op. cits.

Strelnikov: Pincher, *Inside
Story*.

Soviet Intelligence: Corson,

Suvorov, Freemantle, Barron, Pincher *op. cits*.
Berlin: Schlesinger, Mander, Cate, Jean Smith *op. cits*.

CHAPTER 8: The Minister for War: A Screw of Convenience

Interviews: Intelligence sources; Robert Harbinson 1987; Paul Mann 1987; Mandy Rice-Davies 1985.
MI5 & Ward: West, Pincher *op. cits*; *Denning Report*; *Sunday Times* 28/11/82.
Berlin: Schlesinger, Mander, Cate, Jean Smith *op. cits*.
Keeler & Profumo: *Nothing But*; *News of the World* series June 1963, October 1969; *Sunday Pictorial*; *Denning Report*.

CHAPTER 9: An Operation Botched

Interviews: Intelligence sources: Mandy Rice-Davies 1985; R. Barry O'Brien 1987; Johnny Edgecombe 1987.
MI5 & Ward: West, Pincher *op. cits*; *Denning Report*; *Sunday Times* 28/11/82.
Berlin: Schlesinger, Mander, Cate, Jean Smith *op. cits*.

Penkovsky: Wynne, Penkovsky, D. Martin, Verrier, Knightley *op. cits*. *Neue Zürcher Zeitung* 28/11/82; *New York Times* 2/7/61, 10/6/82; Pincher, Kelleher chapter 6 *op. cits*.
Keeler & Profumo: *Nothing But*; *Mandy*; *News of the World* series June 1963, October 1969; *Denning Report*; unpublished Drury interview 1963.

CHAPTER 10: The Loyal Englishman, and the Man in the Mask

Interviews: Michael Bentine 1986; Max Robertson 1986; Hod Dibben 1986; Mandy Rice-Davies 1986; Roy East 1987; Lord Dudley 1987; Dr Ellis Stungo 1987.
Ward letters to Foreign Office: *Nothing But*; Ward memoir; *Denning Report*.
Berlin: Schlesinger, Mander, Cate, Jean Smith *op. cits*.
Man in the Mask: Novotny manuscript, 'The Government Chief Whip (Retired)'; *Mandy*; Mandy Rice-Davies interview 1985; Minney *op. cit.*; *Hansard* 16/12/63, *Denning Report* Debate; interviews: Dibben; Earle; East.
Keeler: *Nothing But*; Edgecombe interview 1987.

CHAPTER 11: Not the End of the World

Interviews: Michael Eddowes 1979, 1987; William Shepherd 1986; Alfred Wells 1986; Johnny Edgecombe 1987; Andrew Tully 1987; Mandy Rice-Davies 1986.

Penkovsky: Verrier, Wynne, Deacon (*Oldfield*) *op. cits*.

Ward & Missile Crisis: Ward memoir, *Denning Report*, Crawford, Craig *op. cits*.

Cuba: Detzer, Salinger, Cohen, Nunnerley, Eddowes, Macmillan, Roberts *op. cits*.

Novotny manuscript, 'The Government Chief Whip (Retired)'.

CHAPTER 12: Disaster Looms

Interviews: Pelham Pound 1979; Johnny Edgecombe 1987; Michael Eddowes 1979, 1987; Nina Gadd 1986; William Shepherd 1986; Frederic Mullally 1987; Warwick Charlton 1987; Logan Gourlay 1987; Lord Dudley 1987; Sir Edward Tomkins 1987; Bronwen Astor 1987; Peter Earle 1987.

John Lewis file supplied by Labour Party Headquarters, 1987.

Interviews: Roger Whipp 1987 (stockbroking analyst);

Miss D. Golding (Wigg's secretary) 1987.

Divorce: *Times* 3/12/54; interviews: Charlton, Gourlay, Mullally.

Phone call: *Unsolved* magazine, no. 17; Pincher (*Too Secret*), p. 377; copy of CIA document, Appendix E, Eddowes (*Oswald File*); Letter Tommy Friend 1986; Wigg *op. cit*.

CHAPTER 13: Profumo at Bay

Interviews: Mandy Rice-Davies 1985; Nina Gadd 1986.

Chapter is largely based on interpretation of: *Denning Report*; Ward, 'Notes for an Autobiography'; Profumo, House of Commons Debate 17/6/63 and *Denning Report* Debate 16/12/63; Egremont, Keeler, Rice-Davies *op. cits*.

Bruce: Department of State doc. 15/6/63.

American knowledge: interviews, Wells 1986; Bossom 1987; Second American 1987; Mrs Robin Dalton 1986; Corbally – questions answered in writing through solicitor, 1987; Burdett letter.

Ambassador Bruce: journals, seen at Virginia Historical Society by permission of Mrs Bruce; FBI (BOWTIE) file 65–68218.

Kerby: Pincher *op. cits*; Roth, Deacon (*Russian Secret Service*), *New Statesman* 28/11/86, 5/12/86; *Spectator* 6/12/86.

CHAPTER 14: Truth in a Tight Corner

Interviews: Trevor Kempson 1987; Johnny Edgecombe 1987; William Shepherd 1987; Roy East 1987; Charles Bates 1986; Pelham Pound 1980; Michael Eddowes 1979, 1987.

Chapter is largely based on interpretation of: *Denning Report*; Ward, 'Notes for an Autobiography'; House of Commons Debate 17/6/63 and 16/12/63; Irving, Hall and Wallington; Crawford *op. cits*.

CHAPTER 15: The White House Trembles

Interviews: Johnny Edgecombe 1987; Ronna Riccardo 1987; Michael Eddowes 1979, 1987; Charles Bates 1986; Archibald Roosevelt 1987; John McCone 1986; Walter Elder 1986; Alfred Wells 1986; Mandy Rice-Davies 1985; Warwick Charlton 1987; Courtney Evans 1986; letter William Burdett 1987.

FBI (BOWTIE) file series 65–68218, original release

1983, documents released 1986 and 1987, State Department file from London Embassy released 1987; CIA file on Novotny and Towers, released 1986; Air Force Department and Department of Defense file, diclosed through FBI BOWTIE release.

Kennedy and Macmillan; Detzer; Bradlee, Davis, Joesten; O'Donnel, Schlesinger (*JFK*), Wills, Dunleavy, Parmet, *op. cits*; *Time* magazine 29/12/75.

CHAPTER 16: The World of Suzy Chang

Interviews: Charles Bates 1986, 1987; Courtney Evans 1986; Arnold Miller 1987; Glen Costin 1987; Alastair and Sheila Revie 1986; Barbara Pistalo 1987; Donald Stewart 1987; Chang 1987.

FBI BOWTIE file series 65–68218, original release 1983, docs. cleared 1986, 1987.

Chang: Immigration and Naturalisation Documents, INS A 1372612, relating to Chang released 1987; interviews: Costin, Revie's, Pistalo, Miller, Riccardo, Stewart, Earle, Chang. Davies case in British press, March–May 1963.

Skybolt: Evans, Bradlee *op. cits*; *Guardian*, *New York*

Times, *Newsweek*, *New York Journal-American*, *Daily Mail*, 1–14/7/63.

CHAPTER 17: Damage Control: the Denning Inquiry

Interviews: Roy East 1987; Hod Dibben 1987; Peter Earle 1987; Michael Eddowes 1979, 1987; Warwick Charlton 1987; Dr Eric Dingwall 1980; Hod Dibben 1986.

Chapter is based on US State Dept. file from London Embassy on Profumo Affair, released 1987; Defense Dept. documents from London Embassy, as released in FBI (BOWTIE) file 1983; Evans, Denning *op. cits*; *Denning Report*.

CHAPTER 18: Smokescreen: the Trial of Stephen Ward

Interviews: Pelham Pound 1980, 1987; James Burge 1987; Roy East 1987; Thomas O'Shea 1987; R. Barry O'Brien 1987; Harry Stevens 1987; Robert Harbinson 1987; Michael Pertwee 1986; Bronwen Astor 1987; Bobby McKew 1987; Ronna Riccardo 1987; Rice-Davies 1985.

Trial transcripts released for the first time, in Feb. 1987, by Lord Chancellor's Dept. The transcripts, which are incomplete, include testimony of Christine Keeler, Mandy Rice-Davies, Stephen Ward, Vasco Lazzolo, Sylvia Parker and Frances Brown. Kennedy, Playfair, Charlton, Jackson, Napley *op. cits*, and outline for proposed account by Pelham Pound (unpublished). The authors are grateful to Ludovic Kennedy for permission to quote from his excellent book *The Trial of Stephen Ward*.

Suicide: interviews Mangold, Pound, doctors; Mullally, 'Look Back in Anger', *Penthouse* magazine, date unclear (70s); *Evening Standard* 9/8/63; *Daily Telegraph* 10/8/63; *Sunday Telegraph* 4/8/63; *Daily Mail* 1/8/63; *Evening News* 3/8/63.

EPILOGUE The Rich Wot Gets the Pleasure

Profumo: *Daily Mail* 22/4/77; *Sunday Telegraph* 8/4/79.

Keeler: *Sunday Times* 19/5/85; *Sunday Express Colour Magazine* 23/1/83.

Rice-Davies: Rice-Davies interview 1985.

Ivanov: letter from Brian Freemantle 1986; *Time* magazine and UPI 18/7/63.

Lewis: Warwick Charlton interview 1987; *The Times* 15/1/70.

Astors: interview Lady Astor 1987.

MI5: letter Wagstaffe 14/3/87; *Sunday Times* 28/11/82.

Denning: *Today* magazine 23/1/87; *Sunday Times* 21/4/77 and 2/12/82; Critchley letter, 24/2/86; *Daily Telegraph* 3/4/64.

Novotny: Hod Dibben interview 1986; report on inquest by Anthony Frewin 21/3/83.

Gulliver: files of Anthony Frewin; *Evening Standard* 9/8/63.

Brooks: interview Nicholas Luard 1981; *Daily Telegraph* 23/3/64; *Evening Standard* 25/3/64; *News of the World* 5/4/64.

Brown and Tailford: interview Brian McConnell 1981 and 1986; Du Rose, McConnell, Kennedy *op. cits*, and *Daily Express* 27/11/64.

POSTSCRIPT A Final Mystery: the Last Hours of Stephen Ward

Interviews: Angus Labunski 1987; Serge Paplinski 1987; Yvonne Rytter 1987; Bryan Wharton 1987; Tom Mangold 1987; Paul Mann 1987, 1988; Michael Bentine 1987; Pelham Pound 1980; MI6 Operative 1983, 1987.

Communications with Noel Howard-Jones 1987; Bill Lang 1987; Dr Harvey and Dr E. N. Coomes 1987.

Documentation: Critchley letter 24/2/86; Trial transcript; *Sunday Mirror* 17/5/87; *Evening Standard* 9/8/63; *Daily Telegraph* 10/8/63; *News of the World* 1/8/63; *Daily Mail* 1/8/63; 'Just Like the Blitz' by Derek Lambert (Hamish Hamilton 1987).

BIBLIOGRAPHY

Abel, Ellie, *The Missile Crisis* (Bantam, 1968)

Allason, Rupert (Nigel West), *The Branch: A History of the Metropolitan Police Special Branch 1883–1983* (Secker & Warburg, 1983)

Allen, Charles, with Dwivedi, Sharada, *Lives of the Indian Princes* (Arena, 1986)

Astor, Michael, *Tribal Feeling* (John Murray, 1963)

August, Frantisek, and Rees, David, *Red Star over Prague* (Sherwood Press, 1985)

Baker, Bobby, *Wheeling and Dealing: Confessions of a Capitol Hill Operator* (W. W. Norton, 1978)

Baron, *Baron* (Frederick Muller, 1956)

Barron, John, *The Secret Work of Soviet Agents* (Corgi, 1975)

Barron, John, *KGB Today: The Hidden Hand* (Coronet, 1985)

Barrow, Andrew, *Gossip 1920–70* (Pan, 1980)

Bartok, Eva, *Worth Waiting For* (Putnam, 1959)

Bayliss, John, *Anglo-American Defence Relations 1939–84* (Macmillan, 1984)

Bentine, Michael, *The Long Banana Skin* (Wolfe, 1975)

Bentine, Michael, *The Door Marked Summer* (Granada, 1981)

Bird, Eugene, *The Loneliest Man in the World: Rudolph Hess in Spandau* (Secker & Warburg, 1974)

Birmingham, Stephen, *Jacqueline Bouvier Kennedy Onassis* (Fontana, 1979)

Block, Jonathan, and Fitzgerald, Patrick, *British Intelligence and Covert Action* (Zed Press, 1983)

Booker, Christopher, *The Neophiliacs: A Study of the Revolution in English Life in the Fifties and Sixties* (Collins, 1969)

Boothroyd, Basil, *Philip: An Informal Biography* (Longman, 1971)

Boyle, Andrew, *The Climate of Treason* (Coronet, 1980)

Bradlee, Ben, *Conversations with Kennedy* (Quartet, 1976)

Buckle, Richard (ed.), *Self-Portrait With Friends: The Selected

Diaries of Cecil Beaton 1926–74 (Weidenfeld & Nicolson, 1979)

Campbell, John, *F. E. Smith, First Earl of Birkenhead* (Jonathan Cape, 1983)

Cate, Curtis, *The Ides of August: The Berlin Crisis of 1961* (Weidenfeld & Nicolson, 1978)

Caute, David, *The Great Fear* (Secker & Warburg, 1978)

Cecil, Lord David, *The Young Melbourne* (World Books, 1955)

Charlton, Michael, *The Price of Victory* (BBC, 1983)

Charlton, Warwick, *Stephen Ward Speaks* (Today, Odhams Press, 1963)

Churchill, Sarah, *Keep on Dancing* (Weidenfeld & Nicolson, 1981)

Clutterbuck, David, with Devine, Marion, *Clore, The Man and his Millions* (Weidenfeld & Nicolson, 1987)

Cohen, Warren, *Dean Rusk* (Cooper Square, 1980)

Collis, Maurice, *Nancy Astor: An Informal Biography* (Faber & Faber, 1960)

Collis, Maurice, *The Journey: Reminiscences 1944–68* (Faber & Faber, 1970)

Connell, Jon, and Sutherland, Douglas, *Fraud: The Amazing Career of Dr Savundra* (Hodder & Stoughton, 1978)

Coote, Colin, *Editorial: The Memoirs of Colin Coote* (Eyre & Spottiswoode, 1965)

Coote, Colin, *The Other Club* (Sidgwick & Jackson, 1971)

Corson, W. R. and Cowley, R. T., *The New KGB: Engine of the Soviet Power* (Harvester Press, 1986)

Cowles, Virginia, *The Astors* (Weidenfeld & Nicolson, 1979)

Craig, Mary, *Longford: A Biographical Portrait* (Hodder & Stoughton, 1978)

Crawford, Iain, *The Profumo Affair* (White Lodge Books, 1963)

Croft-Crooke, Rupert, *The Dogs of Peace* (W. H. Allen, 1973)

Davis, John H. *The Kennedy Clan* (NEL, 1985)

Deacon, Richard, *A History of the Russian Secret Service* (NEL, 1975)

Deacon, Richard, *'C': A Biography of Sir Maurice Oldfield* (Macdonald, 1985)

Dempster, Nigel, *HRH The Princess Margaret: A Life Unfinished* (Quartet, 1981)

Denning, Lord, *Lord Denning's Report* (Cmnd 2152, HMSO, 1963)

Denning, Lord, *The Due Process of Law* (Butterworths, 1980)

De Feu, Paul, *Let's Hear It for the Long-Legged Woman* (Angus & Robertson, Australia, 1975)

Detzer, David, *The Brink: The Cuban Missile Crisis of 1962* (J. M. Dent, 1980)

Dickie, John, *The Uncommon Commoner: A Study of Sir Alec Douglas Home* (Pall Mall, 1984)

Dobson, Christopher, and Payne, Robert, *The Dictionary of Espionage* (Grafton Books, 1986)

Donner, Frank J., *The Age of Surveillance* (Knopf, 1980)

Dors, Diana, *Behind Closed Doors* (Star, 1979)

Dunleavy, Stephen and Brennan, Abse, Peter, *Wild, Wild Kennedy Boys* (Pinnacle, New York, 1981)

Du Rose, John, *Murder is My Business* (W. H. Allen, 1971)

Egremont, Lord, *Wyndham and Children First* (Macmillan, 1968)

Eddowes, Michael, *November 22nd: How They Killed Kennedy* (Neville Spearman, 1976)

Eddowes, Michael, *The Oswald File* (Clarkson N. Potter, 1977)

Evans, Harold, *Downing Street Diary: The Macmillan Years 1957–63* (Hodder & Stoughton)

Evica, George Michael, *And We Are All Mortal* (University of Hartford, 1978)

Finmore, Rhoda Lee, *Immoral Earnings or Mr Martin's Profession* (M. H. Publications, 1951)

Fisher, John, *Burgess and Maclean: A New Look at the Foreign Office Spies* (Robert Hale, 1977)

Freemantle, Brian, *The Fix* (Corgi, 1986)

Frischauer, Willi, *Margaret: Princess without a Cause* (Michael Joseph, 1977)

Frolik, Josef, *The Frolik Defection: Memoirs of an Intelligence Officer* (Corgi, 1976)

Fryer, Peter, *Private Case, Public Scandal* (Secker & Warburg, 1966)

Gelb, Norman, *The Berlin Wall* (Michael Joseph, 1986)

Glenton, Robert, and King, Stella, *Once upon a Time: The Story of Antony Armstrong-Jones* (Anthony Blond, 1960)

Goodman, Jonathan, and Will, Ian, *Underworld* (Harrap, 1986)

Gordon, Charles, *The Two Tycoons* (Hamish Hamilton, 1986)

Gosling, John, and Warner, Douglas, *The Shame of the City: An Enquiry into the Vice of London* (W. H. Allen, 1960)

Gould, Tony, *Inside Outside: The Life and Times of Colin MacInnes* (Penguin, 1986)

Graham, Philip, and Fisher, Heather, *Consort: The Life and Times of Prince Philip* (W. H. Allen, 1980)

Grantley, Lord, *Silver Spoon* (Hutchinson, 1954)

Green, Shirley, *Rachman* (Hamlyn Paperback, 1981)

Grigg, John, *Nancy Astor: Portrait of a Pioneer* (Sidgwick & Jackson, 1980)

Hamblett, Charles, and Deverson, Jane, *Generation X* (Tandem, 1964)

Hancock, Robert (Douglas Howell), *Ruth Ellis: The Last Woman to be Hanged* (Weidenfeld & Nicolson, 1985)

Harrison, Rosina, *Rose: My Life in Service* (Cassell, 1975)

Heald, Tim, *Networks* (Coronet, 1985)

Hersch, Burton, *The Mellon Family: A Fortune in History* (William Morrow, 1978)

Hopkins, Harry, *The New Look: A Social History of the Forties and Fifties in Britain* (Readers Union, Secker & Warburg, 1964)

Horan, James, *The Right Image* (Crown Publishers, 1967)

Howard, Anthony, and West, Richard, *The Making of the Prime Minister* (Jonathan Cape, 1965)

Humphry, Derek, and Tindall, David, *False Messiah: The Story of Michael X* (Hart Davies, McGibbon, 1977)

Hutchinson, George, *The Last Edwardian at No. 10: An Impression of Harold Macmillan* (Quartet, 1980)

Hyde, H. Montgomery, *A Tangled Web: Sex Scandals in British Politics and Society* (Constable, 1986)

Irving, Clive, Hall, Ron, and Wallington, Jeremy, *Scandal '63: A Study of the Profumo Affair* (Heinemann, 1963)

Israel, Lee, *Killgallen* (Dell Publishing, 1980)

Jackson, Stanley, *The Old Bailey* (W. H. Allen, 1978)

Joesten, Joachim, *The Dark Side of Lyndon Baines Johnson* (London, 1968)

Judd, Denis, *Prince Philip: A Biography* (Michael Joseph, 1980)

Kassis, V., *Caught in the Act* (Progressive Publishers, Moscow, 1977)

Kaufman, William, *The McNamara Strategy* (Harper & Row, 1964)

Kavaler, Lucy, *The Astors: A Family Chronicle* (George G. Harrap, 1966)

Kearney, Patrick J., *The Private Case* (Jay Landesman, 1981)

Keeler, Christine, and Meadley, George, *Sex Scandals* (Xanadu, 1985)

Keeler, Christine, with Fawkes, Sandy, *Nothing But* (New English Library, 1983)

Kelleher, Catherine, *Germany and the Politics of Nuclear Weapons* (Columbia University Press, 1975)

Kennedy, Ludovic, *The Trial of Stephen Ward* (Gollancz, 1964)

Knightley, Philip, *The Second Oldest Profession: The Spy as Bureaucrat, Patriot, Fantasist and Whore* (André Deutsch, 1986)

Kollek, Teddy, *For Jerusalem, A Life* (Weidenfeld & Nicolson, 1978)

Lane, Peter, *Prince Philip* (Robert Hale, 1980)

Lane, Sheldon, *The Spying Game* (Mayflower-Dell, 1967)

Langhorne, Elizabeth, *Nancy Astor and her Friends* (Arthur Barker, 1974)

Leaman, G., *The Horn Book* (University Books, 1964)

Leslie, Anita, *Cousin Randolph: The Life of Randolph Churchill* (Hutchinson, 1985)

Levin, Bernard, *The Pendulum Years: Britain and the Sixties* (Jonathan Cape, 1970)

Levy, Norma, *I, Norma Levy* (Blond & Briggs – withdrawn)

Lewis, David, *Sexpionage: The Exploitation of Sex by Soviet Intelligence* (H. Hanau, 1976)

Lord, John, *The Maharajahs* (Hutchinson, 1972)

Lucas, Norman, *The Great Spy Ring* (Mayflower, 1968)

Lucas, Norman, *Britain's Gangland* (Pan, 1969)

McConnell, Brian, *Found Naked and Dead* (New English Library, 1974)

Maclaren Ross, Julian, *Memoirs of the Forties* (Penguin, 1984)

Maclean, Donald, *British Foreign Policy Since Suez* (Hodder & Stoughton, 1970)

Maclean, Fitzroy, *Take Nine Spies* (Weidenfeld & Nicolson, 1978)

Macmillan, Harold, *Pointing the Way* (Macmillan, 1972)

Macmillan, Harold, *At the End of the Day* (Macmillan, 1973)

McTaggart, Lynne, *Kathleen Kennedy* (Weidenfeld & Nicolson, 1984)

Mader, Julius, *Who's Who in the CIA* (Berlin, 1968)

Malone, Peter, *The British Nuclear Deterrent* (Croom Helm, 1984)

Mander, John, *Berlin, Hostage for the West* (Penguin, 1962)

Margaret, Duchess of Argyll, *Forget Not* (W. H. Allen, 1975)

Martin, David, C., *A Wilderness of Mirrors* (Ballantine, 1981)

Martin, Ralph G., *A Hero for Our Time: An Intimate Story of the Kennedy Years* (Macmillan, 1983)

Masters, Anthony, *Nancy Astor: A Life* (Weidenfeld & Nicolson, 1981)

Miller, Compton, *Who's Really Who* (Blond & Briggs, 1983)

Minney, R. J., *The Biography of the Hon. Anthony Asquith, Aristocrat, Aesthete, Prime Minister's Son and Brilliant Film Maker* (Leslie Frewin, 1973)

Morgan, Janet (ed.), *The Backbench Diaries of Richard Crossman* (Hamish Hamilton and Jonathan Cape, 1981)

Morrison, Majbritt, *Jungle West 11* (Tandem, 1964)

Mure, David, *Practice to Deceive* (Sphere, 1979)

Mure, David, *Master of Deception* (William Kimber, 1980)

Mure, David, *The Last Temptation* (Buchan & Enright, 1984)

Napley, David, *Not Without Prejudice* (Harrap, 1982)

Navasky, Victor S., *Naming Names* (John Calder, 1982)

Nicol, Jean, *Meet Me at the Savoy* (Museum Press, 1952)

Nicolson, Nigel, *Harold Nicolson Diaries and Letters 1930–39* (Collins, 1966)

Nunnerley, David, *President Kennedy and Britain* (Bodley Head, 1972)

O'Donnel, Kenneth, and Powers, David F. with McCarthy, Joe, *Johnny, We Hardly Knew Ye: Memoirs of John F. Kennedy* (Little, Brown, 1972)

Parmet, Herbert S., *JFK: The Presidency of John F. Kennedy* (Penguin, 1984)

Penkovsky, Oleg, *The Penkovsky Papers* (Fontana, 1967)

Penrose, Barry, and Freeman, Simon, *Conspiracy of Silence: The Secret Life of Anthony Blunt* (Grafton Books, 1986)

Pertwee, Michael, *Name Dropping* (Leslie Frewin, 1974)

Roberts, Brian, *Randolph* (Hamish Hamilton, 1984)

Pincher, Chapman, *Inside Story: A Documentary of the Pursuit of Power* (Sidgwick & Jackson, 1978)

Pincher, Chapman, *Their Trade is Treachery* (Sidgwick & Jackson, 1982)

Pincher, Chapman, *Too Secret, Too Long* (Sidgwick & Jackson, 1984)

Pincher, Chapman, *The Secret Offensive* (Sidgwick & Jackson, 1985)

Playfair, Giles, *Six Studies in Hypocrisy* (Secker & Warburg, 1969)

Power, James, *Against Oblivion* (Fontana, 1981)

Powers, Robert, *The Man Who Kept the Secrets: Richard Helms and the CIA* (Weidenfeld & Nicolson, 1979)

Rice-Davies, Mandy, with Flack, Shirley, *Mandy* (Sphere, 1980)

Rice-Davies, Mandy, *The Mandy Report* (Confidential Publications, 1964)

Roberts, Chalmers, *First Rough Draft* (Praeger, 1973)

Roth, Andrew, *Sir Harold Wilson: Yorkshire Walter Mitty* (Macdonald & Janes, 1977)

Rositzke, Harry, *The KGB: Eyes of Russia* (Sidgwick & Jackson, 1982)

Salisbury, Harrison E., *The Coming War Between Russia and China* (Pan, 1969)

Salinger, Pierre, *With Kennedy* (Garden City, 1972)

Sampson, Anthony, *Anatomy of Britain* (Hodder & Stoughton, 1963)

Schlesinger, Arthur, *A Thousand Days: John F. Kennedy in the White House* (Mayflower Dell, 1967)

Schlesinger, Arthur, *Robert Kennedy and His Times* (Futura, 1979)

Sinclair, David, *The Astors and Their Times* (J. M. Dent, 1983)

Slater, Frank, *Getting a Likeness* (Seeley Service, 1952)

Smith, Jean Edward, *The Defense of Berlin* (Oxford University Press, 1963)

Smith, R. Harris, *OSS: The Secret History of America's First Intelligence Agency* (University of California Press, 1972)

Sorenson, Theodore C., *Kennedy* (Harper & Row, 1965)

Strong, Sir Kenneth, *Intelligence at the Top* (Cassell, 1968)

Sullivan, William C., *The Bureau: My Thirty Years in Hoover's FBI* (Norton, 1979)

Summers, Anthony, *Goddess: The Secret Lives of Marilyn Monroe* (Gollancz, 1985)

Suvorov, Victor, *Soviet Military Intelligence* (Hamish Hamilton, 1984)

Sykes, Christopher, *Nancy: The Life of Lady Astor* (Granada, 1979)

Tangye, Derek, *When the Wind Blows* (Michael Joseph, 1980)

Tully, Andrew, *White Tie and Dagger* (William Morrow, 1967)

Ungar, Sandford J., *FBI* (Atlantic Monthly Press, 1976)

Van den Bergh, Tony, and Marks, Laurence, *Ruth Ellis: A Case of Diminished Responsibility* (Macdonald & Janes, 1977)

Verrier, Anthony, *Through the Looking Glass: British Foreign Policy in the Age of Illusions* (Jonathan Cape, 1983)

West, Nigel, *A Matter of Trust: MI5 1945–72* (Weidenfeld & Nicolson, 1982)

West, Nigel, *Molehunt* (Weidenfeld & Nicolson, 1987)

West, Rebecca, *The Meaning of Treason* (Penguin, 1965)

Wigg, Lord, *George Wigg* (Michael Joseph, 1972)

Wighton, Charles, *Dope International* (Four Square Books, 1964)

Wills, Gary, *The Kennedys: A Shattered Illusion* (Orbis Publishing, 1983)

Winn, Godfrey, *The Positive Hour* (Michael Joseph, 1970)

Wright, William, *The Von Bülow Affair* (Arlington Books, 1983)

Wyatt, Woodrow, *Confessions of an Optimist* (Collins, 1985)

Wynne, Greville, *The Man from Odessa* (Granada, 1983)

Wynne, Greville, *Wynne and Penkovsky (The Man from Moscow)* (Corgi, 1985)

Young, Kenneth, *Sir Alec Douglas-Home* (J. M. Dent, 1970)

Young, Wayland, *The Profumo Affair: Aspects of Conservatism* (Penguin, 1963)

Ziegler, Philip, *Mountbatten* (Collins, 1985)

INDEX

ALSO AVAILABLE FROM
HODDER AND STOUGHTON PAPERBACKS